Vignettes & Adventures

Vignettes & Adventures

THOMAS G. DAVIS

PRIMIX
PUBLISHING
THE WRITE CHOICE

Primix Publishing
East Brunswick Office Evolution
1 Tower Center Boulevard, Ste 1510
East Brunswick, NJ 08816
www.primixpublishing.com
Phone: 1-800-538-5788

Published by Primix Publishing: 01/27/2025

ISBN: 979-8-89194-414-5(sc)
ISBN: 979-8-89194-415-2(e)

CONTENTS

The Author and His Remarkable Achievements & Prestigious Recognitions

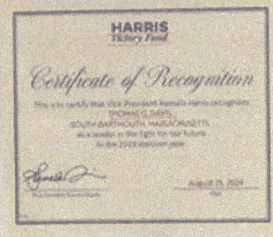

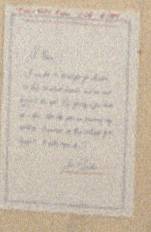

GRADUATE FROM
HIGH SCHOOL & COLLEGE

> INCREASE YOUR KNOWLEDGE.

> ENRICH YOUR LIFE.

> BROADEN YOUR HORIZONS.

> OBTAIN AN INTERESTING, CHALLENGING
AND SATISFYING JOB.

> EARN A HIGH INCOME.

> ENJOY A NICE LIFESTYLE.

NEW BEDFORD SCHOOL DEPARTMENT
& SOUTHCOAST EDUCATIONAL
IMPROVEMENT FOUNDATION

Graduate from High School and College

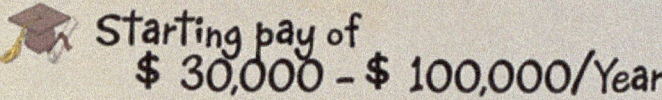 Starting pay of
$30,000 – $100,000/Year

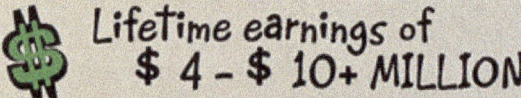 Lifetime earnings of
$4 – $10+ MILLION

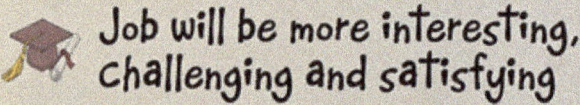 Job will be more interesting, challenging and satisfying

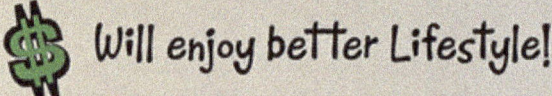 Will enjoy better Lifestyle!

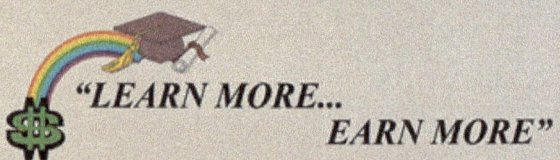 *"LEARN MORE...*
EARN MORE"

New Bedford School Department
and
Southcoast Educational Improvement Foundation

GLOBAL LEARNING CHARTER SCHOOL

- GRADES 5-12; 475 STUDENTS; FREE

- ADMISSION BY LOTTERY

- HIGH EXPECTATIONS FOR ALL STUDENTS

- SMALL CARING ENVIRONMENT & FREE TUTORING

- LONGER SCHOOL DAY

- LEARNING MADE INTERESTING BY WORKING ON PROJECTS & BACK AND FORTH CONVERSATIONS WITH TEACHERS

- MANY FUN ACTIVITIES

- COLLEGE & CAREER FOCUS FROM DAY 1; INTERNSHIPS FOR JUNIORS & SENIORS

- DUAL ENROLLMENT PROGRAMS WITH UMASS DARTMOUTH & BCC

- VERY HIGH ATTENDANCE, GRADUATION, COLLEGE ENROLLMENT & PARENT PARTICIPATION RATES

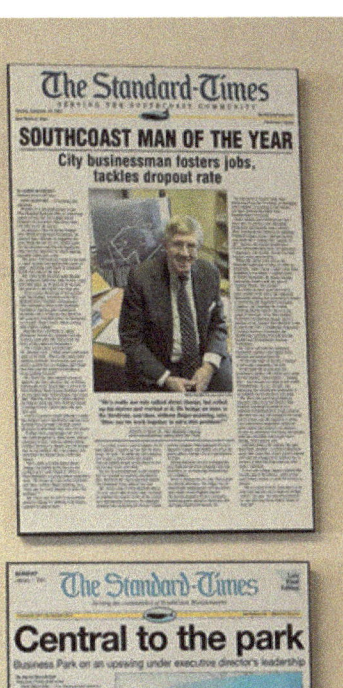

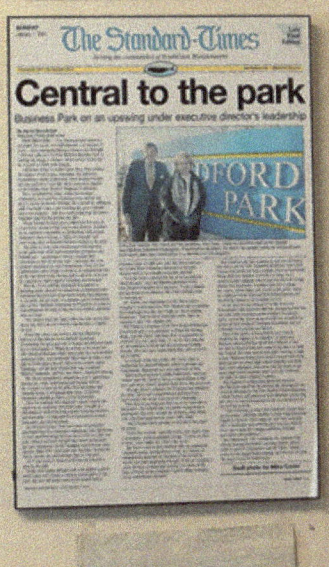

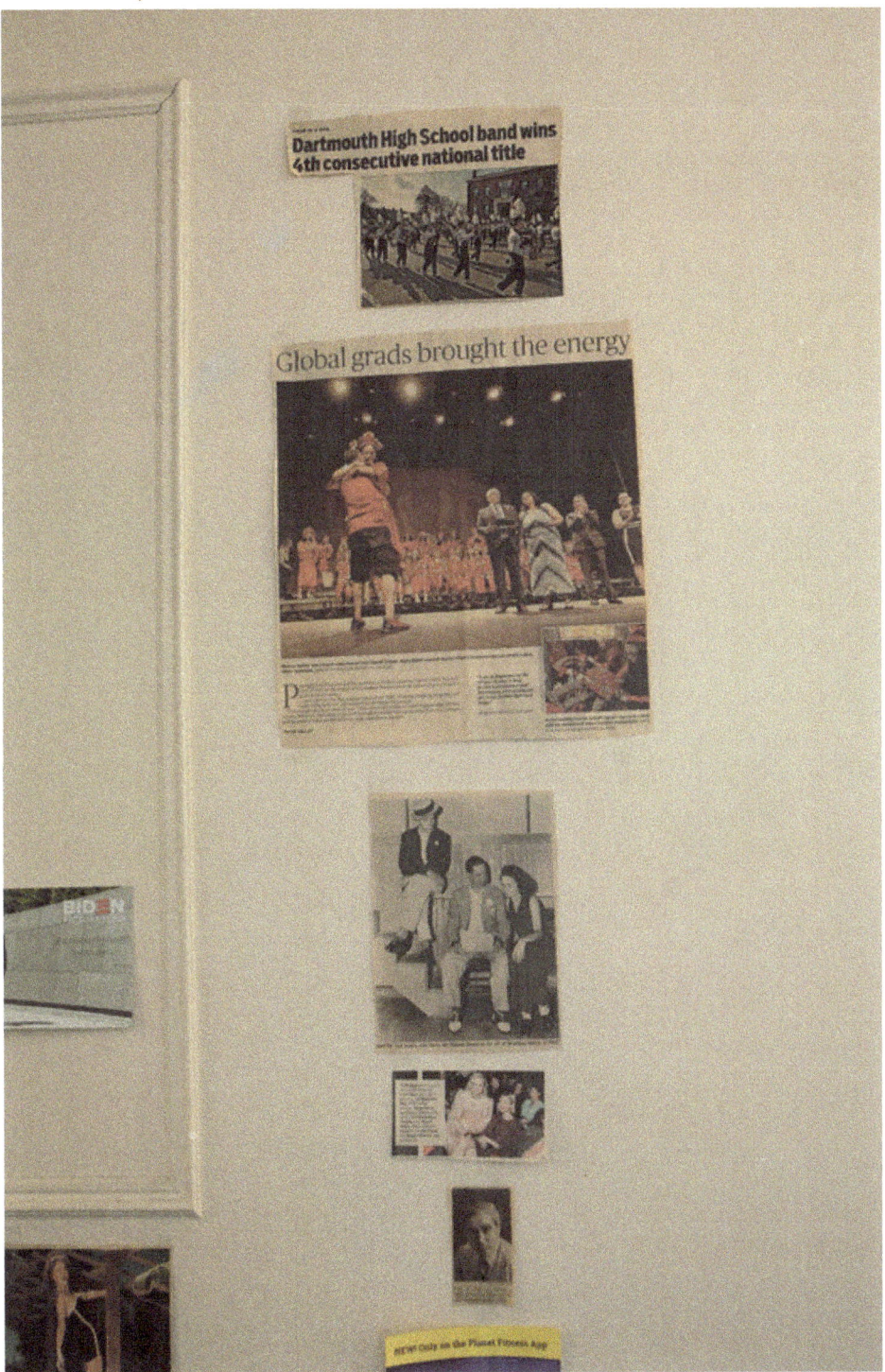

Vignettes of the Life of Thomas Garfield Davis

(FROM 1940 TO 2020)

PROLOGUE

I am Writing a Number of Short Vignettes on My Exciting and Diverse Life, Highlighting My Adventures, Accomplishments, and Mishaps, which Hopefully will be of Interest to Tommy, My Son; Christie, My Daughter; Tommy's Sons (Nick and Henry); and Christie's Son (Kingston).

1. Born in Governor's Mansion

My Father, after obtaining a PhD in Education Administration from Columbia University, became Deputy Secretary of Education for Vermont and was Responsible for Community Relations and Public Affairs.

Early on, He Established a Strong Personal and Professional Relationship with Governor George Aiken.

The Governor Lived and Worked at the Governor's Mansion in Montpelier. The Mansion was Four Stories, with the Public Rooms on the First Floor, the Offices of the Governor's Senior Staff on the Second Floor, and the Third and Fourth Floors were for the Personal Residence of the Governor.

However, Governor Aiken, who was Very Frugal, told my Father he Only Needed One Floor for His Personal Residence. And Thus, He Offered One of the Floors to My Father and Mother without any Rent Provided My Father Would Also Serve the State as His Director of Public Relations without Any Extra Pay.

My Father Accepted the Offer and Moved There in 1939 and Stayed Through My Birth on February 12, 1940, which is Abraham Lincoln's Birthday, but had to Leave in 1941 After George Aiken was Elected to the US Senate.

Senator Aiken Became a Very Distinguished and Highly Respected Senator and Served for Thirty-four Years. He Became Known for his Opposition to Senator McArthy and the Vietnam

War and His Advocacy for Trying to Improve Relations with the Soviet Union.

Importantly, My Father Placed a High Priority on Maintaining Good Relations with His High School and College Friends and Everyone He Worked Closely with in Ohio; New York City; Hollywood; Vermont; Washington, DC; Puerto Rico; and Chicago.

In this regard, He Maintained a Close Relationship with Senator George Aiken, who Helped Him Obtain a Senator Administrative Position at George Washington University in 1946 and Provided Our Family with Front- or Second-Row Seats at Many Washington, DC, Special Holiday and Political Events.

2. WHO IS GARFIELD?

*R*egarding My Middle Name of Garfield, President James A. Garfield from Ohio was a Relative of My Mother's Family in Ohio.

Garfield was Born in a Log Cabin in 1831 in Moreland Hills, Ohio. His Father Died when he was two years old, and he grew up in Poverty in the Household of His Strong-willed Mother.

Poor and Fatherless, Garfield Escaped by Reading all of the Books he could find. He Became a Strong Student and Graduated from Williams College in Massachusetts as Class Salutatorian and Gave a Commencement Address.

After an Early Career in Teaching and Law, He Joined the Union Army in 1861 as an Officer and was Quickly Promoted to Major General and Fought in Three Famous Battles from 1861 to 1863.

At the Same Time, He also Became Involved in Ohio Politics and was Elected to the US House of Representative as a Republican in 1863 to Represent Ohio's 9th District. He Rose Rapidly through the Political Ranks and Chaired the House Appropriation's Committee. Banking Committee, and Military Affairs Committee.

At the 1980 Republican National Convention, Senator Elect Garfield Attended as Campaign Manager for Secretary of Treasury John Sherman and Gave the Presidential Nomination Speech For Him. While Neither Sherman nor His Rivals, Ulysses S. Grant and

James Blaine, Could Muster Enough Votes to Secure the Nomination, the Delegates Chose Garfield as a Compromise on the 36th Ballot.

Garfield Conducted a Very Low-key Front-Porch Campaign for the Presidency and Narrowly Defeated Democrat Winfield Hancock.

In His Inauguration Address on March 4, 1981, and Early on in His Presidency, Garfield was an Exceptionally Strong Proponent of Equal Rights for African Americans.

Unfortunately, on July 2, 1981, Garfield was Shot by a Segregationist at the Railroad Station in Washington, DC, and Died Several Months Later.

3. WORKING FOR THE *WASHINGTON EVENING STAR* IN 4TH GRADE

*E*arly On and Throughout my Childhood and Adult Life, I Liked to Work Hard, Make Lots of Money, and Live Well.

As a Young Child, I did not like to have to rely on my Parents to buy for me some but not all of the Recreation and Sports Items I Desired.

While Living in Bethesda, Maryland, and just starting Fourth Grade, I Learned that the Newspaper Boy for Delivering the *Washington Evening Star* in Our Neighborhood would have to give up the Job shortly because his family was moving to Another State.

That Same Day, I waited at the spot where the papers were dropped off for the Delivery Boy and Asked the Delivery Truck Driver If I could Take Over the Job. After checking with his Supervisor, the Delivery Truck Driver Told Me the Next Day that I could have the Job. And He Gave Me a List of the Names and Addresses of the fifty Subscribers on the Route and a Write up on What My Duties Would Be.

Even Though I was only nine years old, I Took on the Job with Great Enthusiasm, which Involved Delivering the Newspapers from a *Washington Evening Star* Wooden Paper Wagon After School was Over, Every Afternoon from Monday through Friday, and on Sunday Mornings to fifty Households. I also had to Collect the Newspaper Subscription Fees at the End of Every Month, which Sometimes

Involved More than one Visit to a Household, and then Turn Over the Checks and Cash to the Delivery Truck Driver After Deducting my Monthly Pay of Twenty-five Dollars Plus Tips of Five to Ten Dollars.

I was Very Good at Saving my Earnings. And After a Year, I was able to Purchase a Raleigh English Bicycle and a Professional Model of the Rawlings Marty Marion Shortstop Glove. I also became a big Movie Fan and went to a Nearby Movie Theater Almost Every Saturday to see a Western or Adventure Film, Walt Disney, and Amos 'n' Andy Cartoons, and a First-Class Worldwide News Summary.

I kept the Newspaper Job Until the Start of 7th Grade, when my Father Obtained a New Senior Administrative Job at the Chicago Campus of the University of Illinois.

4. Aunt Dorothy and Mary the Man

Aunt Dorothy, My Father's Spinster Sister, would come to visit us in Vermont and then Bethesda, Maryland, Every Year After Driving Non-Stop from California. She would Arrive Exhausted and Sick and would have to Spend a Week in Bed, which was a Big Strain and Irritant for my Mother.

As a Health Teacher, she would Criticize my Mother for Not Serving Healthy Breakfasts of Steak, Eggs, and Freshly Squeezed Orange Juice and for Waiting Much Too Long before Buying New Shoes for my Sister and Me, which caused Me to Have Hammer Toes.

Thus, My Mother Despised Aunt Dorothy and was Very Mean to her. This Caused Lorraine, My Sister, to also be Mean to Aunt Dorothy.

However, I was Nice to Aunt Dorothy as I Enjoyed Her Stories about how Wonderful California and the Wild West was. As a result, when she sent a Large Carton of Presents to Our Family at Christmas, I made out by Far the Best, with Many Presents such as Cowboy Clothes, Pretty Western Stones, Photographs of US Military Planes, and Indian Head Pennies etc.

When Aunt Dorothy Died in her early seventies when I was Working for Exxon, She Willed her House in Apple Valley, California, and all of her Savings to Me Alone. However, I did not think this was the Right Thing To Do. So, I Managed to Take Over the Settlement of Her Estate in California and Divide the Proceeds from Selling her House and Her Savings Equally Between My Father, Sister, Brother, and Me after Paying the California Estate Taxes.

When Aunt Dorothy was Working as a Health Teacher in Philadelphia, before Moving to California, she met Mary Conley, who was also a Health Teacher and an Athletic Coach for Girls High School Teams. They became Good Friends and Lifelong Companions.

Mary Conley was Amazing. She was Very Active in Sports. She Won Second Place in the Women's National Bowling Championships. She also Joined One of the Early Women's Professional Soft Ball Teams in Philadelphia and Became a Major Star Both as a Pitcher and a Batter.

She came to the Attention of Connie Mack, the Great Philadelphia Athletics Baseball Coach and Owner, who was Known for Stunts such as Sending a Midget Up to Bat as a Pinch Hitter When the Bases were Loaded so that a Walk for the Midget would Force in a Run.

Connie Mack Hired Mary Conley for one Baseball Game Against One of the Famous New York Yankee Teams. She Entered the Game as a Relief Pitcher in the Eighth Inning and Struck Out Lou Gehrig, Babe Ruth, and Red Rolfe with Her Underhand, Whiplike Fastball Pitches.

When I saw Mary Conley for the First Time in Vermont, When She was Visiting Our House with Aunt Dorothy, According to My Mother, I Asked Her, "Why Do You Have Hairs On Your Chinny-Chin-Chin?"

5. TURTLE PENS

As a Young Boy Living in Bethesda, Maryland, I became Interested in a lot of Pet Animals, but Most of All Turtles.

Maryland is known as the Terrapin State, due to its Large Number of Ornate Box Turtles and Beautifully Marked Freshwater Painted Turtles.

To House my Turtle Collection, I Built a Large Turtle Pen in the Back of Our Large and Deep Backyard. I Erected a Wire Stake Fence which was Two Feet High and One Foot Below the Ground. I also Installed a Good-Sized Plastic Water Pool for the Painted Turtles.

On Trips in the Car into Wooded Areas, I would always be Looking Out the Window for Box Turtles Crossing the Road. When Seeing One, I Would Ask My Father to Stop the Car so I could Fetch it for my Turtle Pen. Also, I Liked to Walk with My Father Along the Banks of the nearby Chesapeake and Ohio Canal with a Net at the End of a Long Pole. When I would see Painted Turtles Basking in the Sun on a Log Near the Shore, I would quietly Sneak Up Close to the Water's Edge and Try to Net One of the Painted Turtles when they Plunged into the Water. While my Success Rate was only about One Painted Turtle for Every Four Attempts, I did after One Year Net enough small Painted Turtles to Fill Up the Water Pool Inside my Turtle Pen.

Of course, with the Turtle Pen came a Lot of Responsibilities. I had to Feed the Turtles Every Day, Make Sure the Box Turtles had

Fresh Drinking Water, Clean Out the Painted Turtle Pool Once a Week, and Bury all of the Turtles Each Winter at the Bottom of a Huge Leaf Pile so that They Would Survive During the Cold Weather Months. Also, when Our Family was Away on Vacations, I had to get one of my Boyhood Friends to Take Care of the Turtles, for a Small Fee.

Word of My Carefully Maintained Turtle Pen for Sixty Turtles Spread Throughout Our Neighborhood and Town so much that the *Washington Post* did a Feature Story with Pictures of the Turtle Pen and Me in Their Sunday Edition.

When Our Family Moved to Evanston, Illinois, in 7th Grade, I had to Give Up Collecting Turtles as Illinois is not a Big Turtle State. However, I did Return all of My Turtles in Bethesda, Maryland, to Their Natural Habitats in the Woods or the Canal.

6. "You Ought to See My Uncle Joe When He Is Getta Mad"

*I*n 8th Grade in Evanston, Illinois, We were Allowed to Select One Elective Course to Attend Each Semester Over and Above the Required Courses.

I Selected a Course in Acting and Effective Speaking. This Course was Very Important to Me Then and Later in Life as it Helped Me Get Over My Initial Stage Fright and Become an Outstanding Public Speaker.

Initially, I Entered a Large Poetry Reading Contest in 8th Grade and Recited with an Italian Accent a Poem Entitled "You Ought to See My Uncle Joe When He Is Getta Mad." I Received a Big Ovation from the Audience and Was Awarded Second Place.

7. Terrified by Ghost at Mrs. Kroniker's Estate

*I*n Our Evanston, Illinois, Neighborhood, My Parents Became Good Friends with a Northwestern Professor and His Wife. They had a Summer Cottage in Door County, Wisconsin, which was Perched on a Ledge halfway down a Steep Granite Cliff Overlooking Their Private, Rocky Beach on Lake Michigan. They Invited My Parents to Stay There for Two Weeks Every Summer During My Middle School and Early High School Years.

To get to the Cottage, My Father had to Drive One Mile on a Dirt Road Through the Woods to the Top of the Steep Cliff and We all had to Climb Down the Cliff on a Primitive Trail to the Ledge for the Cottage.

There were only Two Summer Houses within Half a Mile of Our Cottage. Both were Large Estate Houses on the Top of the Cliff. One was South of Our Cottage and Owned by a Doctor with Five Kids. The Other was North of Our Cottage and Owned by Mrs. Kroniker, who was a Widow in Her Eighties and a Heiress to the Kuppenheimer Clothing Company Fortune.

In the Nearby Town, Mrs. Kroniker was Rumored to be a Witch as she Always Wore a Head-to-Toe Black Cape During the Hot Summer Months, Walked with a Cane, and was Driven Around in a Large Rolls Royce by a Chauffeur who also Wore a Large, Black Cape.

During the Days, My Sister and I would get together with the Five Kids From the Doctor's Estate House. Near the End of our Last Summer's Stay in the Cottage, I Talked the Doctor's Five Kids Into Walking After Dinner to Mrs. Kroniker's Estate House to see what it was like.

It was the Early Evening and Just Starting to Get Dark. After Walking a Half Mile on a Cliff Top Trail to Mrs. Kroniker's Estate, We Stopped Behind a Huge Bush Where We Could See the Estate House. There were a Small Group of People Having Dinner in a Screened-In Porch and Being Serenaded by a String Quartet.

We then Heard a Whistling Sound from what we Thought was a Servant Walking a Dog Around the Estate House. The Whistling Sound Got Closer and Closer to Us and Stopped on the Other Side of the Large Bush where We Were Hiding. However, We Could Not See Anyone.

Shortly thereafter, on the side of the Estate House Facing Lake Michigan, We Heard the Large, Wooden Third Floor Shutters Being Opened. And We Saw Mrs. Kroniker's Head Leaning Out of the Shutters, with Her Very Long Grey Hair of About Two Feet Blowing Out Towards Lake Michigan.

Immediately, We all Became Very Frightened and Ran as Fast as we could along the Clifftop Trail Back to Each of Our Summer Houses. The Next Morning, Without My Sister, I got Together with the Five Kids From the Doctor's Summer Estate, And We Decided to try to Visit Mrs. Kroniker's Estate again but from the Rocky Beach Rather than the Cliff Trail.

When We Arrived at the Base of the Cliff below Mrs. Kroniker's Estate, We Discovered a Steep, Rocky Trail going up to the Estate House. The Doctor's Kids were Reluctant to Go Up the Steep Trail but Agreed to Go only if I Led the Way, Which I did.

As soon as I just Barely Reached the Top of the Steep Trail, with only My Head in View from anyone at the Estate House, I Heard a Man in a Deep, Scary Voice Yelling, "Go Away, Go Away, Go Away."

I Immediately Turned Around and Scampered down the Steep

Trail as Fast as I could and Sought Refuge in a Large Cave at the Base of the Trail where I Found the Five Doctor's Kids Waiting For Me.

And, at the same time, Someone Began Pushing Small Boulders from the Top of the Steep Trail down Towards the Cave Entrance. After Shaking and Huddling in the Cave for about Twenty Minutes, We All Left and Returned to Our Respective Summer Houses.

None of Us Ever Tried to Visit Mrs. Kroniker's Estate Again! However, I did see Mrs. Kroniker once in Town. She was wearing the Long, Black Cape and Getting into the Back of a Large, Black Rolls Royce Driven by Her Chauffeur, who was also Wearing a Black Cape.

8. Dental Career Ends in 10th Grade

As a Young Boy, I had Terrible Teeth and was Always going to the Dentist for Examinations and Fillings.

Thus, Early On, I Thought that Becoming a Dentist would be a Financially Rewarding Career.

And I Realized that I needed to take All of the High School Science Classes and Do Well in Them if I Wanted to Become a Dentist.

As a Freshman at Evanston Township High School, I took Biology and Received a B+ in the Course.

However, as a Sophomore, I Took Chemistry and Hated It from Day One. Halfway Through the Course, I had Received Ds in all my Quizzes and Exams. And, Since I had A's or B's in Most of My Other Courses, I Reached the Conclusion that I Needed to Drop Out of the Chemistry Course Just Before the Dropout Deadline so as Not to Have a Poor Grade in Chemistry Adversely Impact my Overall Outstanding High School Academics Record.

When I arrived for the Chemistry Class the Day of the Dropout Deadline, to My Astonishment, the Chemistry Teacher had Posted on the Wall Beside the Blackboard a *Sunday Parade Magazine* Article by University of Illinois Chicago Professor Edwin W. Davis, My Father, Entitled "Persistence Pays," and Recommended That Everyone in the Class Read It.

As a Result, Throughout the Class that Morning, I agonized

Back and Forth about Whether or Not to Drop Out of Chemistry, which would be Very Embarrassing to Me Given My Father's Article.

Nevertheless, when the Bell Rang at the End of the Class, I Decided That it would be in My Best Long-Term Interest to Drop Out of Chemistry so as to Maintain my Strong Academic Record of Receiving Mostly A's and B's at Evanston Township High School.

However, I Never Told My Father or Mother what I had done that day. And Fortunately, the Semester Report Card which was Sent to My Parents Never Listed the Chemistry Course Which I Had Dropped.

9. Overwhelmed by Grand Canyon

During the Summer after My Junior Year in High School, My Parents Took My Sister, Brother, and Me on a Nice Driving Vacation to See Most of the Top Western National Parks.

The Last Park We Visited was the Grand Canyon in Arizona. However, when we Arrived There in Mid-July, the Temperature was 110 Degrees. While there are Nice Views from the Northern Rim of the Canyon into the Canyon, I wanted to Hike to the Colorado River at the Bottom of Grand Canyon. However, Due to the Extreme Heat, Neither my Sister, Brother nor Parents Wanted to Take a Long Hike, and the Horseback Trips Into the Canyon Had Been Cancelled that Day Due to the Heat.

Thus, I Set Out in the Morning by Myself with One Water Bottle, a Sandwich, a Camera, and a Hiking Stick.

While it was an Extremely Long Hike to the Colorado River, I wanted to Accomplish my Objective. My Hike Down the Very Steep Canyon was Fairly Easy, and I had a Big Smile on My Face when I Dipped my Feet into the Colorado River After a Hike of Three Hours.

However, Climbing Back Up the Steep Canyon in the Afternoon in Almost Record Heat was Awful. I Ran Out of Water Before I had Even Reached the Halfway Point Going Up. And My Hiking Pace Slowed Considerably Due to the Steep Trail and Heat Wave.

Fortunately, I did Finally Reach the Northern Rim of the Canyon at six thirty p.m. But I was in Terrible Condition, Suffering from Heat Stroke and Severe Dehydration.

When My Father Saw Me, He Realized the Seriousness of My Condition and Drove Me to the Emergency Room of the Nearest Hospital.

I Ended Up Spending Two and a Half Days in the Hospital and Did Not Fully Recover Until the End of Our Long Drive Back to Evanston, Illinois.

However, Much Later in Life, when I was Working as a Cargo Salesman for Exxon and Traveling Back from California, I Decided to Try to Tackle the Grand Canyon Again. Thus, I Booked a Flight from Los Angeles to an Airport that was Close to Grand Canyon.

But, in Mid-May, the Weather Conditions were much more Favorable for a Hike into the Canyon. While the Temperature at the Rim of the Canyon was a little below Freezing, and there was a Foot of Snow on the Ground at or Near the Canyon Floor, the Temperature was Spring-like, and the many Different Varieties of Cacti were in Full Bloom and Beautiful.

Also, I was much better equipped this time, with Lots of Water and Food and Two Hiking Sticks.

And, Using Better Judgment, I Decided to Turn Around when I could see the Colorado River Rather than Hiking Down Another Hour to the River Itself.

It was Still a Tough Hike Back Up to the Northern Rim. But this time, I was able to Fully Recover from the Strenuous Hike After Soaking in a Hot Tub for One Hour at the Nice Luxury Hotel on the Canyon Rim.

10. SHARON EVES AND BIG DADDY

My Girlfriend during my Junior and Senior Years at Evanston Township High School was Sharon Eves, who was a Year Younger Than Me.

She was Tall, Very Attractive, Had A Lot of Nice Friends, and Loved to Dance with Me.

She Lived in a Large Victorian-Style Red Brick Estate House Within a Short Walk From Downtown Evanston; a Good Movie Theatre; the YMCA, which had Juke Box Dances for Teenagers Every Friday Night; and Lake Michigan.

Sharon's Mother Died of Cancer when She Was Very Young, So Her Father Oversaw the Development of Sharon and Diane, Her Younger Sister, Along with Help from a Cook and a Maid.

Her Father Co-Owned a Successful Advertising Business in Chicago, Weighed 275 Pounds, and Looked Just Like and Had The Same, Overflowing Personality as Burl Ives. On Saturday Nights, He Stayed Up Late Watching Movies on TV and Eating Take-Out International Food from Many Different Countries. He Would Quite Often Invite Sharon and Me to Share Some of His Interesting International Food When We Returned from the Movies.

After I Went Off to the University of Michigan, and My Parents Moved to Chevy Chase, Maryland, Sharon and I would See Each Other Just a Few Times a Year by Her Visiting Me at Michigan or My Visiting Her When she was a Nursing Student in Chicago.

However, We Only Saw Each Other Once After Her Father Moved His Advertising Business and Residency to Texas.

Regarding Marriage, Sharon would have been Delighted to Marry Me. However, from a Financially Prudent Standpoint, I did not want to make any Marriage Commitments until I had Completed both Undergraduate and Graduate School and Obtained a Good-Paying Full-Time Job, which did not Occur Until Five Years After I had Graduated from High School.

And Fortunately, Sharon did Meet a Nice Man in Texas and Married Him During my Last Year in College.

11. THE KILLER IS LOOSE

*I*n the Summer just before my Junior Year in High School, My Father Took Our Family on a Nice Vacation Focused Primarily on Northern and Southern California.

In Los Angeles, an Old Friend of My Father at Paramount Pictures, who had become Executive Vice President of Public Affairs, Invited Our Family to Have Dinner and Spend the Night at His Malibu Estate.

After Dinner, He Invited My Sister and Me to either Have Lunch with the Stars at the Paramount Pictures Dining Room the Next Day or Be in a Movie as an Extra. My Sister, who wanted to be an Actress, Much to my Surprise, Chose to Have Lunch with the Stars. However, I Chose to be in a Movie as an Extra.

The Next Morning, I was driven to a Bank Site in a Los Angeles Suburb. I was told Together with a Group of a Dozen People, to Walk on the Sidewalk in Front of the Bank Looking Relaxed and Natural. But We Were Not Told What Was Going to Happen Inside or Outside the Bank.

What Then Happened Within Just a Few Seconds After They Started Filming the Scene Was We Heard a Shot from Inside the Bank and Immediately Thereafter Two Men Ran Out of the Front Door of the Bank, Carrying Large Money Bags, and Dashed to a Large, Black Cadillac that had just come to a Screeching Halt in

Front of the Bank. And the Two Men with the Money Bags Jumped into the Back Seat of the Cadillac as it was Starting to Speed Off.

I was very Frightened, Shocked, and Fearful of My Life, Thinking that this was a Real Bank Robbery Rather Than a Movie Scene.

Then After Our Group of Twelve Walk-ons had Recovered from this Terrifying Experience, We were told that we had just Participated in a Major Action Scene For a Movie called *The Killer Is Loose*.

And, much to the Walk-on Group's Surprise and Relief, we were told that They would Not Retry This Action Scene Again That Morning But Could Retry it Again on Another Day.

I then Asked the Casting Director If there were any Other Scenes that were being Filmed that Morning which were close to the Bank. And I was told that the Detective and His Girlfriend, whom were the Stars of the Movie along with the Killer of the Bank Teller, Were going to be in a Movie Scene Two Blocks Away which would be Filmed in Fifteen Minutes.

I Walked to the Scene Site, and much to my Bewilderment, the Serene and Simple Scene of the Detective (Joseph Cotten) and His Girlfriend (Rhonda Flemming) Crossing a Downtown Intersection while having a Conversation was Reshot Ten Times.

When Being Driven Back to Meet My Parents and Brother and Sister, I thought that the Complex and Fast-Breaking Bank Robbery Scene would Definitely Need to be Reshot Many Times. And Thus I Probably Had Little, if Any Chance of Being in the Movie. In Fact, I Never Mailed My Walk-on Payment Form to Paramount Pictures to Collect my Pay of Twenty-eight Dollars.

In February of 1956, *The Killer Is Loose* Opened at a Large Number of Theatres Nationwide.

I Took Sharon Eves, My Girlfriend, to See the Movie in Evanston, Illinois. However, I Never Told Her that I was Filmed for an Action Scene in the Movie Since I Never Felt that the Frist Attempt to Film the Complex Action Scene Would be Successful.

Unbelievably, There I was in the Opening Scene of the Movie, Looking Terrified, Frightened, and Scared in Front of the Bank When the Two Bank Robbers Ran with the Money Bags to the Black

Cadillac that had just Come to a Screeching Halt on the Street in Front of the Bank.

Anyway, so much for the Start and End of My Highly Successful Movie Career in a Film which became a Major Commercial Success.

12. COUNT BASIE AND JOE WILLIAMS AT BLUE NOTE

Starting in 8th Grade, I became Very Interested in Jazz Music and Purchased Lots of Records of the Big, Famous Jazz Bands.

Along with Bill Lindsey, who was a Neighborhood Friend of Mine, Starting in My Sophomore Year of High School, We Both Obtained the OK from Our Parents to Take the Train into Chicago and Go on a Weekend Evening to The Blue Note, which was a Famous Jazz Club, to Hear and See in Person Some of The Famous 1950s Big Jazz Bands.

The Blue Note had a Small Upstairs Gallery for Minors and would only Charge us Twelve Dollars to Enter the Club and Hear the First Session of One of the Great Jazz Bands while Sipping on a Tall Glass of Pink Lemonade.

I Particularly Liked the Count Basie Band, which included the famous Vocalists Ella Fitzgerald and Joe Williams.

Other Favorites of Mine were Duke Ellington, Benny Goodman, Maynard Ferguson, Dizzy Gillespie, and Louis Armstrong.

Incidentally, Bill Lindsey became a Very Successful Radio Music Disc Jockey in Minneapolis after Graduating from College.

13. I'm a Workaholic

After My Family Moved from Bethesda, Maryland, to Evanston, Illinois, at the Start of 7th Grade, I Lost My Good-Paying *Washington Evening Star* Paper Route Job.

However, I took on a Variety of Jobs that Not Only Matched but Exceeded My Paper Route Earnings.

During the Winter in 7th Grade, I Shoveled Snow for Some of Our Neighbors, Sold Christmas Cards Door-to-Door, and Delivered Western Union Telegrams from My Bicycle.

In the Following Spring, Summer, and Fall Months, I Mowed Lawns for some of Our Neighbors, Washed Cars, and Sold Vegetables Door-to-Door from My Father's Large Vegetable Garden.

Beginning in the Summer After My Eighth Grade School Year and Continuing for Four More Summers Until I Entered College, I Caddied at the Nearby Westmoreland Country Club.

I Would Arrive by Bicycle Early Every Morning, so that I would be in One of the First Five Foursomes to Play and thus be able to finish the Eighteen Holes of Being a Morning Caddie In Time to Obtain Another Caddying Job in the Early Afternoon.

I Caddied Six Days a Week since the Golf Course was Closed on Mondays for Maintenance. And, After the First 8th-Grade Summer When Club Rules Would Only Allow Me to Carry One Golf Bag, Due to My Young Age, I was Able to Carry Two Golf Bags at a Time.

As a Result, in my Last Four Summers, I Earned Between Eight and Nine Hundred Dollars a Summer. And, Even After Spending Some of My Earnings on Personal Expenses, I Had Saved Enough Money to Cover 100 percent of College Costs for One and a Half Years.

Due to My Father Obtaining a New Senior Administrative Job with the National Education Association in Washington, DC, at the Start of My Senior Year at Evanston Township High School, My Family Had to Move to Chevy Chase, Maryland.

However, I Felt that it Would Be Better for Me to Complete My Senior Year at the Outstanding Evanston Township High School and Maintain My Strong Grade Point Average so as to Be Accepted at a Top University, Rather Than Having to Adjust to a Totally New High School in Chevy Chase, Maryland.

Thus, I Obtained a Room in Mrs. Vernon W.H.T. Ewin's Estate House in a Lovely Section of Evanston in Return for My Cleaning Her Large House Once a Week. And My Parents Sent Me Monthly Checks to Cover My Food Costs and Other Personal Expenses.

14. A Large Public High School That Excels

I was Fortunate to be able to Attend Evanston Township High School, which had an Excellent Reputation in Terms of Leadership, Having an Outstanding Faculty, and Creating a Curriculum Focused on Preparing Students To Do Well in College.

While I was not an "All-A Student," I had Very Good Grades, Finished in the Top 18 percent of My Class, and Did Well on the Collage SAT Exams.

Thus, I was Accepted at All of the Top Universities that I Applied To, Including the University of Michigan, University of California Berkley, University of Pennsylvania (An Ivy School), and New York University.

Today, Evanston Township High School, Which has an Enrollment of 3,567 Students, is Ranked by US News and World Report as Being in the Top 2 percent of All Public High Schools in the US in Terms of Performance. Eighty-nine percent of the Teachers have Advanced Degrees. The Four-Year High School Graduation Rate is 91 percent. The Advanced Placement Course Participation Rate is 72 percent. And 80 percent of the Graduates Enroll in College. This Strong Performance is Despite Having a Minority Student Population of 55 percent and a Low-Income Family Student Population of 41 percent.

15. I'M AN EVANS SCHOLAR

As a Result of My Five Summers of Caddying Six Days a Week at the Westmoreland Country Club in Wilmette, Illinois, Except when I was on Vacation with My Parents, I was Awarded a Four-Year Evans Scholarship to Attend the University of Michigan, the University of My Choice, by the Western Golf Association.

The Caddie Scholarship Awards are based on High School Grades, Recommendations from Country Club Members where One Caddies, and Financial Need. The Scholarship Covered 100 percent of Out-of-State Tuition and Fees and Housing Costs.

The Evans Scholar Foundation was Founded in 1930 by Chick Evans of Chicago, who became the First US Golfer to Win Both the US Amateur and US Open Professional Championships in the Same Year.

When I was an Evans Scholar, the Evans Scholar Foundation Had Very Nice Scholar Houses that were just like a Fraternity House at Six Outstanding Midwestern Universities. The Evans Scholars Were All Men. At the University of Michigan Scholar House, fifty were from the State of Michigan, six from Illinois, and one from Wisconsin. As meals were not served at the Evans Scholar House, almost all of the Evans Scholars, including myself, had Meal Jobs at Fraternities or Sororities. This Required us to work Monday through Friday both at Lunchtime and Dinnertime in return for Excellent all-you-can-eat Free Meals. However, we had the weekends off.

The Evans Scholar Foundation has Grown A Lot since My University Days and has Maintained a Record of Exceptionally Strong Results.

In 2017/2018, there were 965 Scholars. Their Cumulative Grade Point Average was 3.3. The Four-Year Graduation Rate was 95 percent. And within Six Months of Graduation, 97 percent of the Scholars either Had a Full-Time Job or were Enrolled in Graduate School.

Also, there are now Scholar Houses at eleven Midwestern Universities, all of whom were Ranked by the US News and World Report in the Top 100 of the 300 Best National Universities.

In Addition, the Evans Scholar Foundation Decided to Begin to Expand Outside the Midwest and has Added Scholarship Houses at Universities in Six Other States. And, for the First Time, Scholarships are being Awarded to Female Caddies.

Importantly, in the Last Two Years, the Evans Scholar Foundation Asked Me to Help Get Them Established in Massachusetts. In May of this year, We Awarded Nineteen Four-Year Scholarships to Sixteen Male Caddies and Three Female Caddies, All of Whom Caddied at Country Clubs in Southeastern Massachusetts.

As College Costs have Skyrocketed at Three Times the Rate of Inflation since I went to College, and there is a Major Difference Between Out of State Versus In State Tuition and Fees, The Four-Year Value of the Scholarships that We Awarded Ranged from $155,000 to $255,000, with Northwestern Being the Highest and Illinois Being the Lowest.

16. COURSE SELECTION AT MICHIGAN

The University of Michigan is One of the Largest Universities in the US and Offered Several Thousand Different Undergraduate Courses when I Attended.

Thus, a Very Difficult Decision at the Start of Each Semester was to Decide which Courses to Sign Up For.

At the Start of My Freshman Year, I Decided that I wanted to Obtain a Broad Liberal Arts Education and then go to Graduate School for a Law or Business Degree.

My Father Suggested that it was Most Important to Be in the Courses Taught by the Top Professors in Terms of Academic Prestige and Teaching Ability. Thus, He Recommended that Starting with the Second Semester of My Freshman Year that I Meet Beforehand with the Vice President and Dean of Faculty to Obtain his Input on the Very Best Professors Regardless of What Courses They Taught.

I Followed My Father's Recommendation, and Much to My Surprise, the Vice President and Dean of Faculty Agreed to Meet with Me just Before the Second Semester of My Freshman Year and Many Times Again Before the Semesters of My Sophomore, Junior, and Senior Years.

As a result of the Dean's Input, I Became Exposed to Many of the Great Academic Minds, who were also Captivating Speakers, and Also Received a Very Broad Liberal Arts Education.

Just Before the Last Semester of My Senior Year, One of the

Dean of Faculty's Recommendations was to try to get into Professor Paul McCracken's Course on Business Cycles, since he was a Long-Time Member of the US Presidents Council of Economic Advisors. However, Due to All of the Time that McCracken had to Spend in Washington, DC, He was only able to Teach One Course that Semester on Business Cycles Limited to PhD Students in Business. While I thought that I had a very Low Chance of Being Accepted Into His Class of PhD Students, I was still able to Arrange a Meeting with Professor McCracken. And, Much to My Surprise, He Let Me Into His Course. And I was Overwhelmed when I Received a Final Grade of B+.

Another Major Side Benefit of My Meetings Each Semester with the Dean of Faculty was that I was Appointed by the President's Office to be on the University of Michigan Student Government Council My Junior and Senior Years, which is One of the Most Prestigious Extra Curricular Activities at the University. While Fifteen Members are Elected by the Students, Two are Selected by the President's Office.

17. GRINDING AWAY

At the University of Michigan, I wanted to Obtain Very Good Grades while also Participating in a Number of Student Activities.

In My Freshman Year, I Worked at the *Michigan Daily* Newspaper Selling Advertisements. In Addition to Being on the Student Government Council, I was Active in Intramural Sports all Four Years, was Treasurer of the Evans Scholar House My Junior and Senior Years, and Worked for a Professor for One Year, Doing Research for an Update of his Textbook.

And Despite All of the Above Activities, I Always Went to the Library Between Classes, and After Completing my Meal Job at Night, Studied Most Weeknights and Sunday Nights Until Midnight.

Thus, I was able to Graduate in the Top 18 percent of My Very Smart and Competitive Classmates.

18. Exposure to Jack and Bobby Kennedy

*D*uring My Senior Year of High School at the Start of the Christmas School Break, My Father, who was a Senior Lobbyist at the National Education Foundation in Washington, DC, said that he wanted to Take Me to the US Senate and Introduce Me to Two Men who were not then National Leaders but who would both likely Become National Leaders in the Near Future.

Thus, He Took me early on Monday Morning to the US Senate Building and Introduced Me to Senator John F. Kennedy and Bobby, His Brother. Jack was the Chairman of the Senate Labor Committee and was just Starting a Hearing to Investigate Jimmy Hoffa's Activities as President of the National Teamsters Union. And Bobby was Special Council for the Labor Committee.

I Quickly Became Fascinated with Both Jack and Bobby and Sat Through the Whole Day of the Hearing on Monday and Returned for the Next Four Days until the Hearing was Completed. In Fact, the Five Full Days in the Same Senate Conference Room with Jack and Bobby is still Vivid in My Mind.

Then, Four Years Later, when I was a Senior at the University of Michigan and on the Student Government Council, and Jack was Campaigning to be President, I Invited Jack, via His Campaign Staff, to Give a Speech at the University of Michigan.

I Finally Received with only Three Days' Notice His Planned Visit just Three and a Half Weeks Before the Election and was Told to Have a Very Large Crowd of Students on Hand since Jack Planned to Announce a Major New Initiative Involving Graduating Students that He Would Implement if Elected and which He had Never Talked About Before.

I Arranged for Jack to Speak on a Large Outdoor Platform on the Third Floor of the Student Union. And with the Help of the *Michigan Daily*, His Visit was Highly Publicized.

And, as it turned out, Four Thousand to Five Thousand Students Showed Up. However, as Ann Arbor was the Last Stop That Day of Three State Campaign Visits, Jack Showed Up Three Hours After His Scheduled Appearance at Ten p.m.

Jack Apologized to the Crowd for being so late and was Visibly Overwhelmed by the Huge Turnout Late at Night. To Put the Students in a Good Mood, He Told Them that he had always wanted to Visit Ann Arbor because Harvard University, where He Graduated, is Proudly Known as "The Michigan of the East."

Jack then Announced for the First Time His Plans to Start Up the Peace Corps and Asked for a Show of Hands of the Students Willing to Join the Peace Corps When They Graduated.

After his Inspirational Talk on the Peace Corps, an Exhausted JFK Asked Me if he could Spend the Night at the Michigan Union. And Fortunately, I was able to Arrange for a Good Room even though all but One of the Staff at the Michigan Union's Two Floors of Overnight Rooms had Departed.

In the Next Few Days, We Collected Over Five Hundred Signatures of Students Interested in Serving on the Peace Corps and Sent Them to JFK's Campaign Staff.

Within a Week of Jack's Visit, Several Campus Clothing Stores had Designed, Produced, and Started to Sell T-Shirts and Sweatshirts in the Harvard Crimson Colors Emblazed with "Harvard University, the Michigan of the East." These T-Shirts and Sweatshirts are still Sold on Campus Today.

Also, Currently, at the Start of the First Day of a Two-Week

Orientation Program in Washington DC, for New Peace Corps Members, they are Shown a Film of JFK Announcing His Peace Corps Initiative on the Balcony of the University of Michigan Student Union.

19. Encyclopedia Britannica's Top Summer Salesman

My First Summer Job After Starting College was to Sell Collier Encyclopedias on a Door-to-Door Basis. I did OK in Terms of Sales. But My Territory of Southern Illinois was a Terrible Strain on Me as I had to Drive There in the Afternoon from Chicago and Most often would not get back to Chicago Until After Midnight.

However, in the Next Two Summers, I Landed a Much Better Job Selling the Very Prestigious Encyclopedia Britannicas in Washington, DC, which was in Close Proximity to My Parents Home in Chevy Chase, Maryland.

I would arrive at the Encyclopedia Britannica's Nice Division Headquarters on Connecticut Avenue in Northern Washington, DC, at ten thirty a.m. Every Weekday Morning for a Sales Meeting. At the End of the Meeting, I would be Given Telephone Company Green Sheets that Contained the Names, Addresses, and Phone Numbers of Residents Living in My Assigned Washington DC, Sales Territory. I would then call A Lot of Households from the Encyclopedia Britannica Office so as to Obtain Enough Meeting Appointments in the Late Afternoon or Early Evening After Dinner to Fill Up All of My Sales Time for that day.

I ended up doing Extremely Well and Averaged One Sale a Day for My Monday–Friday and Saturday Work Schedule. The Sales Price was $375, which included a Twenty-four-Volume Set of the

Encyclopedia Britannicas, a Nice Wooden Bookcase, and Annual One Volume Updates for Three Years. The Buyer Could Pay the $375 Up Front or Over Twenty-four Months with a Downpayment of Seventy-five Dollars, Plus a Moderate Interest Charge.

My Sales Commission was Fifty-five Dollars Per Sale. However, I also had Expenses for Lunches Near the Division's Sales Office, Car Costs, and Dry-Cleaning Charges for Suits and Dress Shirts.

Since the Hot Summer Season was the Worst of Encyclopedia Britannica's Sales Seasons, They had a Sales Contest Each Summer which Awarded the Top Salesman for Each Division a Very Nice, All-Expenses-Paid Trip to Mexico for Seven Days for the Salesman and His Wife.

I was the Top Salesman that Summer for the Washington, DC; Maryland; and Virginia Division. And I still remember the Trip to Mexico, which was First Class in all Respects and Hosted by Three Senior Executives From Encyclopedia Britannica.

The Next Summer, I was Not the Top Salesman for My Division but still Received a Thousand-Dollar Bonus for Being One of the Five Top Summer Salesmen in My Division.

Apart from the Very Good Money that I Earned Selling Encyclopedia Britannicas, By Far the Biggest Benefit was that I Learned How to Be an Outstanding Salesman and Know When and How to Close a Sale, which was Extremely Helpful to Me During My Future Business Career.

20. LAW SCHOOL OR GRADUATE BUSINESS SCHOOL

*E*arly in the Second Semester of My Senior Year at Michigan, I Decided to Apply to Law School. And I was Accepted at Four Top Law Schools (i.e. Michigan, Virginia, Pennsylvania, and New York University).

However, In April, I began to Question Whether I Wanted to be in Law School for Three Years Compared to About One Year if I Enrolled in a Graduate Business School for a Master's Degree.

Thus, I Applied to a Number of Top Business Schools that Offered MBA Degrees and was Fortunate to be Accepted to Harvard, Wharton, Northwestern, and New York University.

Harvard was Very Tempting. However, They Required that I Work for One Year Before Enrolling Since I was only Twenty-two Compared to an Average Age of Twenty-eight for their MBA Students. And They Would Not Give Me Any Course Credits for the Economic and Business Courses that I Took at Michigan. And Thus, It would Take Me a Full Two Years to Obtain Their MBA Degree.

Thus, I Decided to Enroll in Northwestern's MBA Program, which was Rated as one of the Top Six Graduate Business Schools. While Their MBA Program was Also Two Years, By Taking Two Extra Classes for Each of Their Three Tri-Semesters, and with Course Credits for the Economic and Business Courses that I Took at Michigan, I would be able to Graduate with an MBA Degree in One Year Plus a Summer School.

Also, Northwestern Provided Me with a Continental Grain Merit Scholarship, which Covered My Tuition and Room Costs at Abbott Hall.

21. Chicago Date with Mafia Boss's Daughter

At Northwestern, Since I was Taking Two Additional Courses Each Tri-Semester, it was basically an All-Work-and-No-Play Experience.

Virtually Every Night, along with Saturdays and Sundays, I Studied at Northwestern's Very Quiet Law Library, which was Located along with the Graduate Business, Medical, and Dental Schools at Northwestern's Chicago Campus Near Lake Michigan and Just North of the Downtown Area.

Thus, I only Remember One Exception to My All-Work-and-No-Play Life at Northwestern's Graduate Business School.

At the Law Library, I Became Well Acquainted with a Law Student who First Invited Me to Have Thanksgiving Dinner at His Parents Nearby High-Rise Luxury Apartment Building Opposite Lake Michigan in the Gold Coast Area of Chicago.

The Law School Student Subsequently Invited Me to Join Him for a Saturday Night on the Town and said he would Fix Me Up with a Friend of His Girlfriend.

I Met My Law School Friend and His Girlfriend at his Parents' Apartment, and he Drove Me in His Parents' Car to Pick Up My Date.

We Arrived at My Date's Residence, in Chicago, Near the Ice Hockey Stadium, which was almost the size of an Entire City Square

Block and was Behind a Twenty-Foot High and Very Thick Stone Wall. Rather Than Trying to Enter the Residence Past a Very Large and Strong Driveway Security Gate, My Law School Friend Rang a Bell Outside the Gate.

And My Date Arrived After Ten Minutes on the Other Side of the Gate in an Armored Security Vehicle. Then I Quietly Asked my Law School Friend about the Background of My Date's Parents and was Told that Her Father was the Boss of a Large and Powerful Chicago Mafia Family. And, There were a Half-Dozen Lions Roaming the Grounds Between the Estate House and the Stone Walls.

After Overcoming the Shock of whom I was Dating that Night, we went to the Headquarters of the Playboy Club and Later to the Gaslight Club and Had a Wonderful Time.

However, After Driving Back to the Outside Security Gate of My Very Attractive Date's Estate Residence, I was Afraid to Even Give her a Quick Peck Kiss on Her Cheek when I said Goodnight.

And I Was Afraid to Ever Date Her Again.

22. COLLECTING JOB OFFERS

*D*espite Having a Big Course Overload at Northwestern, I was able to Graduate in the Top 18 percent of My Very Strong MBA Class.

Northwestern Had an Excellent Program for Helping Students Obtain Good Full-Time Jobs with Excellent Companies. It was Headed Up by a Retired CEO From a Major Company and a Young, Hard-Working Assistant.

They Invited Top Companies from Coast to Coast to Come to Campus to Interview Graduating Students. The Companies would first be Asked to Send a One-Page Description of the Type of Jobs that They were Seeking to Fill and a One-Page Description of the Company along with Their First, Second, and Third Choices for Interview Dates.

Graduating Students would Read the Job and Company Descriptions and, If Interested in Being Interviewed, would Write Their Name on the Sign-Up Sheet and Provide Their Resume to the Campus Job Placement Office.

The Campus Job Placement Office would Send to the Company One Week Before Their Interview Date the Names and Resumes of the Graduating Students that They would be Interviewing.

As a Finance Major, I Decided to Focus on Arranging for Interviews with Large International Companies that Had Openings for Financial Analyst Jobs and Wall Street Firms, Mutual Funds, and Banks that Had Openings for Security Analyst Jobs.

I Spent A Lot of Time Reading the Materials Posted on the Descriptions of the Companies and the Types of Jobs They were Seeking to Fill.

I Signed Up for Thirty-Minute Interviews with Twenty-five Companies. And, I was Invited to Visit the Headquarters of Seventeen Companies for a Full Day of In-Depth Interviews, with All of My Travel Expenses Paid for By the Companies.

Before Making Any Visits, I Made a Very Wise Decision to Borrow One Thousand Dollars from the Northwestern Business School and then went to Brooks Brothers in Chicago and Purchased Two Business Suits, Several Nice Dress Shirts and Ties, a Pair of Business Shoes, and a Light Spring Outer Coat.

I Ended Up Making Fifteen Full-Day Visits to Companies, Banks, and Wall Street Firms in Chicago, Minneapolis, Detroit, Cleveland, and New York City and Received a Dozen Offers.

Most Importantly, What Impressed the Company Interviewers the Most was that, Based on My Work Experiences Starting with the *Washington Evening Post* Delivery Job in 4th Grade and Continuing with Five Years of Caddying at the Westmoreland Country Club and My Two Successful Summers Selling Encyclopedia Britannicas, I was a "Hard Worker and was Highly Motivated to Make Money." And Thus, I would be an Ideal Employee for Their Business.

23. Standard Oil Company of New Jersey in Rockefeller Plaza

*N*ear the End of May, It was a Very Difficult Job Acceptance Decision for Me to Make Between One of the World's Largest Mutual Fund Companies Based in Minneapolis, General Mills in Minneapolis; the Northern Trust Investment Bank in Chicago; and The Standard Oil Company of New Jersey based at 30 Rockefeller Center in New York City.

Also Influencing My Decision was the Location of the Four Companies. And as I had Fallen in Love with Manhattan after Spending a Full Week There being Interviewed by Five Companies, I Decided to Accept a Position with the Standard Oil Company of New Jersey, which later changed its name to Exxon, as a Financial Analyst in Their Controller's Department.

I was Initially Put Through a Fifteen-Month Training Program, Spending Three Months in Each of Five Controllers' Department Divisions. I Worked on Special Projects in the Financial Forecasting, Capital Budgets, Accounts Payable, Accounts Receivable, and General Accounting Divisions.

After the Initial Fifteen-Month Rotational Training Assignment, I was Assigned to the Financial Forecasting Division as a Financial Reporting Analyst.

24. CHURCHES WERE VERY IMPORTANT TO ME

My Father was Episcopalian and My Mother was Southern Baptist. Growing Up, My Parents Alternated Each Year Between Attending Services at an Episcopal Church or a Presbyterian Church.

During My Elementary School Years, I Attended Sunday School at Bethesda Presbyterian Church, Where I First Learned to Memorize The Lord's Prayer.

In My Middle and High School Years, Rather than Attend the Churches My Parents Attended, My Sister and I went to Sunday School at the American Bible Church, a Fundamentalist Church which was located in an Elementary School that was Close To Our Parents' House in Evanston, Illinois.

At The University of Michigan, I Attended the Main Services at a Wide Variety of Churches that Included a Congregational, Lutheran, Catholic, and Episcopal Church.

When I Went Home During College Breaks to My Parents House in Chevy Chase, Maryland, I Attended Services at The Church of Our Savior, which was located in a Brownstone House in the Dupont Circle Area of Washington, DC. The Minister at this Church had an Intellectual Mind and was a Captivating Speaker. And, to Become a Member of this Church, One Had to First Attend Bible Study Classes at the Church for Two Years.

For Christmas Services, Our Entire Family Attended the Wonderful Christmas Eve Services at the Episcopalian Washington National Cathedral in Washington, DC.

While at Northwestern, I First Attended a Service at the Fourth Presbyterian Church on Michigan Avenue Just North of Chicago's Financial District. Elam Davies, the Head Pastor at the Fourth Presbyterian Church, which had a Membership of about 5,400, was Very Inspirational; Served There For Twenty-three Years; and Was Included In *Time Magazine*'s List of Seven Star Preachers in America and Other Lists Of the Top Ten Preachers in America. After My First Visit, I Attended the Main Service at Fourth Presbyterian Every Sunday During My Full Year at Northwestern's Graduate School of Business and Never Went to Another Church.

Last, But Not Least, I Attended and Participated in Two Billy Graham Rallies at a Large Professional Baseball and Football Stadium in Washington, DC, and One Billy Graham Rally at a Sports Stadium in Chicago.

25. FIRST APARTMENT ON 61ST STREET AND PARK AVENUE

When Moving to Manhattan to Start My First Full-Time Job with Standard Oil Company of New Jersey, since I did not know Anything about the Wide Variety of Residential Neighborhoods in the Huge Island of Manhattan, My Father Advised Me to First Stay at the Old, Famous West Side YMCA on West 63rd Street for Several Months while I Scouted Out Various Residential Areas for a Nice Place to Live.

That was Wonderful Advice. And I Located a Nice Apartment in a Residential Area on East 61st Street just One Building East of Park Avenue in a Historically Attractive Nineteenth-Century Brownstone Owned by a Lady from Argentina.

I Rented on a Month-to-Month Basis a Walkup Apartment on the Fourth Floor of the Five-Story Brownstone with a Living Room and Dining Area, a Bedroom, a Small Kitchen, a Bathroom, and Windows Looking Out Onto East 61st Street.

Importantly, This Location was only Thirteen Blocks From Standard Oil's Two Headquarters Office Buildings in Rockefeller Center.

26. My Fair Lady

After My First Workday, I returned to my New Apartment and Stood for a While on a Small Outdoor Balcony on the Second Floor of the Brownstone Building and Watched the World Go By on East 61st Street.

After About Thirty Minutes of Eye-Gazing, I noticed a Beautiful, Tall Brunette Lady in a Gucci Dress Pass By, who Looked Just like Jackie Kennedy. I Gazed at Her Until She Reached Lexington Avenue and Turned Left Out of My Sight.

And, Lo and Behold, the Next Weekend when I was doing My Laundry in the Basement of the Brownstone, She showed up with Her Laundry. Thus, I Started Up a Conversation with Emily Adee and Found Out that She Lived on the Third Floor of the Same Brownstone as Me and Shared an Apartment with Ingrid, a Medical Research Assistant from Denmark, and Barbara Livingston, who had a PhD in Art History and Lectured on Art History at the Metropolitan Museum of Art.

I did not see Emily again for several weeks, but I ran into Barbara Livingston and Asked Barbara Out for a Dinner Date, which went just so-so. A Week Later, I ran into Emily and Asked Her Out to see a Movie. Our First Date went Extremely Well.

And we subsequently Established a Bond of Mutual Interests such as Going to Foreign Restaurants, Seeing European Avant-Garde Movies,; Walking in Central Park, Attending Off-Broadway Plays, and Enjoying Parties.

27. Penthouse on Central Park West

I Discovered Very Quickly that My Monthly Payments for Renting an Apartment in the Exclusive Area of 61st Street and Park Avenue were Eating Up One-Third of My Monthly Take-Home Pay From Standard Oil of New Jersey.

Thus, I began to Look at Other Apartments that were being Advertised for Rent in Manhattan.

An Ad that Caught My Eye was a Penthouse Apartment on 24 West 69th Street.

After I Contacted the Real Estate Listing Agent, I Found Out that an Executive Vice President from McCann Erickson, a Large International Advertising Agency, had Just Lost His Job and Was Seeking to Save Money by Subletting his Very Large Penthouse Apartment to Two Individuals. He had Lined Up One Male and was Seeking to Line Up a Second Male to Maximize his Sublet Income.

When I Frist Saw the Penthouse Apartment on the 12th Floor of a World War I Building, I was Overwhelmed.

It had Two Large Terraces with Views of Central Park and the Midtown Manhattan Skyline. There was a Separate Living Room and Dining Room and an Entrance Hall, all with Parquet Floors. It also had Two Separate Bedrooms and Bathrooms and a Large Kitchen. And Every Major Room had an Antique French Phone and Piped-In Music.

Thus, I sublet the Penthouse Apartment for Half of the Monthly Rent.

The Other Subletter was Tom Adair, a Principal Soloist Ballet Dancer with the American Ballet Theater who had previously been with the Ballet Rousse de Monte Carlo. He had been a Star Football Halfback for the Texas Longhorns, whose Coach Got Him to Take Ballet Lessons during the Off Season to Improve his Dexterity and Coordination. He was also Related to Red Adair, who Started Up a Very Successful Company to Help US and Foreign Oil Companies Extinguish Terrible Fires at Their Crude and Natural Gas Fields.

Tom Adair was Six Feet, Three Inches, Always Dressed in a Business Suit, Had a Girlfriend from the Ballet Company, and Did Not Seem Anything like Other Male Ballet Dancers. Thus, He Only was Given Very Masculine Dancing Roles.

After Subleasing the Penthouse Apartment, I Found Out that it was the Penthouse Apartment Used in the Filming of *The Apartment* Movie in 1960 which Won Five Oscars and Starred Jack Lemmon and Shirley MacLane.

28. HELD UP AT GUNPOINT

After Moving into My New Penthouse Apartment, I soon Discovered One Major Downside of Living in the Westside of Upper Manhattan.

And that was "Personal Safety."

Late at Night After Attending a Party, as I was Walking to My Penthouse Apartment Building, a Big Man wearing a Nice Winter Overcoat Walked Towards Me with His Right Hand in the Side Pocket of His Overcoat, and he Appeared to Be Holding a Revolver. He Stepped Directly in Front of Me and Asked for My Wallet.

Having had One Too Many Drinks at the Party, I Reached into My Pants Pocket and Instead of Taking Out My Wallet, I Took Hold of My Comb and Threw it High Into the Air. When the Man Looked Up to see what I was Throwing into the Air, I Quickly Dashed Between Two Parked Cars. As the Man Started Swearing, I Ran Down the Street While Ducking My Head so that the Cars Would Shield Me from Any Bullets.

On Another Very Cold Winter Night, the Doorbell of My Penthouse Apartment Rang at nine p.m. As this is an Odd Time for a Visitor, without Opening the Door, I looked through the Peephole and Saw a Muscular Man wearing only a Summer Short-Sleeved Shirt and Cargo Shorts who was Holding onto a Gym Bag with the End of a Rope Protruding from the Bag. Without opening the Door, I Asked the Man What He Wanted. He Replied that he was Soliciting

Cash Donations to Support the Firemen's Annual Christmas Party. I Yelled at the Man to Leave as I was Going to Call the Police. He then Ran Down the Hallway Stairs and Disappeared.

Also, I was Informed by the Owner of the Liquor Store at the Other End of My West 69th Street Block that He Had Decided to Close His Store at six p.m. Every Night Rather than Stay Open Until nine p.m. as He Had Been Held Up Ten Times in the Last Six Months.

Finally, What Led Me to Decide to Relocate to a Safer Area of Manhattan was that a Young Man who was living in an Apartment Across the Street From My Building was Robbed, Shot, and Killed One Weekday Morning at seven a.m. as He Was Walking Out of His Building To Go To Work.

29. GETTING MARRIED

*E*mily and I Stopped Dating During the Winter Months, Although I Helped Her Obtain a Job as a Computer Programmer at Standard Oil of New Jersey as she was Dissatisfied with Her Secretarial Job at IBM.

Early in the Spring, Emily and I Started Dating Again.

Late in the Spring, We Went on a Hiking Trop to Bear Mountain in Upstate New York which was a Two-Hour Bus Ride from Manhattan. And After Returning to Manhattan that Evening, We Really Jelled Together for the First Time. This In Turn Led to Getting Together Virtually Every Night After Work, Doing Lots of Interesting Things on the Weekends in Manhattan, and Taking One-Day Trips Outside of New York City.

In short, We Became Engaged on a Weekend Trip to New London, Connecticut, to Stay with Mrs. Kasem-beg, who was Emily's Very Interesting Russian Professor at Connecticut College.

And, Lo and Behold, We Were Married in the Late Fall in Sands Point, Long Island, where Emily's Mother Lived. Her Mother was Shopping Editor for *Town and Country Magazine* in Manhattan. Her Father was a Corporate Lawyer for IBM, but died of a Heart Attack when Emily was in High School, and Genevieve, Emily's Sister, was Six Years Younger Than Emily.

At the Wedding, Three of My Groomsmen were My Best Friends From Evanston Township High School, The Evans Scholar House at the University of Michigan, and Northwestern University's Graduate School of Business. My Fourth Groomsmen was Don Davis, My Brother, who was Eight Years Younger Than Me.

We Mutually Decided that Rather than Take a Short One-Week Honeymoon, We Would Postpone Our Wedding Trip and Take a Three-Week European Trip the Following Summer to France, Italy, Switzerland, and Germany.

And the Night After Our Nice Church Wedding and Party, We Moved for the First Time into a Lovely Gramercy Park Apartment with a Nice View of the Park and the Lovely, Old, Historic Brownstones Surrounding the Park. We Had Just Partially Furnished the Apartment with a Few Nice Pieces from Emily's Mother and a Few Purchases by Ourselves.

30. Avant-Garde Life in Manhattan

*I*n Manhattan, For the First Time in My Life, I Experienced A Lot of Avant-Garde Activities.

I went to see all of the Movies Directed by Ingmar Bergman of Sweden, Federico Fellini of Italy, Harold Pinter of England, and Roman Polanski of Poland.

I Attended Many Off-Broadway and Off-Off-Broadway Plays in Greenwich Village, but went to see only a Few Broadway Plays and Musicals.

I Enjoyed Hanging Out at Coffee Houses on the Weekends in Greenwich Village; Eating at Italian, French, Spanish, and Russian Restaurants; and Having an Ale with Limburger Cheese at McSorley's Tavern on The Lower East Side, which was the Oldest Tavern in Manhattan.

My Favorite Museums Were the Metropolitan Museum Of Art, Frick, Guggenheim, American Museum Of Natural History, and Cloisters in Upper Manhattan Overlooking The Hudson River.

One Could Encounter Me Playing Chess in Washington Square Park in Greenwich Village or Attending Wednesday Amateur Night Performances at the Apollo Theatre in Harlem.

I also Relished Seeing Rudolph Nureyev's and Margot Fonteyn's Wonderful Ballet Performances when the Royal Ballet was Performing at Lincoln Center and Hearing Joan Sutherland's Beautiful Soprano Voice at the Metropolitan Opera House.

31. SECOND-ACTING ON BROADWAY

Stan Summers, a Church Friend of Mine, Got Me to Try Out Second-Acting on Broadway.

This Involved Hanging Out at a Bar Across the Street from a Broadway Theatre that was Having a Play which was Sold Out. At the Break Between the First and Second Acts, Attendees would Pour Out onto the Sidewalk and Street. We would then Enter the Theatre with the Large Crowd Just Before the Start of the Second Act Without Any Theatre Attendants Asking for Tickets.

We would Stand at the Back of the Theatre Until the Curtain was Opened for the Start of the Second Act. We would then Look Around the First Floor of the Theatre Until We Spotted Two Empty Seats Together. We would then Dash Down the Aisle and Sit in the Two Empty Seats that had been Vacated by Two Ticket Holders, Probably due to Illness or Not Liking the Play.

This Worked Out Twice for Us. However, on the Third Try, After we had Sat Down Together in Two Empty Seats, the Two Ticket Holders Arrived about Five Minutes After the Start of the Second Act. And we had to Quickly Leave, Looking Embarrassed that we had been Sitting Without Tickets in Someone Else's Seats.

Thus, I Never Tried Second-Acting Again!

32. Huge Oil Deal with Nelson Bunker Hunt

At Standard Oil of New Jersey, I Frist Worked in all Five Divisions of the Controller's Department, Including Being Group Head of the Financial Forecasting Section.

I was then Transferred to the Market Planning Unit of Standard Oil's International Division and After Two Years Became a Junior Sales Representative and then a Senior Sales Representative in I Cargo Sales Department.

I was Responsible for Sales of Tanker Loads of Standard Oil's Foreign Crude Oil, for which it had a Surplus Above its own Refining Needs, to Large US Companies Located West of the Mississippi, Including Chicago.

I Discovered By Myself that I could also Generate Profits for Standard Oil not just by Selling Standard Oil's Crude Oil to Other Companies for Their Refineries, but by Purchasing Light, Low-Sulfur Crude Oil From Other Companies, since Standard Oil had a Surplus of High-Sulfur Heavy-Crude Oil from the Persian Gulf, but Not Enough Light, Low-Sulfur Crude Oil to Refine so as to meet the Accelerating Market Demand For Mogas, Jet Fuel, and Low-Sulfur Fuel Oil in the European Market.

As Hunt Oil in Dallas, Texas, was in My Territory, and They had a Surplus of Light, Low-Sulfur Crude Oil from Libya Above

Their Own Refinery Requirements, I Approached Them About Purchasing Some of Their Libyan Crude Oil.

Hunt Oil's Libyan Crude Oil Exploration and Production Company was Owned by Nelson Bunker Hunt, who was one of the Three Sons of the Famous H.L. Hunt, who Won in a Poker Game the Exploration Rights to what became One of the World's Largest Oil Fields in East Texas.

My Dealings with Nelson Bunker Hunt soon became a Family Affair as H.L. Hunt and His Three Sons all had Offices Next to Each Other on the Top Floor of a Dallas Office Building, And They All Consulted with One Another Before Making Major Business Decisions.

H.L. Hunt Focused Primarily on Exploring and Producing Crude Oil in the US and in Trying to Influence American Politics in an Ultra-Conservative Direction. Lamar Hunt Acquired the Kansas City Chiefs Profession Football Team and Founded the American Football League. He also Owned a Professional Basketball Team and a Professional Soccer Team. Herbert Hunt Built a US Refining and Marketing Company from Scratch. And Nelson Bunker Hunt Concentrated on Acquiring Oil Exploration Concessions in North Africa on the North Sea and on Trying to Establish a Monopoly Position in the World's Silver Market.

After a Year of Negotiations, I Concluded a Huge Contract with Nelson Bunker Hunt to Acquire Two Hundred Thousand Barrels a Day of His Light, Low-Sulfur Libyan Crude Oil for Three Years. The Total Purchase was Equivalent to 9.2 Billion Gallons of Crude Oil.

33. Gored in Amazon

At Standard Oil of New Jersey, Which Later Changed its Name to Exxon, I Liked to Take Adventuress Vacations Outside the US After One Year. I was Entitled to Three Weeks of Vacation and to Four Weeks After Five Years of Service.

On One of My Trips, Emily and I Went Down the Amazon River, Starting Near Its Source in a Dugout Canoe Made from a Tree Trunk. And After Some Arduous Travel Days, we switched to a Small, Motorized Boat with Screens that could be Attached to its Sides as we had to Travel Through a Hostile Native Territory where the Natives were known to use Blow Guns to Shoot Poisonous Darts at People. Fortunately, we had no Encounters with Hostile Natives.

In Columbia's Only Tiny Port on the Amazon, We Stayed for Several Days at a Hunting Camp in a Primitive Native Farming and Hunting Area.

While Taking a Trail Hike One Day, We Encountered a Boa Constrictor which was Twenty-five Feet Long. On Another Day's Hike, while Starting to Cross a Deep Creek on a Large Fallen Tree Trunk, a Native Shouted at Us that the Creek was Full of Man-Eating Piranhas. I then Stopped My Crossing Immediately, Dropped to My Hands and Knees on the Tree Trunk, and Crawled Back to where I Started.

On Another Days Hike By Myself, a Motorboat gave me a Ride Across a Tributary of the Amazon to the Other Side so that I could continue My Hike. However, when Returning to the Tributary River Late in the Afternoon, there was no Motorboat in Sight.

I then saw a Thatched Roof Hut Near the Water. I Peeked in the Entrance to the Hut and saw a Beautiful, Young Native Girl. I tried to Explain to Her that I Needed a Canoe Ride Back Across the Tributary River. However, she spoke No English. Then I Diagrammed in the Dirt in Front of Her Hut that I needed a Canoe Ride Back Across the Tributary River to the Other Side. Without Saying Anything, she Led Me to the Riverbank where she had a Canoe Hidden in the Reeds and Paddled Me Back to the Other Side of the Tributary River.

On the Last Day, Emily and I Rented Motor Bikes to Take a Long Trip on a Dirt Road. When coming back from our Trip, while we were Biking Up a Steep Hill, Several Natives Appeared at the Top of the Hill Road and were Driving a Large Herd of Male Cattle with Long Curved Horns Down the Hill Road.

One of the Bulls at the Front of the Herd Charged Toward Me. I then Quickly Drove My Motorbike to the Edge of the Road and Tried to Hop Off the Motorbike on to a Hilly Bank Away from the Bull. However, It Caught the Lower Part of My Right Leg with its Horn. The Result was I was Bleeding Profusely, and the Motorbike was Badly Damaged.

Fortunately, a Small Truck Came By Shortly and Took us and the Motorbikes Back to where we had Rented the Bikes and Near Where we were Staying. While I was Expecting to have to Pay a lot of Money to Repair the Badly Damaged Motorbike, the Owner of the Bike Rental Place Told Me that he had Insurance that Would Cover the Repair Costs.

34. Narrow Escape at Rio Soccer Match

As part of a Three-Week South American Vacation, Emily and I Spent a Week in Rio de Janeiro Flanked by Beautiful Hills, Islands, and Ipanema Beach.

On a Sunday Afternoon, We Attended a Soccer Match Between the National Teams of Brazil and Argentina.

With Only Three Seconds to Play, Argentina Scored a Goal to Break a Tie. Having Known About Violent Reactions by the Fans at Soccer Matches in Europe and South America, I Instantly Realized the Potential for a Clash Between the Brazilian Fans in the Stands on Our Side of the Field and the Argentina Fans on the Other Side of the Field.

Thus, I Immediately Took Emily's Hand and Told her to Run with Me to the Nearest Exit.

A Fight Quickly Broke Out Between the Two Teams on the Field, And the Brazilian and Argentina Fans on Both Sides of the Field Started Racing Down the Aisles to Get to the Field.

Emily and I Made It Out Just in Time as we Subsequently Learned that Twenty-six Brazilian Fans were killed and Over Two Hundred Injured in the Stampedes and Fighting Between the Brazilian and Argentina Fans.

35. Entering Church To "Take the A Train"

As I Like Going to Church and Learned About Many Interesting and Different Church Services in Manhattan, I would Quite Often Attend Two Services on Sundays.

Firstly, I would almost Always Go to the Madison Avenue Presbyterian Church on Madison Avenue and 73rd Street to Hear the Captivating Sermons Packed with the Life Experiences of David Read, Their Scottish Preacher who also had a Weekly TV Show. He had Served as a Military Chaplain for the British in World War II and was Taken Prisoner by the Germans Early in the War and Spent Five Years in a Prisoner of War Camp.

Regarding Other Churches, I Attended My First five p.m. Sunday Jazz Religious Service by Reverend John Gensel at a Large Lutheran Church in Midtown Manhattan. I Arrived about Fifteen Minutes Late. As I Opened the Large Front Door of the Church, I Heard Booming Big Band Jazz Music for "Take the A Train" with None Other Than Duke Ellington Conducting.

Duke Ellington and a Few Other Members of His Band Gave Testimonials, Read the Required Bible Readings, and Participated in the Speaking of the Prayers.

Later, I Found Out That Reverend Gensel Ministered to Jazz Musicians in Many Wonderful Ways. He Attended Their Performances in the Wee Hours of the Night, Married Them,

Baptized Their Children, Presided at Their Funerals, and Counseled and Supported Them in Times of Trouble.

Another Church I Attended was St. Clement's Episcopal Church on West 46th Street and 10th Avenue. Their Minister was Sidney Lanier, who Gave a Twelve Noon Service for Theatre and Movie Actors and Actresses. He also Founded the Off-Broadway American Place Theatre at the Church, which Attracted Big Crowds Including Emily and Me and Andy Warhol. Due to the Popularity of the American Place Theatre and the Critical Acclaim of Their Productions, They Had to Subsequently Move the Theatre to Broadway.

Also, I Attended the seven a.m. Services at the Judson Memorial Church Adjacent to Washington Square Park in Greenwich Village. Everyone Brought Breakfast Food to Share with Others at Big, Round Tables. Al Carmines, the Minister, Oversaw an Informal Service that Included His Playing on the Piano and Singing Broadway Musical Songs, Many of Which He had Written Himself and Performed on Broadway.

In Addition, I Attended Motivational Services by Norman Vincent Apale, a Famous Preacher Who Wrote a Best Seller Book Entitled *The Power of Positive Thinking*, at a Large Church on Fifth Avenue.

And Emily and I Would Attend Easter Services at the Russian Orthodox Cathedral on Upper Park Avenue.

36. More Big Deals with Oil Titans

*I*n My Exxon Job as Senior Cargo Sales Executive Responsible for Foreign Crude Oil Sales, Purchases and Exchanges with US Companies Located West of the Mississippi and in Chicago, I Did a lot of Deals Over a Two Year Period with Very Large Companies Including Chevron, Amoco, Getty, Signal, and Occidental.

Some Notable Oil Titans that I Dealt with Included John Paul Getty, the Owner and Founder of Getty Oil, and Oscar Hammer, who was CEO of Occidental.

John Paul Getty was Named Several Times by *Fortune Magazine* as the Richest Living American. He Resided Most of the Time in his Sixteenth-Century Tudor Estate in England but Maintained Tight Control of Getty's Operations by Installing Loud Speaker International Phone Systems in Every Executives Office at Getty's US Headquarters in Los Angeles and at Getty's Companies Located Outside the US.

Getty Bargained Very Hard on Every Foreign Crude Oil Purchase from Me Whether It was a Small Deal or a Very Large Deal and Always Tried to Obtain the Lowest Possible Price.

He was also Frugal in Many Other Ways Including Washing His Clothes by Hand Because He did not want to Pay to have Them Laundered. And when his Shirts Became Frayed at the Cuffs, He Would Trim the Frayed Part Off Instead of Purchasing New Shirts.

He Also had a Habit of Writing Responses to My Letters, Cables, and Contracts on the Margins or Back Sides of the Paper and Mailing Them Back to Me Rather Than Using a New Sheet of Paper or Sending a Cable Response.

Armand Hammer, the CEO of Occidental Since 1957, was Another Colorful Character. He Loved to do Short-Term Trades of Foreign Crude with Me. Such as Buying Just One Cargo of Foreign Crude Oil From Me and Quickly Selling it to Another Company's Refinery at a Slightly Higher Price or Conversely Selling One Cargo of Foreign Crude to Me at an Attractive Purchase Price that he had Just Purchased from Another Company at a Slightly Lower Price.

In Addition to Armand Hammer's Astute Oil Trading Reputation, He Amassed a Large Collection of Museum Quality Paintings and Established a Close Relationship with the Soviet Union. He also Married a Famous Soviet Actress who was the Daughter of a Senior Russian General.

Another Unique and Unusual Large Foreign Crude Oil Sale that I Made was the Sale of 29,500 Barrels Per Day of Exxon's Saudi Arabian Crude for Ten Years to the Guam Oil and Refining Company, Whose Two Founders were a Partner in an Oil Consulting Company in Dallas, Texas, and a Lawyer and Lobbyist in Washington. DC.

Bud Gertz from Dallas and Marvin Cole from Washington, DC, Without Knowing Anyone in Exxon's Cargo Sales Department in Manhattan, Walked into Our Office One Day Without an Appointment but Managed to Speak to Brice Sachs, One of the Senior Managers.

Their Pitch Was

They Wanted to Sell Jet Fuel and Marine Diesel Oil to the US Army and Navy Bases in Okinawa from the Nearby Island of Guam, which was a US Territory.

They Would Build a Small Refinery in Guam and Size It at Slightly Less Than Thirty Thousand Barrels Per Day of Capacity, so as to Qualify for a Small Business Set Aside for the US Military Purchase as Well as Purchase Prices for the Jet Fuel and Marine Diesel Oil that were Above Market Prices.

However, Since They Did Not have the Funds to Build the Small

Refinery, They Wanted Exxon to Provide a Significant Direct Loan to Them as well as use Its Connections with Major US Banks to get the Banks to Also Make Significant Loans To Them.

In Return for Exxon's Financing Assistance, They Would Purchase 29,500 Barrels a Day of Light Arabian Crude For Ten Years for Exxon's Crude Oil Producing Concession in Saudi Arabia at a Significant Premium to The Market Price for Crude Oil.

I was Assigned by Brice Sachs to Try to Make This Unusual Type of Crude Oil Sales Deal Happen Which Had Never Been Done Before by Exxon.

While It Took Me Several Years to Line Up the Financing from the Banks and Obtain the Approval For the Deal from Exxon's Very Conservative Executive Committee, I Pulled Off the Complex Deal.

The Refinery was Built on Guam Without Any Problems, and the US Defense Department Honored Its Commitment to Purchase the Jet Fuel and Marine Diesel Oil from the Guam Oil and Refining Company Under a Small Business Set Aside at Premium Prices.

And Both Guam Oil and Exxon Realized Significant Profits from the Deal. And the Banks and Exxon Received Their Interest and Principal Payments from Guam Oil on Time.

37. ALEX ROSE, DAVID DUBINSKY, AND LIBERAL PARTY

When I First Started to Work for Standard Oil of New Jersey in Manhattan, I Also Wanted to Get Involved in Politics.

I Approached the Democratic State Representative for the Silk Stocking District in The Upper East Side of Manhattan about Getting Involved with the Democratic Party.

He Told Me That Because There were So Many Recent College Graduates Starting Jobs in Manhattan that wanted to Work for the Democratic Party, If I Wanted a Meaningful Assignment with Important Responsibilities in the First Two to Three Years other Than Physically Handling Mass Mailings, I Should Contact the Liberal Party.

The Liberal Party was a New York Political Party Headed Up By David Dubinsky, The Long-Time President of the Ladies Garmet Workers Union; Alex Rose, The Astute Head of the Hatters Union; and Reverend Donald Harrington.

They were a Small Political Party, but Very Well Organized, and Could Account for About 20 percent of the Vote in New York City Elections and 10 percent of the Vote in New York State Elections.

While Their Political Positions were Similar to the Democratic Party, They Would Occasionally Support Very Attractive and Competent Republican Politicians, Particularly If the Politician Running for Office Would Offer to Hire Two Liberal Party Members For Senior Administrative Positions In Their Government If They Were Elected.

For Example, The Liberal Party Publicly Endorsed John Lindsey when He Ran For Congress and Later For Mayor of New York City. They Also Endorsed Nelson Rockefeller When He Ran for Governor of New York.

As Virtually all of the Leaders of the Liberal Party were in their Sixties or Older, the Three Top Leaders of the Liberal Party Realized a Need to Recruit and Appoint Younger Party Members to be Officers in The Party.

And Thus, I Was Appointed to be Their Assistant Treasurer, and Henry Stern, a Young Friend of Mine, Was Appointed to be Their Assistant Secretary.

When John Lindsey was Elected Mayor of New York City with the Support of the Liberal Party, I was Offered a Position as Deputy Finance Manager for New York City. However, I Did Not Accept It As I Liked Working For Standard Oil; Was Doing Very Well There; and Wanted To Remain in the Private Sector.

However, Henry Stern, My Friend, Accepted A Position as Deputy Parks Commissioner for New York City and Did An Outstanding Job.

In Central Park He Initiated Free Shakespeare in the Park Plays and Free Concerts by the New York Philharmonic Orchestra and The Metropolitan Opera Company. He Closed Off Car, Bus, and Truck Traffic in the Park on Summer Weekends and Weekdays After Six P.M. In Addition, He organized a First-Rate Touch Football League with Referees Provided by the City and Constructed New Football and Baseball Fields. And He Also Planted a lot More Trees, Bushes, and Flowers.

As a Result of My Officer's Position in the Liberal Party, I was Chosen to be on Bobby Kennedy's Campaign Staff as a Volunteer Campaign Leader For Manhattan when he ran for the US Senate and the Presidency.

What Surprised a lot of People was that Standard Oil Never Objected to My Being Active in the Liberal Party as They Always Focused on Employing the Best and Brightest Business Associates Regardless of Their Political Affiliation, Race, or Religion.

38. Covering Quebec Town with Green Coke from Argentina

*E*arly in My Exxon Career, while I was still in the Market Planning Division, I was Asked to Try and Find a Market For Green Coke, which was a Byproduct from a Newly Installed Coker at Exxon's Refinery in Argentina. The Coker was used to Convert Very Heavy Argentina Crude Oil to Higher-Priced Petroleum Products such as Mogas and Jet Fuel.

Exxon Never Had to Sell Green Coke Before Since They did not have Any Cokers at Their Other Worldwide Refineries.

I Did a lot of Market Research and Found Out that Green Coke could be used to make Aluminum.

Thus, I Contacted a lot of Aluminum Companies. However, only Alcan in Canada showed Any Interest as they had an Aluminum Plant in a Small Town in Quebec on the St. Lawrence Seaway.

After a lot of Negotiations, I Reached Agreement with Alcan on a Multi-Year Sale, Provided that Exxon Delivered the Green Coke to a Port on the St. Lawrence Seaway that Served Their Aluminum Plant.

The Green Coke was like Pieces of Coal, but the Coke Material was Much More Powdery than Coal.

Unfortunately, the Cargo Ship that Esso Argentina Hired to Make the First Delivery of Green Coke to Alcan Encountered a Bad Hurricane on the Voyage. While the Cargo Ship Survived The

Hurricane, Most of the Coke Broke Apart and Became Very Powdery. And, Unfortunately, when it was Unloaded at Alcan's Receiving Port on to an Overhead Uncovered Conveyer Belt to Transport the Green Coke to Alcan's Aluminum Plant, a Very Strong Wind Sprung Up in the Direction of the Small Town of Arvida. And the Result was that a Lot of the Green Coke Ended Up in Powdery Form on the Streets, Buildings, Houses, and Lawns in the Small Town of Arvida.

As a Result, that was the End of Esso Argentina's Green Coke Sales to Alcan in Quebec. However, I did Find Another Market for the Green Coke for Metallurgical Uses in Japan. And I Contracted to Sell All of the Esso Argentina's Green Coke to Sumitomo, which Also Transported the Green Coke in Their Own Cargo Ships to Japan.

39. TOUCHDOWNS AND MORE TOUCHDOWNS

*S*hortly After Moving to Manhattan, I Became Involved in a Touch Football League, which Played Its Games on Saturday or Sunday in Central Park.

The Quarterback of My Team was None Other than Al Henry, who was a Classmate and Close Friend of Mine From Northwestern's Graduate School of Business.

I would Workout in Central Park One Night a Week Just with Al Henry, who had been a First-String Quarterback For a Division I Midwestern University.

Incidentally, Most of the Participants in the Touch Football League Played Football in College and Some were Still Hoping to Make the Pros by Staying in Shape.

As the Games were Quite Competitive, and Blocking was Allowed, Someone Would be Seriously Injured Almost Every Week.

I was a skinny, but Very Fast Wide Receiver and Very Good at Catching Long Passes.

I Ended Up Playing Until Age Thirty-Four When I Cracked Most of My Ribs when I was Playing Free Safety on Defense. This Happened when I was Trying to Break Up a Pass to a Muscular Tight End, But Instead Collided Chest to Chest with My Opponent while Both of Us were Running at Full Speed.

Nevertheless, I Ended My Semi-Pro Football Career by Averaging One Touchdown Per Game. And Because of My Football Success, I Earned the Nickname of Touchdown, which is still Used Today by My Children and Grandchildren when Addressing Me.

40. Winning Over the Russians

*E*mily and I Decided in the Late 1960s to Take a Three-Week Trip to The Soviet Union to see what it was really like as we were Skeptical of all of the Negative Publicity in the US During the Vietnam War and Cold War Period about The Soviet Union.

However, it took us Eight Months to Obtain a Visa from The Soviet Union, which Required that we Specify what Cities we wanted to Visit and the Exact Number of Days that we would spend in Each City.

Also, somehow the US State Department Found Out About Our Travel Plans and Sent Us a Certified Letter Advising Us Not to Take the Trip. However, that Warning made us want to go Even More.

Emily was the Perfect One to have on the Trip with me as she had a Degree in Russian Literature from Connecticut College and Attended a Russian Language Emerson Program at Middlebury College. She also Looked Just like Jackie Kennedy as President John Kennedy and Jackie were still Greatly Admired by the Russians. We also Brought with us Kennedy Silver Dollars to Give to the Russians that Befriended Us.

Our First Stop was For a Week in Moscow. We Stayed at the Metropole Hotel which was only a block from Red Square and was One of only Two Hotels where non-Soviet Citizens Could Stay. We were also Allowed to Eat at Only Six Restaurants in Moscow.

At the Hotel, there was an old lady in her seventies who Sat at a Small Desk by the Elevator on Our Floor and Recorded in a Notebook all of the Times that we left and Returned to Our Room.

On the First Morning after Arriving the Night Before, we Decided to Pull an Old James Bond Trick of Wetting a Few Strands of Our Hair and Putting Them Across the Opening Creases of Our Two Suitcases. And, At the End of the First Day, After Returning From a Full Day of Going to Museums, Churches, and Parks, All of the Hairs were on the Floor, Meaning that a Russian Security Agent Had Opened Our Suitcases to Examine What Was In Them.

On the Second Day, We Decided to Get on a Subway and Ride It for Five Stops and then Get Off Without Any Idea of Where We Were Going. It Turned Out that it was a Residential Area with Tall Concrete Apartment Buildings that had been Erected after World War II to Provide Housing for those Russians who had Lost Their Homes during the Bombings by the Germans.

After Getting Out of the Subway and Reaching a Busy Intersection, Several Russians Approached Us and Asked if we were Lost as there were no Museums or Churches in that area. The Initial Russians were soon Joined by Many Other Russians as they were Curious About Seeing Americans for the First Time in Their Neighborhood. And This Resulted in about Forty-five Minutes of Back-and-Forth Conversations in Russian with Emily about why we were Visiting Russia and what was life like in America.

And, as Quite a Surprise to us, One Lady Invited us to Have Tea with her in her Apartment the next day, which we Graciously Accepted. And a Student at Moscow University Told Us About an American Jazz Dance Party that was Being Held on Saturday Night at one a.m. in an Alley at the University. As we Both Loved to Dance, we Accepted His Invitation and Stayed Until the End of the Dance Party. And I always remember Dancing with a lot of Vivacious Russian Coeds. However, when Returning to our Hotel at three thirty a.m., the Few Hotel Workers Still Behind Their Desks in the Lobby looked Flabbergasted as to why we were coming back to the Hotel so late at night as Restaurants and Bars in Moscow Could Only Stay Open Until eleven thirty p.m. And, They all Jumped on

Their Phones Immediately to Report our Late Arrival to Russian Police and Security Agencies.

The Next Day, while walking in Gorky Park, there were lots of Loudspeakers with Recordings Criticizing Life in American and America's War to Try to Conquer North Vietnam.

And, in the Park, we were Approached Separately by a Small Group of Chinese Students and African Students who were attending Moscow University. Each of the Small Groups Asked us to Meet with a Larger Group of Chinese and African Students the Next Day in the Park at a Specific Time, which we Agreed to.

The Soviet Union had been making a Major Effort to Develop Alliances with Developing Countries in African, Asia, and Latin America so as to Obtain Their Support in Their Cold War With the United States. Thus, They Provided Scholarships to Students from These Countries to Attend Universities in Moscow. However, the African Students Told Us That They Were Discriminated Against by the White Russians and Formed a Negative Opinion About Life in the Soviet Union. And the Chinese Students Told Us that Moscow University was No Better than the Large Universities in China and also Were Disappointed with Life in Moscow, due to all of the Restrictions on non-Soviet Citizens. Unfortunately, we Found Out Right Away After Leaving the Soviet Union that all of the Chinese Students Were Ordered to Return to China Soon After Our Meeting with Them as a Result of Their Negative Statements About Universities and Life in the Soviet Union.

One Night in Moscow, we went to a Restaurant in the Prestigious National Hotel for Dinner and Dancing. Like the few Other Restaurants that didn't have a Prohibition on Serving non-Soviet Citizens, They had Mostly Large Long Tables to sit at. And thus we Joined a Table with Ten Other Russians.

A Man from one of the few Small Tables for just Two People came and Asked Emily to Dance. After the Dance, He sent over a Carafe of Vodka, which I was Reluctant to Accept but Agreed to Due to the Urgings of the Russians at Our Table. A Short Time Later, he came to our Table and asked me to Step Out into the Hallway.

He then asked me to Provide him with some US Dollars, So He Could Convert Them Into Lots of Russian Rubles in the Foreign Exchange Market Due to the Extremely Low International Ratings of the Soviet Union Currency. I Declined, so He Returned to Our Table and Asked Emily for some Dollars. She Declined. He then Got Very Mad and Went Stomping Back to His Table for Two where he was Sitting With a Lady Friend. He Picked Up a Glass Vase with some flowers and Slammed It Against the Dinner Table. Unfortunately, a Long Shard of Glass from the Badly Broken Vase Entered the Inside of His Wrist, which caused His Blood to Spurt Up About Six Feet to the Ceiling of the Restaurant. The Russians at Our Table all saw what Happened and Yelled at Emily and Me to Leave the Restaurant Immediately For Our Own Safety. When Emily said, "What About Our Dinner Bill?" The Russians at Our Table said They Would all Share the Costs of Our Dinner. So We Sprinted Out of the Restaurant and Quickly Hailed a Taxi to Take Us Back to Our Hotel.

In Moscow, We Also Enjoyed Going to a Performance of the Ballet Rouse De Monte Carlo Starring None Other than Rudolph Nuveyev and Morgot Fontaine. And not to be Forgotten was an Intellectual Discussion We Had at a Meeting with the Prestigious Moscow Writers Association and Our Trips Every Night to Witness the Changing of The Guards at Red Square.

On the Last Morning of Our Stay in Moscow, I Accidently Knocked Over a Large, Beautiful Porcelain Washing Basin on to the Floor of Our Hotel Room and Broke it into Several Pieces. The Old Lady by the Elevator Heard the Crash Noise and Burst Into Our Room. She Saw the Beautiful Porcelain Washing Basin Broken on the Floor, Burst Into Tears, and Screamed in Russian that I had Broken the Peoples Beautiful Porcelain Washing Basin. To This Day, I Have Never Gotten Over Breaking the Peoples Beautiful Porcelain Washing Basin.

We Next Flew to Tbilisi, the Capital of Georgia. At one of our Sidewalk Discussions in Russian, a Very Old Man with at least Thirty Metals on his Soiled Suit Jacket Invited Us to Have Lunch with him. We Accepted and Listened to His Stories about Being One of the Founders of the Communist Party. This was Another Wonderful Example of How we Made So Many Friends "Out of the Blue" in Chance Encounters with Russians.

Next we Flew a Long Way to Visit Bukhara and Samarkand in the Central Asian Section of the Soviet Union. Both Cities were on the Famous Silk Road Between China and Europe. Bukhara is Second Only to Baghdad as the Intellectual Center of the Islamic World. It was also a Center of Trade, Scholarship, Religion, and Culture, Stretching Back for Thousands of Years. In a kind of Admiring Trance, we Walked the Town's Maze of Blue-Domed Mosques, Mosaic-Tiled Courtyards and Inns where Travelers could stay with Their Animals. In Samarkand, we were Overcome with the Beauty of a Vast Labyrinth of Blue Tiled Honeycomb-Vaulted Mausoleums. And I Loved Seeing the Elders of the Town Talking to Each Other Around an Ancient Water Well while Smoking Their Pipes.

Next was a Long Flight back to Moscow and Then a Train Ride to Leningrad, Formerly Known as St. Petersburg, on the Baltic Sea. While There, We Met a Soviet Journalist who Invited Us to a Special Event Three-Hour Movie on Overcoming the Attempted Seizure of Leningrad by the Germans For 872 Days During World War II. Most of the Film was Shot During the Brutal Soviet Winters, And we could really Experience what it was like for the Russians to be Surrounded On All Sides By Thousands of German Troops and Tanks as We Were Visiting Leningrad During the Winter, and the Theatre Showing the Film Had Turned Off the Heat.

The Last Soviet City We Visited was Kiev, the Capital of Ukraine. One Late Afternoon, We Visited Their Pioneer Palace, which Exists in Many of the Major Soviet Cities and Functions as a Wonderful After-School Program for School-Age Children Focused on Sports and Learning Arts and Crafts. However, Only Members of the Communist Party Could Send Their Children to the Pioneer Palace.

We asked to see the Inside of the School. And, Unbelievably, the Lady Principal Took Us on a Forty-five-minute Tour and Showed Us all of the Sports and Craft Areas While the Students were there.

Also, we Had a Wonderful Back-and-Forth Conversation with Her Focused on Schooling in America and the Soviet Union. At the End of the Tour, the Principal Told Us that she had the Day Off the Next Day and Offered to Take Us on a City Tour to Visit Parts of Kiev that Visitors were never shown. We Accepted and Spent a Half Day with Her, Visiting a Catholic Convent, an Underground Political Organization, and a Mausoleum Built Five Hundred Feet Below the Ground which Housed Bodies of Famous Ukrainian Communists in Full View.

On Our Last Day in Kiev, Before Leaving the Soviet Union to Fly to Belgium on an Aeroflot Jet and Then on a European Jet to New York City, we went to One of the Few Restaurants in Kiev for Lunch that Allowed non-Soviet Visitors.

As Usual, we Sat Down at a Long Table. And soon afterwards, a Stocky, Well-Built Russian Wearing a Beautifully Tailored Grey Italian Suit Sat Down on the Other Side of the Table From Us. He Immediately Stared at Us with His Piercing Steel-Gray Eyes and Started to Question Us In English in a Rapid Staccato Manner as to What Our Purpose was in Visiting the Soviet Union and Whom Did We Meet With During Our Trip.

Emily and I Realized After About Fifteen Minutes that He was Interrogating Us. So She Tried to "Break the Ice" by Telling Him a Joke in Russian. He Burst Out Laughing. And Then for the Remainder of Our Lunch, we had a Nice Back-and-Forth Conversation About Life in Russia and Where Each of Us Had Traveled.

At the End of the Lunch, when Emily and I Stood Up to Leave, the Russian Also Stood Up and Extended His Hand to Shake Hands with us. We Then Exchanged Business Cards.

And who was the Russian Interrogator? He was None Other than The Chief Justice of The Soviet Supreme Court. Obviously, I Believe that Our Visit and Bizarre Efforts Over Three Weeks to Become Friends With a Wide Variety of Soviets in Six Different Cities Piqued The Interest of the Soviet Security Agencies. However, I also Believe that the Chief Justice Concluded at the End of Our

Lunch that we were Not Visiting the Soviet Union to Cause Any Discord with The Soviet Government.

In Summary, We Had Won Over Many Russians by Being a True Friend of Russia and the Russians.

And Upon My Return to Exxon, My Message to the Senior Leaders of the Cargo Sales and Marketing Departments Who Wanted To Expand Exxon's Business Into More Countries, was that We Could Get Along with the Russians and do Business With Them. This Led Initially to Exxon Deciding Within Two Years of My Return to Establish Wholesale and Retail Market Positions First in the Large Eastern European Communist Countries of Poland, Czechoslovakia, Hungary, and Yugoslavia. And After Being Successful in Eastern Europe, Exxon Decided to Establish Business Positions in The Soviet Union, with an Initial Focus on Oil and Gas Exploration.

41. Giving Security Head the Slip

Upon Returning to Our Apartment on East 73rd Street and Lexington Avenue in New York City on a Friday Night, Emily and I Decided to Visit the Metropolitan Museum of Art the Next Day.

Shortly After Walking Through One Gallery After Another, We Both Noticed That There was a Very Tall Man, of at Least Six Feet, Five Inches, Dressed in a Business Suit, with a White Shirt and Tie, that was Always Entering The Gallery We Were In Just as We Were Leaving It to Go to the Next Gallery.

That Saturday Night, We Met for Dinner at an Italian Restaurant in Greenwich Village with Our Good Friends Rand and Suzanne Carpenter. When Leaving the Restaurant, I Noticed that there was a Very Tall Man Trying to Hide Behind a *New York Times* Newspaper Directly Across the Street from the Restaurant.

The Carpenters Invited Us to Come to Their Apartment in Greenwich Village for a Nightcap, Which We Accepted. However, After Walking Across Several Intersections To Go to the Carpenters' Apartment, I Noticed the Tall Man Walking One Half Block Behind Us on the Opposite Side of the Street. I Realized Right Away that He was the Same Man Who was Tailing US at the Metropolitan Museum of Art.

I Told the Carpenters that Emily and I were Being Tailed by a US Securities Agent as a Result of Our Trip to Russia. And Then I Told

Emily and the Carpenters to Proceed to Their Apartment. However, I Would Walk Away in a Different Direction and, After Ditching the US Security Agent, I Would Meet Them at Their Apartment.

And Fortunately, I Remembered a New York Subway Ditching Trick From a Movie that I Had Seen the Prior Year.

As I Had to Walk Quite a Few Blocks to the Express Stop of the Lexington Avenue Subway on East 14th Street, I Noticed That the Tall Man Was Still Following Me.

I Entered the Subway Station and Boarded the Express Train Going North. After Entering One of the Subway Cars, I Saw the Tall Man Entering the Subway Car Just Behind Mine. At the First Express Stop Going North on East 34th Street, there was No Express Train on the Other Side of the Platform Stopped to Go Southward. So I Could Not Attempt My Ditching Trick. However, at the Next Express Stop Going Northward on East 42nd Street, Another Express Train Going Southward on the Other Side of the Platform Had Come to a Stop at the Same Time as My Train Going Northward. So, Just as the Exit Door on My Train was Starting to Close, I Dashed Out and Barely Made it to the Other Side of the Platform Just as the Entrance Door on the Southbound Train was Closing.

Fortunately, I made it onto the Southbound Express Train. However, the Tall Security Man Had Also Tried to Dash Out From the Northbound Train to an Adjacent Car From Mine on the Southbound Train. However, He Just Missed the Closing of the Entrance Door and His Shouts to Reopen the Door were to No Avail. So, I stayed on the Southbound Express Train to a Different Express Stop on East 4th Street and Walked to the Carpenters' Apartment with No One Tailing Me.

Unfortunately, I Learned that the Very Tall US Security Man, who was Employed by the CIA and Worked at a small CIA Office in Rockefeller Center Near Exxon's Two Buildings, Shot Himself in the Head and Died.

42. LUNCHES AT 21 CLUB

*I*n My Job as a Senior Cargo Sales Representative for Exxon at the Headquarters of Their International Division in Manhattan, Most of the Large US Companies I dealt with had International Cargo Sales and Purchase Representatives.

And to Find Out if there were any Mutually Attractive Sales, Purchases, or Logistics Exchanges to Pursue, we would have Lunch Together on a Alternating Host Basis.

I Liked to Take My Customers to the Famous and Exclusive 21 Club which was Located just One Block from Exxon's Building in Rockefeller Center.

I would always sit at a Table in Their Large Second-Floor Dining Room. On Many Occasions, I would see Aristotle Onassis, who sat at a Corner Table on the Second Floor with just One Guest so He could Observe what was going on Around Him. I would also sometimes see Jackie Kennedy-Onassis in Their First-Floor Dining Room.

The Second Floor was also Frequented by Senior Officers from Large Companies and Famous Wall Street Merger and Acquisition Deal Makers such as Felix Rohatyn of Lazard Freres.

I also liked to go to Lunch at some of the Exclusive French Restaurants with Wonderful Food such as Lutece, Lafayette, and La Cote Basque.

My Luncheon Tabs, with a Cocktail, Half a Carafe of Wine, Dessert and a Large Tip, were Extremely High. Early on, as I was

Concerned about the Bills, I checked with the Vice President of Exxon's International Cargo Sales Department as to whether or not it was OK to Take My Customers to the 21 Club. He Responded that he Worried More About Some of the Other Exxon Cargo Sales Representatives that Seldom Took Their Customers to Lunch at Nice Restaurants than He Did about Paying the High Lunch Bills for the Very Successful Cargo Sales Representatives Like Me who went to Lunch A Lot at Nice Restaurants and as a Result did a lot of Profitable Business for Exxon.

43. Drinking Cow's Blood and Milk

At Exxon, I was known as the Man with the Iron Stomach as I was Willing to Eat and Drink Anything Offered To Me Outside the US, such as Poisonous Fish in Japan, Fried Tarantulas in the Amazon Jungle, and Kava Root Drinks in Fiji.

As a Result, I was Asked to Accompany a Group of Exxon Oil Exploration Executives on a Visit to Meet with a Chief of a Large Native Tribe in Kenya to Negotiate a Lease on a Large Portion of His Tribe's Farmland for a Crude Oil Exploration Project.

We Met the Chief Shortly After Breakfast Outside His Large Tent, As was the Chief's Tradition when Meeting Important New Visitors for the First Time. He Stepped Forward from His Group of Tribal Elders with a Large Gourd Filled with Cow's Blood and Milk and Offered it to the Head of Exxon's Crude Oil Exploration Delegation.

The Head of Exxon's Delegation Looked Horrified as He Had Not Been Made Aware of the Chief's Welcoming Tradition.

Sensing a Major Disaster in Exxon's Attempt to Obtain the Chief's Agreement for a Crude Oil Exploration Lease, I Immediately Stepped Forward Towards the Chief, Smiled, and Extended Both of My Hands to Receive the Gourd. I Then Managed Somehow to Drink All of the Cow's Blood and Milk from the Large Gourd, which was Awful. And I Almost Vomited.

The Chief Seemed Pleased and Went Back to His Tent. To My

Horror, He Came Back Out with Another Large Gourd Filled with Cow's Blood and Milk and Stepped Forward to Offer It to Me.

However, I knew that I would Vomit if I Tried to Drink Another Large Gourd Filled with Cow's Blood and Milk. Thinking quickly on My Feet, I Had Our Tribal Translator Tell the Chief That I Loved the First Drink of Cow's Blood and Milk, But I Could Not Accept Another Gourd of the Chief's Precious Drink as I had Just Come From Having a Very Large Breakfast and My Stomach was Bulging.

Fortunately, the Chief Understood. And, as a result, He Signed an Agreement for Exxon to Lease a Large Portion of the Tribe's Farmland for a Three-Year Crude Oil Exploration Project.

Unfortunately, After Almost Three Years of Trying to Discover a Large Crude Oil Field on the Tribe's Farmland, Exxon Gave Up as All of the Exploration Wells Were Dry.

44. NIGHT OUT AT KENYAN DANCE CLUB WITH LORD DENNING AND MISS TORONTO

On a Three-Week Vacation Trip to Kenya, Uganda, and Tanzania, Emily and I Stayed One Night at a Guest House of the Owner of a Large Tea Plantation in Kenya.

We Had Dinner that Night with the Owner of the Tea Plantation. We were also Joined by Two Other Guests who had Arrived Separately to the Tea Plantation. One was Lord Denning, who was the Son of the Founder of Rolls Royce and was Returning to London From South Africa Via Kenya For a Few Days of Game Park Visits. The Other Visitor was a Beautiful and Vivacious Blond Lady From Ottawa who had Recently Won the Miss Toronto Beauty Contest.

Near the End of the Dinner, I Asked the Owner of the Tea Plantation whether there were any Interesting or Exciting Things that Emily and I could do that Night in the Town, which was Located in the Center of Kenya's Tea Plantation Area. He Responded that there was a Large Dance Club Located on the Main Floor of a Former Colonial-Era Opera House.

Emily and I Liked the Idea as we Both Loved to Dance. And We Persuaded Lord Denning and Miss Toronto to Join Us. And the Tea Plantation Owner Arranged for One of His Workers to Drive Us to the Dance Club at ten p.m. and Pick Us Up at Midnight.

In Entering the Car, Emily and I were Astonished to See Lord Denning Dressed in a Scottish Kilt.

After Being Dropped Off, We Entered the Beautiful Former Colonial Opera House. And We Immediately Saw that the Large Dance Floor was Jam-Packed Not with the White Owners of the Tea Plantations but only with Black Kenyans. Emily and I Immediately Thought that Lord Denning and Miss Toronto Would Turn Around and Dash Out to Try to Catch the Tea Plantation Owner's Car so that they could Return to the Guest House. However, Much to Our Surprise, They Did Not Leave.

For the First Time in My Life, I Felt What it was Like to Be a Minority as a White Person and Seemed at First to be Reluctant to Dance. However, when the Music Shifted to Rock and Roll, which Emily and I Love, We Joined In and Had a Great Time on the Dance Floor. I Enjoyed Having a lot of Dances with Miss Toronto. And we were Mesmerized Watching the Kenyans Dance, and they also Gazed at Us Out Of Curiosity.

Lord Denning Did Not Participate in the Rock and Roll Dancing With Us. However, Near the End of the Evening He Asked the Band Conductor to Play a Scottish Tune and Requested that all the Kenyans Leave the Dance Floor so that They Could Watch a Scottish Dance Jig Performed by Lord Denning and Miss Toronto.

All of the Kenyans Complied. And Lord Denning Began the Scottish Dance Jig at One Corner of the Dance Floor with Miss Toronto at the Opposite Corner. They then Separately Danced to the Center of the Dance Floor, Embraced, and Performed a Wonderful Scottish Dance Jig for About Ten Minutes. At the End of Their Scottish Jig, the Kenyans all Jumped To Their Feet and Gave Them a Long Standing Ovation Along with Lots of Catcalls.

Both Emily and I and Lord Denning and Miss Toronto Left the Dance Club at Midnight Having Thoroughly Enjoyed the Evening and Feeling Exhilarated and Happy About Our Experiences Dancing at the All Black Kenyan Dance Club.

45. Sammy Struck from Orange County, California

In My Cargo Sales Job at Exxon, Most of My Customers were Large US Energy Companies, who were also Involved in Oil Exploration, Production, Refining, and Marketing Outside the US.

There were also a Few Small Oil Brokers in My Territory who Bought and Sold Cargoes of Oil on a Short-Term Basis.

A Particularly Colorful Broker was Sammy Struck from Orange County, California, whose Small Company was Named "Struck Oil."

In One of My Early Trips to Los Angeles to Meet With Getty Oil, Occidental Petroleum, and Signal Oil, I also Arranged to Meet Sammy Struck for Breakfast at My Luxury Hotel in Beverly Hills.

Just Before Our Appointed Meeting Time, I Received a Call in My Hotel Room From Sammy Struck's Secretary. She Explained that Sammy had been out Very Late at Night with a Group of Oil Brokers and would be about One Hour Late For Our Breakfast Meeting.

I Responded That Was Still OK as I was Very Much Looking Forward to Meeting Sammy for the First Time.

As Soon as I Hung Up My Room Phone, It Rang Again, And, Lo and Behold, it was Sammy Struck, Who Said He had just Arrived in the Lobby of My Hotel for Our Breakfast Meeting.

I Asked Sammy How I Would Recognize Him as the Lobby was Very Crowded at that Time in the Morning. Sammy Responded that he was Wearing an Orange Suit Jacket.

I went down to the Lobby, And There was Sammy, Wearing an Orange Suit Jacket Along with an Orange Tie, an Orange Pair of Pants, and Orange Socks.

I had a Very Interesting Breakfast with Sammy Struck, who was a Colorful Character in Every Respect.

And Fortunately, or Maybe Unfortunately, I Only Did One Small Short-Term Oil Trading Deal with Sammy During My Five Years in Exxon's Cargo Sales Department.

46. My Manhattan Buddies

*I*n Manhattan, My Early Male Friends were Fellow Graduates of Northwestern's Graduate School of Business. There was Al Henry, Who Worked For City Bank: Eliot Bernat, Who Worked For a Madison Avenue Advertising Agency; Jeff Weiss, Who Worked For Colgate; and Matt Sterling, Who Worked For IBM.

Also, I Made Quite a Few New Friends at the Madison Avenue Presbyterian Church on the Corner of Madison Avenue and 73rd Street. They had a Very Active Young Adults Group that Played Volleyball on Wednesday Nights at Their Large Recreation and Meeting Center next to the Church. The Young Adults Group also took Weekend Hiking and Cultural Trips About Twice a Month.

Through the Church, I Became Good Friends with Dave Erickson and Paul Hollos, Both of Whom Had Recently Graduated with MBAs from Harvard.

Also, I Became Acquainted with Stan Summers at the Church Who Founded the St. Clements Film Association; Wrote and Illustrated a Best-Selling Children's Book; and Produced a Movie For New York Public Schools with Large Numbers Of Minority Students which Highlighted the Many Accomplishments of Famous African Americans in the US.

In Addition, I Made a lot of Good Friends with New MBA Employees at Exxon who Worked in the Finance Area With Me.

I would Meet Frequently for Lunch With My Male Friends.

We Liked to Eat at a Jewish Deli on 7th Avenue; a Small French Restaurant on East 55th Street; a *New York Times* Cafeteria on East 42nd Street; and a Lunch Room at a Large Episcopal Church on Park Avenue. Also, During Nice Weather, We Liked to Buy a Sandwich and Beer at a Deli and Have Lunch on a Bench in Central Park.

Other Activities with My Male Friends Included Going Out For a Few Beers on Friday Night; Playing Tennis in Central Park and Randalls Island; and Taking Weekend Trips to the Jersey Shore in the Summers.

A Particularly Good Friend, Who Worked at Exxon in Finance and Then Left to Become a Security Analyst with a Wall Street Firm, was Pierre Brull. We were Both Excellent Chess Players and Would Meet on Sunday Afternoons at His Apartment on East 72nd Street to Play Chess.

Pierre Brull Introduced Me to Phil Erard, Another Frenchman, who was a Merger and Acquisitions Deal Maker on Wall Street and Also an Active Technical Mountain Climber and President of The New York Alpine Club. I went on Many Hikes with Phil Erard in the Catskills Mountains After Spending Two Weekend Nights at the Auberge Des Quatre Saisons, which was a Lovely French Inn with Excellent Food.

I also went out on Many Double Dates with My Manhattan Friends to Small Italian and Spanish Restaurants and to See James Bond and Foreign Avant-Garde Movies.

47. RUSSIAN EASTERS WITH SVETLANA KASEN-BEG

*E*mily had Remained Very Good Friends with Svetlana Kasen-beg, who was Her Russian Language Professor at Connecticut College.

Svetlana Kasen-beg would always Invite Us Each Year to Celebrate Russian Easter at Her Large Farmhouse Near New London, Connecticut, along with a Large Group of Her Connecticut College Associates, Relatives, and Friends.

On the Saturday Night Before Russian Easter, Everyone would Go Off to Attend an Easter Service with lots of Pageantry at a Russian Orthodox Church, which was a One-Hour Drive From Svetlana Kasen-beg's Farmhouse. After the Easter Eve Service, we would Return to the Farmhouse to Feast on a Wonderful Russian Dinner, with Lots of Vodka.

On Russian Easter Sunday Mornings, Those Who Stayed at the Farmhouse would Have a Very Nice Breakfast and Then Participate in an Easter Egg Painting Contest Judged by a Connecticut College Art Professor. And, to My Astonishment, I Somehow Managed to Win the Easter Egg Painting Contest on My Last Russian Easter Visit to Svetlana Kasen-beg's Farmhouse.

48. OUTCHEATING THE TURKS

*E*mily and I Took a Three-Week Vacation Frist Visiting Athens and the Lovely Greek Isles for Two Weeks and Then Planned to Go To Istanbul For a Week.

In Athens, We Stayed at a Pensione Run By a Very Nice Greek Lady. Our Third-Floor Suite had a Bedroom and a Sitting Room and an Outdoor Balcony with Wonderful Views of the Acropolis. Everyone in Athens and at the Surrounding Archeological Sites were Very Nice to Us.

On our Greek Cruise, We Loved all of the Beautiful Greek Islands that we stopped at for a Day's Visit. At Mykonos, it was so Attractive with its White-Washed Houses on Hillsides with Flowering Gardens and Windmills that we Decided to Remain for Two Additional Days by not getting back on Our Cruise Ship and Managing to Secure a Cabin on the Next Cruise Ship Owned by the Same Company to Take Us Back to Athens.

We Then Flew to Istanbul for a Planned One-Week Stay. In Securing a Taxi to Our Hotel, the Taxi Driver Did Not Turn on the Meter. So I Asked Him to Turn the Meter On. He Responded that it was Broken. When We Arrived at the Hotel, He Wanted Dollars for the Fare, which seemed Awfully High to me, Rather Than Turkish Currency so He Could Exchange the US Dollars for Turkish Currency on the Black Market for a Higher Rate than the Official Turkish Government Exchange Rate.

When Checking In at the Hotel's Front Desk, I Asked to Confirm the Nightly Rate So I Could Check it With My Reservation Voucher. When the Hotel Clerk Told Me What the Nightly Rate was, I was Astounded to Hear that it was 33 percent Higher Than the Rate on My Reservation Voucher. I Strongly Complained but was Told that the Hotel Owner Had Just Raised the Nightly Rates.

We then went out to Dinner After Unpacking Our Two Suitcases. When I Got the Bill for the Dinner, It Seemed Much Higher Than I had Calculated from the Menu. So I Asked to See a List of Each Item that We had Ordered Along With the Price for Each Item. The Waiter Went Away and Came Back After Five Minutes with an Itemized List of the Charges. While I Couldn't Read Turkish, the Number of Food and Drink Items on the Itemized List was twelve, Whereas I Remembered Only Ordering eight Items.

After Complaining Loudly to the Waiter, He Came Back After a Ten-Minute Delay with a List of Only Eight Items Along with the Bill for Each Item. However, when I Added Up the Itemized Charges to Compare Them with the Total Bill, I Discovered, with Much Angst, that the Restaurant had Made a Significant Addition Mistake in Their Favor. The Waiter Again Disappeared for Over Ten Minutes and Finally Returned with a Total Bill that Had Corrected the Addition Mistake. I Then Paid the Total Tab with Turkish Currency Note that was Larger Than the Total Bill. When the Waiter Returned with My Change, I Quickly Discovered that I had Been Short Changed. After a Long Argument with the Waiter, He Left and Returned with the Correct Change.

Emily and I Returned to Our Hotel and Went to Our Room. Unbelievably, We Discovered that all of Our Clothes that we had Unpacked and Placed in Bureau Drawers or Hung Up in the Closet on Hangers Were Gone. We Raced Down to the Hotel Desk to Find Out to Our Astonishment that All of Our Clothes had been sent to a Laundry to Either Have Them Washed or Dry Cleaned.

Fortunately, All of Our Clothes were Returned by four p.m. the Next Day. But we were stuck with a Very Large Laundry and

Dry-Cleaning Bill. However, After My Loud Complaints, the Hotel Clerk Reduced the Bill by 50 percent.

And That was the Final Straw, as Everyone that we Had Been in Contact With in Istanbul Had Cheated Us or Tried to Cheat Us.

Thus, I Went to a Nearby Travel Agency and Booked a Flight Out the Next Day at Noontime to Return to Athens and Then Connect on a Flight to the Beautiful Greek Island of Corfu.

When we Entered a Taxi to Take Us to the Airport, I Asked the Taxi Driver to Turn On the Meter. He Responded That it Was Broken.

When We Got to the Airport, the Taxi Driver Told Me What the Charge Would Be. I Then Told Emily to Take Her Suitcase and Go to the Ticket Counter For Our Airline. I Then Took From My Wallet a Large Bunch of Small-Denomination Turkish Bills and Handed Them to the Taxi Driver and Then Raced with My Suitcase Into the Airport Terminal to Meet Emily at the Airline Ticket Counter.

A Few Minutes Later, the Taxi Driver Came Into the Airline Terminal and Saw Me at the Ticket Counter. He Rushed Up and Screamed In a Loud Voice That I Had Given Him Only 25 percent of the Fare.

I Yelled at the Taxi Driver that it was all His Fault Since He Did Not Turn on the Taxi Meter.

Emily and I Managed to Get on the Plane and Subsequently had a Wonderful Time for the Next Five Days in the Beautiful Island of Capri with Lots of Friendly Greek People. And No One Tried to Cheat Us.

49. QUEEN ELIZABETH AND PRINCE PHILLIP

*E*mily and I Spent a Wonderful Eight-Day Vacation During the Winter in Grenada. At the Time of Our Trip, Grenada was Celebrating its Becoming a Member of the British Commonwealth of Nations.

There were Ceremonies, Athletic Events, Parades, and a Special Saturday Night-Long Dance Event Called "Jump Up."

When We Arrived at Grenada's Only Jet Airport on the Eastern Side of the Island, we had to Take a Taxi Over a Steep Mountain Range to Arrive at the Islander Hotel on a High Hill Overlooking the Beautiful Historic Capital of St. George with Its Pastel-Colored Houses and Large, Photogenic Harbor Filled with Classic Sailing Schooners.

Just After Crossing the High Mountain Range, Several Grenada Police Vehicles Stopped Us and Asked Our Taxi Driver to Pull Over to the Side of the Road and Stop for Fifteen Minutes Before Proceeding, But We Had No Idea Why We Had to Stop.

However, We Soon Found Out. A Large Motorcade of Rolls Royces and Police Security Vehicles Approached Us Going in the Same Direction as We Had Been Going. And Who Was in the First Rolls Royce? None Other than Queen Elizabeth and Prince Phillip. They were Attending the Celebration and Flew in From the UK to the Same Airport Where We Landed. And, as we Soon

Found Out, They were Being Driven to Board the Large Royal Yacht Just Outside of St. George's Harbor, which was Accompanied and Protected by a British Destroyer.

Two Nights Later, The Owner of Our Islander Hotel, Who Had Been the Long-Time Conductor of the London Symphony Orchestra, Hosted a Cocktail Party for the Queen and Prince Phillip Along with all of the Officers of the Royal Yacht. While Queen Elizabeth and Prince Phillip Only Stayed a Short Time at the Party, We Stayed and Had a Wonderful Time.

50. Meeting the Real James Bond With Butterfly Net

Emily and I Met the Real James Bond While Having Breakfast One Morning on the Terrace of the Islander Hotel in Grenada.

The Real James Bond, who was a British-Educated Ornithologist, was Admired by Ian Fleming for One of His Many Bird Books Called *Birds of the West Indies*.

Ian Fleming Chose to Name the Main Character in All of His Adventure Books James Bond, after the British Ornithologist, as He Thought the Name was Very Masculine.

However, when Emily and I Saw the Real James Bond Appearing Out of the Bushes Early in the Morning with a Small Notebook and Binoculars Around His Neck and a Butterfly Net in One of His Hands, We Formed a Much Different Impression.

The Real James Bond was only about Five Feet and Five Inches Tall, Weighed Not Much More Than a Hundred Pounds, and Was Extremely Frail and Effete in Appearance.

51. Encountering Sean Connery at London Disco

*I*n My New Job at Exxon International as Manager of the Tanker Planning Division in the Supply and Transportation Department, I Had to Travel to London About Once Every Two Months as London was the Headquarters of Companies that Owned and Chartered Out Oil Tankers to International Oil Companies.

I Would Always Try to Plan My Trips to London so that I Could Enjoy the Sights and Activities that This Great Capital City Offered on the Weekends by Scheduling My Business Meetings on Either Monday and Tuesday or Thursday and Friday.

One Saturday Night, After Having a Lovely Chicken Tandoori Dinner at an Indian Restaurant, I went to the Popular Pheasantry Disco on Kings Road in Chelsea to Enjoy Their Live Rock and Roll Band Music and to Hit the Dance Floor.

While I was Watching the Other Dancers From the Sidelines, Sean Connery, Who Had Already Starred in a Number of Films as James Bond, Came Into the Dance Floor Room By Himself.

He Appeared to be Drunk. He Immediately Spotted a Beautiful Blond on the Dance Floor Dancing with a Young, Well-Built Male Partner. Rather Than Waiting for the Music to Stop, He Rushed on to the Dance Floor and Tried to Break In Between the Blond and Her Dance Partner.

The Well-Built Male Dance Partner of the Blond Initially

Stepped Back a Few Steps. However, He Appeared to Be Very Agitated About Sean Connery Trying to Steal His Blond Dance Partner. He Then Stepped Forward Towards Sean Connery and Took One Roundhouse Swing, Hitting Sean Connery in the Jaw and Knocking Him Down Flat on His Back to the Dance Floor.

And That was the Last Time that I Ever Saw the Movie *James Bond* at the Popular Chelsea Disco.

52. BORA BORA AND MOOREA

*E*mily and I Took a Beautiful Two-Week Vacation to Visit the Prettiest and Most Interesting South Pacific Islands, which Included Western Samoa, American Samoa, Fiji, New Hebrides, and Bora Bora, and Moorea in Tahiti.

In Moorea, We Stayed at a Pensionne Cottage Owned By a French Lady and Rented Motor Scooters to Enable Us to See the Entire Island.

Bora Bora was the Most Beautiful Island that I Have Ever Seen, with Two High Mountains Surrounded on All Sides with Lovely, Calm Turquoise Waters. Soft, White Sand Beaches and Palm Trees. And Almost All of the Houses, Resorts, and Buildings were Thatch Roofed.

We Stayed at a Lovely Bora Bora Inn, Enjoyed Great Snorkeling Every Day, and Also Succeeded in Climbing Bora Bora's Highest Peak.

53. ғRIGHTENED BY FIERCE NATIVES IN TANNA, NEW HEBRIDES

At the End of Our Pacific Island Trip, Emily and I Visited the Much More Primitive Island of Tanna in the New Hebrides.

The Trip to Tanna Started Out Well as We Were Brought to a Very Nice Guest House on a Ranch Owned by an Australian Family.

On Our First Excursion the Next Day to Try to Climb to the Top of an Active Volcano, We Saw for the Frist Time a Tribe of Very Fierce-Looking Natives Who were Known To Be Cannibalistic Up Until the Early Twentieth Century. The Tribesmen wore No Clothes, Shoes, or Hats Except For Handmade Bark Belts with Penis Holders.

The Volcano was Considered by the Natives to be a Sacred Property of One of the Ancient Gods of Tanna. So We Had To Be Escorted to the Top of the Volcano by a Group of Fierce-Looking Tribesmen.

As Soon as we Got Near the Top of the Volcano, We Heard the Sound of Explosions, And Then We Saw Rocks Being Spurted Out of the Top of the Volcano Along With a Lot of Smoke.

The Tribesmen Yelled and Motioned At Us to Run Back Down the Volcano as Fast as Possible as They Sensed that the Ancient God was Mad at Them For Bringing Us To Near the Top of the Sacred Volcano.

We Quickly Obeyed!

And When We Returned to the Nice Ranch Guest House, Emily

and I Decided to End Our Trip to the Island of Tanna and Fly Back to Port Vila, the Capital of New Hebrides, which was a Much Safer and More Modern Place To Be.

In Port Vila, We Stayed at a Five-Star Resort on a Calm Bay with a Nine-Hole Golf Course, Tennis Courts, and Access to a River for Canoeing.

54. DO-IT-YOURSELF DIVORCE

After About Ten Years of a Very Happy Marriage With Emily, I Decided that I Wanted to Have Children.

However, Emily was Very Adamant On Not Wanting to Have Children as Both of Her Parents Had Pounded Into Her Head That Children Were a Nuisance and Prevented Them From Being Able to Enjoy Life to the Fullest.

In Addition, Emily Wanted to Focus on Having a Very Successful Professional Work Career at IBM or Elsewhere.

Thus, We Mutually Decided to Get a Divorce, But Without Spending a Lot of Money on Lawyers.

So, After a Lot of Legal Research at the Main New York City Library on Fifth Avenue, I Drafted a Divorce Agreement.

In Terms of Splitting Up Our Assets, Which Consisted of Cash in Bank Accounts; Common Stocks in an Investment Account; and a Lot of Very Nice French Antique Furniture, Paintings and Wedding China Gifts, We Both Decided Without Any Rancor To

Divide the Cash and Stocks Based on Each of Our Respective Share of Our Total Salaries During Our Ten Years of Marriage. My Share Worked Out To Be 55 percent and Emily's was 45 forty-five.

Split Up the Antique and Other Furniture, Paintings, and Wedding China Gifts By Making a Complete List of All of the Important Items and Then Alternating Our Picks, With Emily Getting the First Pick.

After Typing Up the Divorce Agreement and Agreeing on the Split Up of Our Assets, We Flew to Haiti and Obtained a Divorce at a Haitian Divorce Court Recognized by the State of New York.

Most Importantly, We Both Split Up Happily With No Hard Feelings. And, To This Day, We Continue Communicate With Each Other Via Email on Our Vacation Travels, Work Accomplishments, and Political Views etc.

Also, Shortly After Finalizing The Divorce, I Came Down with a Terrible Case of Pneumonia During the Winter and Was In Bed for Almost Four Weeks With a Very High Fever and Terrible Coughing Fits. However, Emily's Mother, Who was a Senior Editor of *Town and Country Magazine* on Madison Avenue in Manhattan and Who Lived in Manhattan, Brought Me a Large Bowl of Wonderful Hot Soup Every Day at Lunchtime.

55. Evenings at Elaine's on Second Avenue and 88th Street

After the Split Up, I Enjoyed Spending Several Nights a Week at Elaine's Tavern on Second Avenue and 88th Street.

Elaine, Who Weighed Over Two Hundred Pounds, was a Very Popular Figure. And Her Large Bar and Italian Restaurant was a Hangout For Newspaper and TV Reporters; Upper-Level Politicians; Wall Street Merger and Acquisition Advisors; and the Producers, Directors and Stars of Movies, Broadway Plays, Operas, and Lincoln Center Classical Music Performances.

Woody Allen was Always at a Small Table Near the Entrance of Elaine's, Having Drinks and Dinner Mostly By Himself.

I Would See Felix Rohatyn, the Famous Wall Street Deal Maker from Lazard Freres and Savior of New York State From Bankruptcy, Quite Often Having Dinner With Important Merger and Acquisition Clients, and On Two Occasions Dining with the Governor of New York.

George Plimpton, the Highly Regarded Founder and Editor of *The Paris Review*, who Also Published Two Best-Seller Vignette Books on the Accomplishments, Adventures, and Mishaps in His Life, and Who was an Active Member of the Explorer Club, was at the Bar Virtually Every Night. George Would Arrive at Elaine's on Bicycle From His East 72nd Street Apartment on the East River.

For Me, Every Night at Elaine's was Exciting, and I Became a Good Friend of Elaine.

56. ATTEMPT TO DATE JACKIE O

*I*n Traveling To and From Work From My East 73rd Street Apartment to Exxon's Headquarters in Rockefeller Center, I Would Always Walk Home From Work Up 5th Avenue or Madison Avenue as I Found This to be a Great Tonic at the End of the Work Day.

When Going to Work in the Cold Weather Months, I Would Take the 5th Avenue Bus. However, in the Nice Spring, Summer, and Fall Months, I Would Walk to Work on the Central Park Side of 5th Avenue.

On One Morning, I Spotted this Very Beautiful Lady Walking Down 5th Avenue About a Hundred Feet in Front of Me.

I Picked Up My Pace so as to Catch Up With Her. When I Just Came Along Side of Her, I Immediately Asked if She would like to Join Me for a Glass of Wine After Work.

She Turned Her Head Quickly to Look at Me, and We Both Burst Out Laughing. I Then Realized That the Beautiful Lady was Jackie Kennedy-Onassis, And Jackie Realized That I Didn't Know Who She Was When I Was Walking Up Behind Her.

I Apologized to Jackie for Accosting Her Suddenly, And She Realized That I Had Not Meant to Harm Her in Any Way.

So We Ended Up Having a Very Nice Conversation Walking Down 5th Avenue to Central Park South.

When I Asked Her What She Was Planning to Do That

Morning, She Told Me that She Was Having Breakfast with Two Lady Friends at the Lenox Hotel on Central Park South. And Then She Had a Bookstore Date at ten a.m. on 5th Avenue With Rudolph Nureyev, Who was in NYC to Perform With the Royal Ballet at Lincoln Center

So Much For My Brief But Eventful Date With Jackie O!

57. Exxon's Senior Strategic Planning Advisor

After Completing My Job as Exxon's Tanker Planning Manager in Their International Division, I Landed a Very Important Job as Senior Strategic Planning Advisor in The Strategic Planning Division of Exxon's Corporate Planning Department.

I was Responsible For Coordinating the Preparation of Exxon's Annual Five-Year Strategic and Investment Plans and Profit Forecasts By All of Exxon's Petroleum Affiliates in Ninety Countries; Its Regional Petroleum Holding Companies for Europe, Asia, Africa, Latin America, Canada and The United States; Its Functional Petroleum Plans For Exploration and Production; Refining, Marketing, and Supply and Transportation; and Its Plans For Nuclear Energy, Coal, and Renewable Energy.

The Most Challenging Part of the Job was to Consolidate about 150 Strategic and Investment Plans and Profit Forecasts Into One Overall Exxon Corporate Strategic and Investment Plan and Profit Forecast.

Another Important Part of My Job was To Identify Corporate Issues that Needed to be Addressed by Exxon's Headquarters Staff or By Individual Regional Companies and Country Affiliates.

The Final Step in the Whole Corporate Planning Process, which Took About Six Weeks, was to Review the Consolidated Exxon

Strategic and Investment Plans, Profit Forecasts, and Follow-Up Issues With

Exxon's Corporate Planning Task Force

Exxon's Strategic Planning Committee

Exxon's Investment Committee

Exxon's Executive Committee

And Lastly, Exxon's Board of Directors

While it Wasn't Part of My Initial Job, I Designed a New One-Year Planning and Stewardship System, Had It Approved by Exxon's Senior Management, and Coordinated the Initial Implementation of it.

Needless to say, I was Exceptionally Busy With This Gargantuan Job and Had to Come to the Office on Many Saturdays and Sundays when I wasn't Away on Vacations.

58. TEARING CALF AT PLAYBOY CLUB RETREAT

One Fall the Corporate Planning Department Decided to Have a Corporate Planning Retreat for the Corporate Planning Managers of the Larger Regional, Country, and Non-Petroleum Energy Affiliates.

It was Held at a Playboy Club Conference Center in New Jersey.

Unfortunately, I Returned to the Office After the Three-Day Retreat on Crutches with a Badly Torn Calf Muscle.

While I Explained to Everyone that I Tore My Calf while Playing Tennis, No One Believed Me.

Those Who knew me Well Believed that I Either Tore My Calf on the Dance Floor with a Playboy Bunny or when Chasing a Playboy Bunny Around the Playboy Conference Center.

In Truth, All Three of the Above Causes of My Injury Were Correct!

59. MISS BASEBALL AND THE NEW YORK YANKEES

I Got to Know Jill Dargeon, A Beautiful, Tall Blond Classmate of My First Wife at Connecticut College, Quite Well.

She Loved Baseball and was Related to one of the Senior Vice Presidents of the New York Yankees.

And, I was Quite Often Able to Secure Two of Exxon's Four Box Seats Behind Home Plate for Sunday Afternoon Games.

So, On Many Occasions, I Invited Jill Dargeon to Join Me. She Would Always Bring a Four-Pack of Beer in an Ice Container. And I Would Treat Her to a Hot Dog and Popcorn.

Getting to Yankee Stadium was Easy as All We Had to Do was to Ride an Express Subway Train For Fifteen Minutes From West 86th Street and Central Park West in Manhattan to the Bronx Stop for Yankee Stadium.

And These Were Memorable Times For Seeing the Famous Yankee Stars Such as Mickey Mantle, Roger Maris, Yogi Berra, Phil Rizzuto, Whitey Ford, and Many Others.

As Jill Dargeon was Dating Danny Selznick, a Famous Hollywood Movie and TV Producer and Director, I Only went out on a Date with Her Once in the Evening. And That was for Dinner at P.J. Clarke's on Third Avenue and 55th Street.

But. To This Day, I Still Vividly Remember My Many Exciting Trips to Yankee Stadium with Miss Baseball.

60. Margaret Mead's Assistant at Museum of Natural History

After My Divorce From Emily, Matt Sterling, who was a Classmate of Mine at Northwestern's Graduate School of Business and Who Lived and Worked in Manhattan, Fixed Me Up with a Number of His Former Girlfriends.

They Were All Quite Attractive, Interesting to be with, and Very Nice. I Dated Several of Them Quite a Few Times Including One Who Worked at the Foreign Policy Association, One Who was a Security Analyst for Morgan Stanley, and One Who Belonged to a Well-Known Philadelphia Philanthropic and Socialite Family.

In Addition, Matt Sterling Invited Me to Have Lunch at a Second-Floor Pakistani Restaurant on West 46th Street with an Attractive Young Lady Who Worked at the American Museum of Natural History in Manhattan. We Had a Nice Lunch but did not Start to Date Until About a Month Later When I Met Her Again at a Large Cocktail Party Hosted by Matt Sterling in His Nice Upper West Side Apartment on Central Park West.

I Became Fascinated With Liddy Nickerson's Background as She Had Graduated From Arizona University with a Degree in Anthropology; Traveled to Many of the Primitive Pacific Islands; Started Her First Job at the American Museum of Natural History; and Become One of Margaret Mead's Two Assistants at the Museum. And Since She Was an Expert on the People of the Pacific Islands,

She Got the Assignment from Margaret Mead for Designing and then Implementing the Museum's First Peoples of Pacific Exhibition Hall.

Her Father, Albert Nickerson, was a Prominent Oil Man and National Business Leader. After Graduating From Harvard, He Started Working For Mobil Oil and Rose Quickly Through the Ranks to Become President of Mobil and then Chairman and CEO of Mobil for Fifteen Years Until His Retirement. In Addition, He Served as Chairman of President Johnson's Business Council; Chair of Harvard University's Board of Governors; President of the Federal Reserve Bank of New York; and a Member of the Board of Directors at Rockefeller University, The Metropolitan Life Insurance Company, and Raytheon.

On Our First Date, I Invited Liddy to Have Dinner With Me at My Lovely Apartment on 73rd Street and Lexington Avenue. I Showed Her Slides From My Amazon River and Russia Trips and Cooked My Famous Chicken Dish From a Best-Selling Cookbook Given to Me By Miss Baseball After My Divorce.

Liddy Then Invited Me to Have Dinner with Her at the Historic Beresford Apartment Building on 811st Street and Central Park West, which is known for its Three Majestic Towers, Very High Ceilings, Fantastic Views of Central Park, and Lavish Lobby. Liddy was Housesitting the Apartment for Morley Safer, the Long-Time TV Reporter for *60 Minutes*, and Jane, His Wife, who also Worked at the American Museum of Natural History, While They Were Staying in Their Summer House in Upstate New York on the Hudson River.

Liddy Cooked a Wonderful Dinner with a Large Striped Bass and Lots of Delicious Side Dishes.

Thereafter, Once a Week During the Work Week, I Would Join Liddy at the Beresford for One of Her Wonderful Dinners. We Both Enjoyed Having a Glass of Chevis Regal on the Rocks Before Dinner, and I Always Brought a High-End Bottle of Red or White Wine For Dinner.

On the Weekends, Liddy and I Liked to Go to the Catskills

Mountains for Hiking and Stay at the Auberge de Quatre Saisons, which is a Lovely French Inn with a First-Class Restaurant.

We Also Traveled Quite a Few Times on the Weekends to South Dartmouth, Massachusetts, and Stay at Her Grandmother's House on Masham Point, which is Flanked on Three Sides By Buzzards Bay.

And, on one occasion, we Traveled to Mid-Coast Maine and Stayed on Clark Island, which Her Parents Had Purchased from a Former Quarry Company Owner Shortly Before Albert Nickerson's Retirement from Mobil.

Clark Island is 174 Acres in Size and is Accessible From the Mainland via a Narrow Land Bar Causeway. It Has Miles of Beautiful Coastal Views, Many Hiking Trails, Cliffs, Apple Orchards, Cleared Fields, Ponds, and a Large Former Quarry Pit that Fills Up with Rainwater, making it Ideal for Swimming Compared to the Frigid Maine Ocean Water.

Liddy and I Became Engaged to be Married in the Fall, when we were Both in the Midst of Planning and Buying Equipment For Our Winter Mount Everest Expedition in December of 1972.

61. Winter on Mt. Everest

*E*arly On in Our Dating, Liddy Agreed to My Idea of Organizing a Small Expedition to Mt. Everest in the Winter of 1972/1973. And She Agreed to Join Me as Co-Leader of the Expedition.

At That Time, There Had Been Very Few Winter Expeditions, and No Successful Winter Expeditions, To Mt. Everest as Weather Conditions were Terrible Due To Temperatures of Up To 50 Degrees Below Zero, Winds Up To a Hundred Miles Per Hour, Frequent Avalanches, and Narrow, But Deep, Crevasses That Were Difficult to See Due To Snow Coverings.

Thus, Our Purpose was Not to Try To Climb to the Top of Mt. Everest But to Find Out What Winter Climbing Conditions Were Like.

As a Postscript, Mt. Everest was Not Climbed in The Winter Until Seven Years After Our Expedition on February 17, 1980, by a World-Acclaimed Polish Climbing Group Known for Their Superior Winter High-Altitude Climbing Skills.

In Planning the Expedition, We Had to First Obtain the Permission of the Nepal Government and Pay a High Fee For a Trekking and Climbing Permit For Both of Us.

Second, We Thought it would be a Good Idea to Hire a Local Expedition Company in Katmandu To Help Us Plan the Best Trekking Route to Take From Katmandu; Advise Us on Where to Camp Each Night; and Hire a Sherpa Guide, Assistant Guide,

Cook, and Porters to Carry Six Hundred Pounds of Our Provisions, Supplies, and Equipment.

We were Fortunate to be able to Hire In Advance of Our Trip Colonel Jimmy Roberts, who was also Edmond Hillary's Supply Manager for His Successful Expedition to Climb Mt. Everest in the Late Spring of 1953.

Third, We Had to Do a Lot of Research on The Equipment, Camping Gear, and Clothes That We Needed; The Appropriate Food to Bring For a Four-Week Expedition; and The First Aid Supplies and Medicine We Needed to Treat Any Accidents or Illnesses During the Expedition.

Fourth, We Needed to Spend Lots of Time Purchasing All of the Equipment, Camping Gear, Clothes, Food Provisions, First Aid Supplies, and Medicine, That We Needed for the Trip.

On Clothing Alone, We Had to be Prepared for Extreme Winter Weather in the Mt. Everest Area.

Fifth, We Decided That it Would Be a Good Idea to Solicit Several Organizations to Sponsor Our Expedition so as to Cover Some of the High Costs of a Winter Expedition to Mt. Everest.

In This Regard, We were Fortunate to get Pan American Airlines and The American Museum of Natural History to Co-Sponsor our Expedition by Paying a Share of the Total Costs.

Our Expedition Began Shortly after Arriving in Katmandu on a Long Flight From New York City with a Change of Planes at New Delhi.

Colonel Jimmy Roberts Met Us the Morning After Our Arrival and Gave Us a Written Report and Maps Covering Where We would Start the Expedition and Where We Would Camp Each Night Before Reaching the Base Camp for Mt. Everest.

He Also Told Us the Background of the Sherpa Guide, Sherpa Assistant Guide, and Sherpa Cook that he had Hired for Our Expedition. And He Explained that We would be Using Twelve Nepali Porters in the First Half of Our 180-Mile Trek to the Mt. Everest Base Camp, Which was in Medium-High Elevations with Less Severe Winter Weather Conditions. However, In the Second

Half of Our Expedition, We would be Switching to Twelve Sherpa Porters, who were Much More Experienced in High-Altitude Climbing During the Cold Winter Months.

The Total Distance by Foot from Katmandu to the Mt. Everest Base Camp was 230 Miles in a North-Easterly Direction.

However, we were Able to Reduce the Trekking Distance to 180 Miles by Traveling on a Road to the Northeast Which Ended Fifty Miles from Katmandu.

We Took Several Trucks Carrying our Six Hundred Pounds of Supplies, Camping Gear, and Climbing Equipment and a Bus Carrying our Nepali Porters and Our Sherpa Guide, Assistant Guide, Cook, and Cook's Helper, to the End of the Road From Katmandu.

Basically, We Trekked in a Northeast Direction Towards Mt. Everest. Each Day, We would have to Cross a Mountain Pass which Increased in Altitude Every Day. This was Very Good for Gradually Acclimatizing to the Much Higher Altitude of the Mt. Everest Area Compared to Katmandu.

We would Camp in Spots Selected By Colonel Jimmy Roberts Which were Most Always in a Valley Downhill From the Mountain Pass but Alongside a Stream that was Ideal For Washing Up and Supplying Water for Cooking and Drinking

The People in the Nepali and Sherpa Villages that we Passed Were Very Friendly Towards Us.

And, Each Mountain Village Had a Buddhist Temple Adorned on the Outside with Colorful Prayer Flags and on the Inside by Wonderful Paintings and Art Works.

At a Famous Buddhist Temple Just Outside of Namche Bazaar, which is the Last Major Village Before Reaching The Mt. Everest Base Camp after a Three-Day Hike, The Head Priest Showed Us the Hairy Skull of a Yeti, Which Was One of the Abominable Snowman that Looks like a Monstrous Ape and Still Inhabits the Highest Himalayan Mountains.

And, on the Fun Side, One Morning We Had a Friendly Snowball Fight with Our Sherpa Porters.

After Eighteen Days of Hiking, we Finally Reached the Base

Camp for Mt. Everest, which had a Very High Altitude of 16,500 Feet.

Just in Front of Our Expedition was a German Expedition. However, a Senior Member of Their Team Died From Altitude Sickness Just Before Reaching the Mt. Everest Base Camp. This Caused Them to Give Up Their Expedition, Turn Around, and Return to Katmandu.

We Spent Six Days Taking Upward Hikes From the Mt. Everest Base Camp in All Directions. Our Head Sherpa Guide Had to be Very Careful to Spot Narrow But Very Deep Crevasses that Had Been Covered by Recent Snowstorms.

We Did Manage to Climb a Mountain on the Opposite Side of the Khumbu Glacier From Mt. Everest and Reached an Altitude of Just Over Twenty Thousand Feet. This Mountain was Famous For Its Incredible Summit Views of Mt. Everest. The Top of Mt. Everest was Not Snowy, but Rocky and Black as the Hurricane-Force Winds Blew Almost All of the Snow off the Top of the Mountain.

There were Always Some Hurricane-Force Winds During Our Upward Hikes. However, with the Sun Out, The Extremely Cold Temperatures were Not So Bad. But at Night, It was Bitterly Cold and Windy.

For Lunch in the Mt. Everest Area, We Always Enjoyed Peanut Butter and Honey Sandwiches on Paratha Indian Flatbread. The Dinners Were Always Cooked and Served Warm By Our Outstanding Sherpa Chef and His Young Sherpa Helper. Breakfast of Hot Porridge and Tea Were Brought to the Entrance of Our Tent Early Each Morning.

The Mt. Everest Base Camp was Very Clean, with No Garbage, Due to the Fact that there were Very Few Expeditions Per Year to Mt. Everest as a Result of the Strict Limits by the King on Granting Trekking and Climbing Visas as He was Concerned that Too Many Western and Other Foreign Visitors to Nepal Would Have an Adverse Impact on the Nepali and Sherpa Culture.

After Our Six Days in the Mt. Everest Area, We Hiked Four Days Southward to Lukla, Which Had an Airstrip. This Enabled Us to Fly Back to Katmandu Along with Our Sherpa Guide, Assistant Guide, Cook, and Cook's Helper in a STOL Plane, which is Famous For Its Short Takeoff and Landing Capabilities. And, Thus, We Did Not Have to Hike For Another Two Weeks Back to Katmandu.

Basically, Our Expedition Was a Success as We Were Able to Observe what Climbing Conditions on Mt. Everest Were Like During the Two Coldest Months of the Year. And Neither Liddy nor I nor Our Two Sherpa Guides, Cook, nor Cook's Helper nor Any of the Twelve Sherpa Porters Were Injured, Hurt, or Became Ill on the Expedition.

While I was 175 Pounds and Fighting Fit When I Began the Four-Week Expedition, When I Returned to Katmandu, I Weighed Only 145 Pounds, Had a Long Beard, But was in Excellent Spirits.

And, As a Totally Unexpected and Wonderful Surprise, the King of Nepal Invited Liddy and I and Our Lead Sherpas to a Lavish Celebration of Our Successful Expedition at His Palace, Which was Attended By About One Hundred Members of His Royal Family, Local Diplomats from Other Countries, and Business Leaders.

Dinner Included Prime Ribs and Baked Alaska. And I Always Will Remember the Gargantuan Fireplace in the Main Room of the King's Palace Which Was About Fifty Feet Long and Ten Feet High.

One of Our Nicest Memories of the Expedition Were Our Many Encounters with the Local Nepalis and Sherpas Who were All Very Friendly and Accommodating Towards Us.

62. TIGER TOPS AND TAJ MAHAL

On the Way Back From Katmandu to New York City, We Made Two Short But Very Interesting Stopovers.

First, We Visited Tiger Tops which is Located in a Nepali National Game Park in Southwestern Nepal.

Getting to Tiger Tops is a Unique Adventure. First We Boarded a Small Old Propeller-Driven DC-3 in Katmandu and Landed on a Dirt Landing Strip about a Forty-Five-Minute Trip on an Elephant to the Tiger Tops Lodge.

We Left the Plane Not By Descending a Staircase to the Ground But By Exiting the Main Passenger Cabin Door on to a Large, Thatched Basket on Top of an Elephant.

The Elephant Walked through The Jungle and Crossed a River Before Letting Us Disembark Not on To the Ground But Into a Tree House Located Very Close to the Tiger Tops Lodge.

During Our Two-Day Visit, We Saw Lots of Rhinos, Elephants, and Beautiful Birds, But Unfortunately No Tigers.

Next, We Flew Back to Katmandu on the DC-3 and Boarded a Jet Plane to New Delhi.

We Focused Our Short Two-Day Trip to New Delhi By Just Visiting Two Wonderful Historic Sites.

The First One was the Taj Mahal, Which is a Beautiful White Marble Mausoleum on the Southern Bank of the Yamura River in the Historic Indian City of Aqua.

Liddy and I Sat Down Just Outside the Gate to the Taj Mahal and Admired Its Natural Beauty For at Least One Hour. The Taj Mahal, Which Took Twenty-one Years to Build in the Seventeenth Century, is known as a Symbol of Everlasting Love Because of the Indian Emperor's Memory, Who Built It, of His Beloved But Decreased Wife.

Our Second Visit was to the Majestic and Very Tall Red Fort, Just North of New Delhi. The Red Fort Encloses a Large Complex of Palaces and Entertainment Halls which were the Main Residences of the Mughlai Emperors.

During Our Visit While Sitting Just Outside the Walls of the Red Fort, a Muscular Young Man Wearing only a Loincloth Began Collecting Money From Other Tourists Sitting Near Us. He then Climbed to the Highest Tower on the Outer Walls of the Fort, And Amazingly, He Made an Aesthetically Beautiful and Perfect Dive of Over One Hundred Feet Into a Small Pool Adjacent to the Outer Wall of the Fort.

Fortunately, He Survived!

63. Getting Married to Liddy

Shortly After Becoming Engaged to Liddy, I was Invited Along With Liddy to Spend a Three-Day Weekend with Her Parents in Lincoln, Massachusetts.

After Work on Friday at Exxon, Liddy's Father and Liddy Met Me at the New Exxon Building Near Rockefeller Center. They Arrived in a Mobil Limousine with a Driver Who Drove Us to Westchester Airport.

Instead of Having to Check In At an Airline Counter, The Limousine Drove On to an Airplane Waiting Area Near the Takeoff Runway. The Limousine Stopped Just Under One of the Wings of a Medium-Sized Mobil Oil Business Jet.

The Wife of One of Al Nickerson's Deceased Harvard Classmates, Who was Exceptionally Friendly, Was Also on the Plane.

On the Plane Trip to a Small Airport North of Boston, We Were Treated to a Drink and Very Nice hor d'oeuvres.

Al and Liz Nickerson Were Exceptionally Nice to Me that Weekend.

Al Drove Me Along with Liddy to His Boyhood Home in Dedham, Massachusetts, which Looked Like an Old Stone Castle on a Large Estate. It is now the Home of the Well-Known Noble and Greenough School, Which is a Coed Day and Five-Day Boarding School For Grades Seven to Twelve Located on 187 Acres Along the Charles River.

Al Also Took Us to Lunch at the Country Club in Brookline, Massachusetts, which is One of the Oldest and Most Exclusive Country Clubs in America and which Liz and Al Thought Would Be a Nice Place for the Luncheon with Special Guests Just Before the Wedding. And Al Took Liddy and I to see the Historic Longfellow's Wayside Inn that was Established in 1716 in Sudbury, which Liz and Al Thought Would Be a Nice Place for a Large Dinner the Night Before Our Wedding.

And, as an Unusually Nice Gesture, Just Before Having Saturday Night Dinner at Al and Liz's Home in Lincoln, Al Brought Out Three Different Bottles of High-End Chilled French Champagne For Liddy and I to Sample and Then Choose Which One We Liked the Best For Our Wedding.

Our Wedding on May 5th of 1973 was Extremely Nice.

I Stayed with My Mother and Father and My Sister's and Brother's Families Along with My Groomsmen at the Historic Concord Colonial Inn, Which was Established in 1716.

My Best Man was Al Henry Who Was a Classmate of Mine at Northwestern's Graduate School of Business; Was a Frequent Weekend Golfing Partner of Mine; and Was Someone Whom I Enjoyed Having a Few Beers with on Friday Evenings After Work.

My Groomsmen Were

Matt Sterling, Who was a Northwestern Graduate Business School Classmate of Mine, Was the One Who First Introduced Me to Liddy, and Whose Sister was a Good Friend of Liddy's From the University of Arizona.

Rand Carpenter, Who Worked With Me at Exxon's Cargo Sales Department and Then Became a Customer of Mine at Occidental Petroleum.

Dave Erickson, Who was a Harvard Business School Graduate whom I Met at Madison Avenue Presbyterian Church and Whom I Met Frequently With For Very Competitive Tennis Matches and Weekday Lunches at Small French Restaurants or in Central Park.

Bert Nickerson, Who Was Liddy's Brother.

On the Day of the Wedding, I Got Up Early in the Morning

and Walked Around Waldon's Pond which was Just a Short Drive From the Concord Colonial Inn.

All of the Arrangements For the Wedding Were Wonderful and Worked Out Flawlessly, Such as

The Friday Night Dinner at Longfellow's Wayside Inn.

The Saturday Luncheon at The Country Club.

The Wedding Itself at The Beautiful Congregational Church.

And The Short Walk Down the Hill From the Church to a Very Nice Reception With Dancing, Food, and Drinks at the Nickersons' House in Lincoln.

After the Wedding, Liddy and I Flew Back to Our Apartment at 155 East 73rd Street, And The Next Day We Flew to Tobago and Later to St. Lucia For a Wonderful Ten-Day Wedding Trip.

64. Texas—First Foreign Assignment

Aㅏfter Spending Eleven Years Working at Exxon's Headquarters at Rockefeller Center in Manhattan, I was Transferred to Esso Eastern in Houston, Texas, which was Exxon's Regional Headquarters for all of its Asian Companies.

It was a Promotional Assignment as I Became the Corporate Planning and Financial Operations Division Manager in Esso Eastern's Finance and Planning Department. Basically, My Primary Responsibility was to Coordinate the Development of Esso Eastern's Five-Year Strategic, Investment, and Financial Plans For all of Exxon's Asian Affiliates.

This was a Big Responsibility as it Involved Overseeing Exxon's Plans in a Highly Diverse Group of Countries which Included Japan, South Korea, Hong Kong, China, Singapore, Malaysia, Thailand, South Vietnam, Cambodia, Laos, Philippines, Indonesia, India, Pakistan, Bangladesh, Nepal, Australia, and New Zealand.

In Just Two Years at Esso Eastern, I Developed a Divestiture Plan which Resulted in Improving Esso Eastern's Financial Performance in Terms of Return on Capital Employed From Being the Worst-Performing Exxon Regional Company to Being the Best-Performing Regional Company.

This Involved Selling Exxon's Affiliates Located in Countries where there were Government Price Controls on Exxon's Marketing Operations. These Price Controls were Structured in Such a Way as to Allow Exxon to Always Make a Very Small Profit But Did Not Allow Exxon to Make an Attractive Return on Its Very Large Refining and Marketing Investments.

Thus, In Just Two Years' Time, We Sold Our Poor-Performing Refining and Marketing Affiliates in India, Pakistan, Bangladesh, Nepal, Laos, Cambodia, and the Philippines to Government-Run Companies.

However, Esso Eastern was Left with Refining and Marketing Affiliates in Eleven Free Market Growth Countries Where it had a Track Record of Earning Very Attractive Rates of Return on Its Investments.

65. New Lifestyle Living and Working in Houston Suburb

*E*sso Easter's Asian Headquarters Office Building was not Located in Downtown Houston But in a Beautiful Campus-Like Setting in Bunker Hill Village, Which was a Very Tiny Western Suburb of Houston, Texas.

Liddy and I also Chose To Buy a House in Bunker Hill Village that was Less Than a Mile from Esso Eastern's Office. It was a Very Nice Spanish-Style Ranch House at the End of a One-Block Cul de Sac. It Had a Beautiful Front Yard and a Backyard with a Swimming Pool. The Property was Separated from One Neighbor By a Live Bamboo Fence and From the Other Neighbor By a High But Tasteful Wooden Fence. And the Front and Backyards Contained a Variety of Fruit Trees and Flowering Cactus Plants.

The House was Much More Spacious Than Our Two-Room Apartment in Manhattan with a Bedroom, Kitchen, and Bathroom. It Had a Large High-Ceiling Living Room with a Fireplace, a Separate Dining Room, Two Bedrooms, Two Bathrooms, and a Large Kitchen and Breakfast Nook. It also Came with a Garage, Along with a Guest Bedroom and Bathroom Above the Garage.

And, Shortly Before Our Move to Bunker Hill Village, I Bought a Mercedes Benz 250 with an Ivory Steering Wheel, Leather Seats, and a Sunroof from an African American Member of the New York Knicks Professional Basketball Team. He was Buying a New

Mercedes and Realized that He Could Get a Better Price for His Used Mercedes By Selling It Himself Rather Than Accepting a Trade-In Offer from the Mercedes Dealer.

As Liddy and I Only Had One Car, on Alternating Workdays We Would Split Use of the Mercedes. On the Workdays When I Didn't Have Use of the Car, Liddy Would Drive Me to Work and Pick Me Up at the End of the Workday. Although on Some Days, I Would Ride My Bicycle To and From Work.

Liddy and I Both Loved Having Pets When We Were Growing Up, And Bunker Hill Village was a Much Better Place for Pets Than Manhattan.

So We Ended Up in Bunker Hill Village with One Bird, Two Cats, One Dog, and Fifty Turtles.

Liddy Brought Her Pet Minor Bird Named Fred From New York City. We Quickly Acquired a Golden Lab Puppy Named Houston, And Liddy Purchased a Baby Tom Cat Named Fred From a Local Kennel and Drove It to Our House in the Front Wicker Basket of Her Bicycle, And We Adopted a Stray Siamese Cat Named Lucy, Which I Found in Our Backyard Garden.

During the Weekends, We Loved Taking Car Trips to Visit and Camp Out at State and National Parks. On Almost Every Trip, We Would See Turtles in the Woods or Basking on Logs Near the Banks of a Stream or Pond.

The Frequent Turtle Sightings Brought Back My Fond Memories as a Young Boy in My Elementary School Years in Maryland of Building a Large Turtle Pen For Turtles That I Had Seen and Captured; Crossing the Road During Car Trips with My Parents; In the

Woods on Camping Trips With My Father, Sister, and Brother; and On Logs Near the Banks of the Chesapeake and Ohio Canal.

Thus, Early On, I Built a Large Fenced Turtle Pen in the Backyard of Our House With Separate Dry Areas for Box Turtles and Desert Tortoises, Water Tubs for Painted Water Turtles, and Mud Pits for Snapping and Mud Turtles.

So, Within Six Months of Moving to Bunker Hill Village, I Had Amassed a Collection of Fifty Turtles.

Also, as there were Many Golf Courses within a Thirty-Minute Drive From Bunker Hill Village, I Played More Golf on the Weekends and Would About Once a Week Play Nine Holes of Golf After Work...

Importantly, While There Were Violent Rainstorms and Thunderstorms Causing Flooding and Tree Damage, I Do Not Remember Even One Snowstorm.

In Summary, Living and Working in Bunker Hill Village was a Totally Different Experience For Me From My Prior Life of Living and Working For Exxon in Manhattan.

66. My Huge Snapping Turtle Attacks Neighbors

I Received a Panicked Phone Call One Early Sunday Morning From Our Neighbor Across the Street, Shouting in a High-Pitched Voice that One of My Huge Snapping Turtles was on the From Steps of Their House and Looking Like It Wanted to Bite Them.

I Then Realized that while My Large Turtle Pen was Staked In By a Six-Foot-High Wire Fence, There Were Two Large Trees Just Inside the Fence of the Turtle Pen. And, Evidently, the Large Snapping Turtle, Which had Very Powerful Claw Feet, Had Climbed Up one of the Trees Just Inside of the Turtle Pen Until it Reached the Top of the Fence. And Then, Without Any Fear, It Had Fallen Six Feet to the Ground.

The Snapping Turtles are in Fact Very Dangerous, With Extremely Strong Jaws Jutting Out From a Long Neck of Six Inches. They have been Known to Bite a Broom Stick in Two and Totally Sever the Arms of Children and Adults.

Also, I Remember My Large Male Snapping Turtle Aggressively Chasing Me Around the Turtle Pen During the Mating Season. And I Also Remember One of My Two Baby Snapping Turtles Biting Off the Head of One of My Small Adult Mud Turtles.

Thus, In Light of the Danger Involved to Others in Having Two Very Large Snapping Turtles and Two Baby Snapping Turtles in My Turtle Pen, I Transported All Four of Them to a Large State Park Not Far From where I Lived and Left Them in a Swampy Area, Which I Am Sure They Would Like Much Better Than My Turtle Pen.

67. DISASTER AFTER DISASTER IN TIERRA DEL FUEGO

Liddy and I Decided to Take a Hiking and Camping Trip To the Beautiful Tierra Del Fuego Area in Southern Argentina and Chile.

Our Jet From Houston and Then Miami Landed in Buenos Aires, the Capital of Argentina. From There, the Only Flight to the Southern Area of Argentina Known as Patagonia was on a Propeller Argentina Military Plane, with Benches For Seating on Each Side of the Plane.

However, the Plane was Several Hours Late in Taking Off and We Didn't Arrive to the City in Northern Patagonia Until Midnight. And When We Went to the Baggage Claim Area to Claim Our Two Suitcases and Hiking and Camping Equipment, Our Baggage Was Not There.

After a Lot of Screaming By Me, They Escorted Me to the Military Plane and Showed Me the Baggage Area. And, Lo and Behold, There Were Our Two Suitcases and Two Large Backpacks With All of Our Hiking and Camping Equipment and Supplies.

When We Arrived at Our Small Hotel After Midnight Where We Had a Reservation, We Were Told That Due to Our Arriving More than Three Hours Late, They Had Given Our Room to Someone Else and Did Not Have Another Room For Us.

However, They Did Allow Us to Sleep on Two Sofas in Their Public Area.

The Next Morning, We Rented a Jeep and Drove to the Needle-Like Peninsula of Punto Tombo That Extended Five Miles Into the Sea. After a Short Trip on a Rough Road, We Encountered Several Thousand Penguins in a Nesting Area. About Half of the Penguins were Close to Their Nests and the Other Half Were in the Water Close to Shore.

I Then Changed into My Bathing Suit and Joined the Penguins in the Water While Liddy Took Many Pictures of Me.

The Next Day, We Were Able to Fly on a Nice Plane to Ushuaia, Which is Argentina's Southern-Most Town in Patagonia.

We Stocked Up on Some Fresh Food Supplies to Supplement the Packaged Camping Meals That We Had Brought From Houston and Drove to a Large Argentina National Park Where We Camped Next to a Stream.

After a Late Lunch, We Took a Short Hike in the Park. However, Upon Returning to Our Tent, We Discovered that an Animal Had Entered Our Tent and Managed To Find and Take Off With Our Large Fresh Steak That We Had Planned to Cook That Night For Dinner.

On the Next Day, We Hiked to the Top of the Highest Mountain in the Park and Encountered Beautiful Glaciers, Managed to Carefully Walk Around Deep Ice Crevasses, and Came Across a Large Herd of Iguanas.

We Then Drove Northward to Calafate, Where We Stayed at a Very Nice Lodge. The Next Day, We Took a Boat Trip on a Large Nearby Lake to View the Perito Moreno Glacier, Which is a Beautiful Two-Hundred-Foot-High Wall of Ice.

Next, We Drove Northward to Los Glaciares National Park to See Fitz Roy Mountain, Which is Very Rocky and Rises Eleven Thousand Feet From a Very Flat Ranching Area.

On Our Way, We Had to Drive Our Car Onto a Small Barge to Be Pulled Across the River on Two Cables as the Bridge Had Been Washed Away By a Hurricane. However, the Men in Charge of the

Barge Crossing Had Just Started Their Lunch and Were Planning to Take Their Usual One-Hour Siesta Before Resuming Their Barge Duties. Nevertheless, Two Hours Later, Our Rental Car and the Two of Us Were Pulled Across the River on the Primitive Barge.

At the Los Glaciares National Park, There was a Nice Tenting Campground where we Spent the Night.

On the Next Day, We Set Our to Climb to the Fitz Roy Base Camp on Two Horses From an Indian Tribe Accompanied By Two Tribal Guides on Their Horses.

However, On the Way to the Fitz Roy Base Camp, We Came to a Narrow but Very Deep Rushing Stream. The Two Tribesmen Gave a Loud War Cry, Hit Their Horses on the Rump, and Jumped Across the Deep Stream.

They Then Motioned for Liddy and Me to Follow. Liddy Did and Completed a Beautiful Jump Across the Stream as She Had Grown Up with Horses at Her Parents' House and Had Competed as a Jumper in Many Horse Shows.

However, I Had Just Taken Riding Lessons For the First Time Several Months Before Our Trip. And I was Scared to Death to Attempt the Jump. But One of the Tribesmen Jumped Back to My Side of the Stream. He Then Motioned Me to Lead My Horse to the Edge of the Stream. And Without My Knowing What Would Happen Next, He Rode His Horse at a Gallop Towards My Horse and Me, Yelled, and Hit My Horse in the Rump. I was Terrified and Quickly Leaned Forward on My Horse and Put Both of My Arms Tightly Around the Horses Neck Just Before My Horse Attempted the Jump.

Fortunately, My Horse was Successful, And I Miraculously Managed Not to Fall Off the Horse During the Jump.

And Liddy and I Had a Very Nice Trip on Our Two Horses Up to the Fitz Roy Base Camp for Climbers Planning to Attempt a Summit of the Mountain.

However, the Two Indian Guides, Rather Than Waiting For Us to Finish Our Lunch, Suddenly Took Off and Left Us.

We Then Became Concerned About Whether or Not We Could

Find the Right Route Back to the Campground and How I Would Get My Horse to Jump the Narrow But Deep Stream.

Fortunately, We Did Find the Correct Route Back to the Campground. However, There was No Way That I was Going to Attempt to Have My Horse Jump Across the Stream. So, I Tied Up My Horse to a Tree and Found a Nearby Walkers-Only Bridge to Cross the Stream. And Liddy Jumped Her Horse Across the Stream and Rode to the Indian Village to Tell Them Where I had Tied Up Their Horse to a Tree. And I Hiked the Rest of the Way Back to the Campground.

After Another Day, We Had to Return Our Rent a Car Back to Calafate.

However, When We Got To the Location of the River That Had the Primitive Barge Crossing By Cable, We Were Told that a Massive Section of the Perito Moreno Glacier Had Broken Off and Fallen Into the Lake. And This Had Caused a Huge Tidal Wave to Form and Cross to the Other End of the Lake and Then Into the River that We Had to Cross. And When the Tidal Wave Reached the Barge Crossing Area, It Caused the Barge to Break Loose From its Mooring, Hit Some Rocks, and Be Totally Destroyed.

We Were Then Told That We Would Have to Drive 150 Miles Northward Where There Was a Bridge Across the River. And After the Bridge Crossing, We Would Have to Drive a Hundred Miles Eastward to Hook Up to a Road That Would Take Us Back to Calafate.

However, Shortly After the Bridge Crossing, One of the Tires in Our Rental Car Blew Out After Hitting a Deep Rut on the Dirt Road. Fortunately, a Very Nice Ranch Owner Stopped His Truck When He Saw Us and Drove Us to His Large Ranch and Fed Us a Late Lunch. He Also Arranged to Have Our Rental Car Towed to the Next Town Where an Auto Repair Garage Would Replace Our Ruptured Tire.

From Calafate, We Stuck to Our Plan of Crossing the Mountains to Visit the Southern Portion of Chile in Patagonia. We were Also Able to Hire a Small Truck with a Driver From Our Hotel.

Astonishingly, We Learned the Day Before Our Trip to Chile that Salvador Allende, the Marxist President of Chile, Had Been Overthrown and Killed in a Military Coup D'état. And, as a Result of This, Both Argentina and the New Government of Chile Had Strengthened Their Troop Presence at the Southern Borders of Their Two Countries as There Had Been Many Military Skirmishes Between the Two Countries In the Past.

And We Were Told That We Might Not Be Able to Leave Argentina or Enter Chile at the Mountain Border Crossing.

When We Reached the Argentina Side of the Border Crossing in the Early Evening, We Had No Problem With Their Customs, Police, and Military Officials.

However, When We Had Just Crossed the Border into Chile, Military Officials Stopped Our Truck and Would Not Allow Us to Continue, And Within Seconds of Being Stopped, a Dozen Very Young Soldiers Charged Down a Snow-Covered Hill Towards Our Truck with Machine Guns Drawn and Pointed Toward Us.

We Were Then Apprehended and Taken to the Chile Customs Building Where We Were Cross-Examined For Two Hours. When the Two Interrogators Realized That We Were Only Entered That Part of Chile to Hike and Camp in Their Beautiful Patagonian Mountains and Had No Political Affiliation with Allende, They Allowed Us to Proceed to the Nearest Town Where We Had a Hotel Reservation.

When We Reached Our Small Hotel at Nine Thirty P.M., The Hotel Manager Told Us That the New Military Government of Chile Had Established a Lot of New Regulations, Which Included Martial Law, and a Curfew of Not Being Allowed Outside After Ten P.M. Thus, We Could Not Go to Any of the Restaurants in the Town For Dinner.

On the Next Day, We Had Decided In Advance to Visit, Camp Out, and Hike in the Torres Del Paine National Park, Which Had Recently Been Selected By National Geographic as One of the Five Most Beautiful Places in the World. It is Known For Its Famed Peaks of Dazzling Rock Pinnacles Rising More Than Ten Thousand Feet From a Turquoise Lake Surrounded by Ice and Snow.

However, When Trying to Leave the Town in Our Truck and Drive to the Park, We Were Stopped at a Military Check Point at the Edge of Town. And We Were Told That We Could Not Proceed Unless We Drove a General From the Army To a City, Which Was Fortunately in the Same Direction as the National Park.

Thus, We Welcomed the General, Who Sat in the Front Passenger Seat of Our Truck. When We Passed By a Coffee House on the Route, He Ordered Us to Stop For One Hour so That He Could Enjoy One or Two Cups of Coffee.

Shortly Thereafter, On the Drive to the North, We Passed By a Large Soccer Stadium, And We Saw, To Our Amazement, Several Hundred Men Dressed in Suits With White Shirts and Ties Standing on The Soccer Field. The General Told Us That They Were Officials From Allende's Marxist Government Which Had to Be Detained, Removed From Their Important Government Positions, and Replaced By Officials Loyal to the New Military Government.

After Dropping Off the General at His Destination, We Entered the Beautiful Paine Towers National Park. First, We Stayed at the Park Lodge and Were Told That the Whole Park Had Been Closed Due to the Change in Governments. However, They Would Allow Us to Camp Next to the Lake Provided We Adhered to the New Evening Curfew Regulations.

And, After Pitching Our Tent, We Were Surprised To Be Joined For Dinner and Later For Sleeping in Our Tent By a Very Friendly German Shepheard, Who Was a Pet of the Lodge Manager.

We Spent a Wonderful Three Days Hiking in the Park to Obtain Good Views of the Most Aspiring Mountain Peaks That We Had Ever Seen. And We Also Enjoyed Seeing Lots of Deer-Like Wild Animals, Flamingos, and Condors.

We Then Traveled Northward On a Bus to Puerto Montt, Where We Could Cross a Large Lake, Travel Back to Buenos Aires, and Take Our Flight Back to the US.

However, On the Sunday of Our Departure From Puerto Montt,

We Learned That the New Military Government of Chile Had Just Promulgated a New Law Preventing Anyone From Leaving the Country Without Written Permission From a Senior Government Official.

Then, After Finding Out That the City Government Office was Closed for the Weekend, I Asked and Found Out Where the Mayor of Puerto Montt Lived.

Liddy and I Then Went to the Mayor's House and Rang His Doorbell. Fortunately, He was Home and Let Us Into His House. We Explained Our Need to Return to Buenos Aires so that We Could Board a Jet on Seats that We Had Reserved To Miami and Then to Houston Where We Had a Home. The Mayor Then Took a Piece of Paper From His Desk with The Mayor's Letterhead on it and Requested in Writing that the Customs Officials on the Chile Side of the Lake Allow Us to Board a Vessel to Cross the Lake to Argentina.

Fortunately, at the Chile Customs Station, They Allowed Us to Board a Passenger Boat to Cross the Large Lake to the Argentina Side.

Then, After a Few Days of Camping in the Mountains of Baralochi, We Arranged for Transportation By Bus to Buenos Aires to Catch the Flight We Had Reserved Back to Houston Via Miami.

However, When Arriving at the Ticket Counter For Our Flight, We Were Told That Our Two Seats on the Jet Had Been Given at the Request of the US Government To the Manager and His Wife of Exxon's Refinery in Campana, Argentina.

Victor Samuelson, Exxon's Refinery Manager, Had Been Kidnapped By Marxist Guerrillas and Held Hostage in the Argentina Mountains For Three Months and Threated With Death Until Exxon Very Reluctantly Paid Their Ransom Request of $14.2 Million, Which was the Highest Ever Paid For an American Kidnapping Victim in a Foreign Country.

As Our Flight Only Had One Available Seat Left, They Managed to Accommodate Both of Us By Having Liddy Fly on Another Jet to New York City and Then Transfer on a Flight to Houston, And

I Would Stay on the Flight That We Had Reserved to Miami and Then to Houston.

After All of the Disasters on Our Trip to Tierra Del Fuego, I Can Say With a Lot of Conviction:

Both Liddy and I are Survivors.

Never Take Things For Granted as There Can Be Many Unpleasant Surprises.

Don't Forget to Thank the Lord on a Daily Basis For Your Safety and Health.

68. Defeating the Chess Master and Grandmaster

Ever Since High School, I Loved to Play Chess.

While Living in the Upper East Side of Manhattan on East 73rd Street, I Would Meet With Pierre Brull, Who Had Worked For Twenty Years in Exxon's Treasurers Department, and Then Held a Job as a Securities Analyst on Wall Street. For Two Games of Chess on Sunday Afternoons at His Manhattan Apartment on East 72nd Street.

Pierre and I Were Both Strong Chess Players Who Were Evenly Matched. And Thus, I Was Only Able to Win Slightly More Than Half of Our Chess Games.

I Also Played Chess With Vladimir Prybylski, Who was a Russian who Worked at the United States Nations Headquarters in Manhattan.

Vladimir Was an Outstanding Chess Player Who Had Achieved the International Chess Title of Chess Master International.

I Always Gave Vladimir a Strong, Drawn-Out Battle on the Chess Board, But Never Won Any Games From Him Until I Defeated Him on a Sunday Night After a Dinner and Lots of Drinks at His West Side Apartment.

Vladimir Became Extremely Angry When I Declared Checkmate. He Shouted Out that "He Would Never Play Another Game of Chess With Me Again."

Near The End of Liddy's and My Three-Week Vacation Trip to Tierra Del Fuego, While We Were Staying For a Couple of Days at Bariloche, Argentina, Before Returning to Houston, Texas, We Had a Nice Lunch at a High-End Hotel in the Mountains of Bariloche.

During Lunch, I Noticed Two Men Playing Chess and Asked If I Could Play the Winner of Their Game. And Both Men Agreed.

And Just Before Starting Our Chess Match, The Winner of His Previous Chess Match Announced That He Held the International Chess Title of Chess Grandmaster.

That Made Me Very Nervous. However, I Ended Up Playing One of My Best Chess Games Ever and Unbelievably Declared Checkmate After More Than One Hour of Our Very Close Chess Match.

Grandmaster is the Title Awarded to Chess Players By the World Chess Organization. Apart From World Champion, Grandmaster is the Highest Title a Chess Player Can Attain. And Once it is Achieved, the Title is Held For Life. International Master is the Next Highest Chess Title and is also Awarded by the World Chess Organization and Held For Life.

After Returning to Liddy's and My New Home in Houston, Texas, I was unable to Form a Personal Relationship with an Active Chess Player and Thus was Forced to Stop Playing Chess.

Nevertheless, I am Still Extremely Proud of My Two Chess Wins Against Two of the Highest Ranked International Chess Players.

69. Rodeos and Cowboy Saloons

On the Weekends While Living in Houston, Texas, Liddy and I Quite Often Would Like to Get into Our C250 Mercedes and Drive to Ranching Areas in Texas.

And, One Weekend, We Visited a Small Texas Town that was Holding a Rodeo. Just Before the Rodeo, We Attended a Nice Barbecue on the Grounds of the Rodeo Stadium. The Rodeo Itself Was Very Exciting to Watch, with Cowboys One After Another on Their Horse Trying to Lasso a Bull Steer that Had Been Released From a Gate Inside a Tiny Steer Pen and Then Having to Leap Off Their Horse On To the Back of the Bull Steer and Wrestle it to the Ground.

In Most Events, the Cowboys Prevailed. But Occasionally the Cowboy Would Just Miss Jumping On To the Bull Steer's Back or Would Be Gored By the Bull Steer in the Cowboy's Attempt to Wrestle it to the Ground.

When I looked at Who was Sitting Around Us in the Spectator Stands of the Rodeo Stadium, I Observed That Virtually Every Male Adult was Wearing a Ten-Gallon Cowboy Hat. And, Since I Was Not Wearing a Ten Gallon Cowboy Hat, I Realized that I Had to Stand Out as an Out-of-Place City Slicker.

On Another Trip to Cowboy Country, Liddy and I Noticed a Saloon in a Small Town. We Decided to Enter the Saloon for a Beer.

In Entering the Saloon, There was Just Like the Movies a Wooden

143

Swinging Door and Hooks on the Wall of the Entrance Hall Where the Saloon's Male Customers Had to Check Their Revolvers.

We Were Also Amazed to See a Number of Large Round Tables with Cowboys Sitting around the Tables Playing Poker While They Were Being Served Drinks by Scantily Clad Western Cowgirls.

And I Realized For the first time that we were in Real Cowboy Country, which Still Existed in the Real Life, Rather Than Just Being Shown in Western Movies.

70. Injured By Go-Go Dancers

Bill Cleveland, Who was President of Exxon's Asian Regional Company in Houston, Texas, Loved to Host Wild and Fun Parties For Employees.

In My First Year with Exxon's Asian Regional Company, I Attended His Christmas Party that Featured a Rock and Roll Live Band with Female Go-Go Dancers.

As I Loved to Dance to Rock and Roll Music, I Hit the Dance Floor With a Number of Exxon's Female Employees and Stayed on the Dance Floor Almost to the End of the Christmas Party.

Unfortunately, I Tripped on the Microphone Cord For One of the Go-Go Dancers and Fell Over Backwards and Landed on My Left Ankle.

The Pain was Awful, and I Could Barely Walk. So, On the Way Home, I Drove to the Emergency Room of the Nearest Hospital.

My Injury was Diagnosed as a "Severe Tear In the Muscle For My Left Upper Ankle." They Put the Ankle in a Boot Cast and Gave Me a Pair of Crutches.

I Had to Use the Crutches for Three Months Until the Severe Ankle Sprain Had Healed.

Nevertheless, I Never Regretted Dancing to the Rockand Roll Band Music at Bill Cleveland's Christmas Party.

71. Entering Wife and Me in AAU Track Meet

After Starting My First Job with Exxon in Manhattan, I Always Liked to Relax After Work by Running For About Thirty Minutes in Central Park.

My Favorite Running Route was Running For Two Large Laps Around the Cinder Track of the Central Park Water Reservoir.

And I Always Had an Objective of Passing Many More Runners Than Those Who Passed Me. Thus, Because of my Competitive Nature, I Became a Very Fast Runner.

In Houston, Texas, I Heard about a Summer AAU Track Meet at Rice University's Football Stadium.

I Talked Liddy into Accompanying Me to the AAU Track Meet. Although Liddy knew that I had Entered Myself in the Men's One-Mile Run, She Did Not Know in Advance that I had also Entered Her in the Women's One-Mile Run.

Liddy Ran First and Did Quite Well and Finished Her One-Mile Run in Just Six-Minutes.

In My Men's One-Mile Run, I saw That Those who Lined Up were Mostly College Track Stars From the University of Texas and Other Southwestern Universities.

Given My Competitive Nature, I was Able to Run with the Lead Pack For the First Half of the One-Mile Run. And, In Fact, at the Halfway Point of the Race, the Lead Pack was Running at a Four-Minute Mile Pace.

However, at the Four-Minute Mile Pace, I Became Totally Exhausted and Out of Breath at the Halfway Point of the Race and Had to Drop Out.

Nevertheless, To This Day, I am Proud of Being Able to Run the Half Mile at an Exceptionally Fast Pace of Two Minutes Flat Even Though I was Thirty-five Years Old.

72. Our Dog Takes Revenge on Head Trainer at Obedience School

*E*arly on While Living in Houston, Texas, We Adopted a Lovely Young Male Golden Labrador Retriever, Whom we Named "Houston," and Who Enjoyed Hiking with Us on the Weekends.

Fairly Soon After Adopting Houston, Liddy Entered Him in a Dog Obedience School Class.

At the Final Obedience Class, the Owners of all of the Dogs were Invited For a Graduation Ceremony.

One By One, the Dogs who Passed the Obedience School Class were Invited Up By the Head Trainer to Announce Their Graduation and Receive a Yummy Treat.

At the End of the Graduation Ceremony, Houston was the only Dog who had not been Invited Up By the Head Trainer to Announce His Graduation and Receive a Yummy Treat.

Being a Smart Dog, Houston Sensed That he had been Left Out of Not Getting a Yummy Treat, so he Walked Up to the Head Trainer, Lifted His Hind Leg, and Peed on the Head Trainer's Pants.

73. Off to Japan With Dog, Cats, Bird, and Turtles

After Transforming Esso Eastern From Being the Worst-Performing Exxon Regional Company to the Best-Performing Exxon Regional Company, I was Promoted to Become a General Manager of a Large Joint Venture Japanese Oil Refining Company that was Headquartered in Tokyo, Japan, with Exxon Owning 50 percent and Japanese Shareholders Owning 50 percent of the Company.

In Houston, Texas, We Had a Large Number of Pets That Included Our Golden Retriever, A Siamese Cat, A Tom Cat, A Minor Bird Named Fred That Talked a Lot in English, and a Few Box Turtles.

When We Arrived at Tokyo's International Airport, We Found Out For the First Time That We Had to Quarantine Our Dog and Two Cats at the Airport Pet Facility For Six Weeks.

Fortunately, We Found Out That the Airport Pet Facility Had an Excellent Reputation For Taking Nice Care of Quarantined Animals. And Before Leaving the Airport to Our Temporary Hotel, We Saw That Our Dog Had His Own Large Indoor Cage with an Open Passageway to a Nice Outside Pen. And Our Two Cats Shared a Similar Large Indoor and Outdoor Pen. And We Were Allowed to Visit Then During the Six-Week Quarantine Period.

74. Living on Prince Konroji's Estate

*O*ur First Priority After Arriving in Tokyo Was to Find a Nice Place to Live.

Exxon Had a Number of Large Business Operations That Were Headquartered in Tokyo Which Included General Sekilyu Seisei, The Oil Refinery Company with Four Large Refineries That I Was Assigned To; An Exxon Oil Marketing Company For Japan; and Other Separate Companies Dedicated to Oil Tanker Construction, Nuclear Energy, and Chemicals.

As a Result of Exxon's Major Multi-Faceted Businesses in Japan, Which Was By Far the Largest Energy Market in Asia, Exxon Had Assigned a Lot of US Expatriates to Senior-Level Managerial Positions with These Companies.

And Exxon Believed That They Should Acquire and Develop Nice Living Areas For the US Expatriates. Thus, When Liddy and I Arrived, We Were Offered a Choice of Living in an Exxon-Owned House in Their Tokyo Housing Compound or in Either of Their Other Two Housing Compounds in a Suburb of Tokyo.

However, Liddy and I Wanted to Live in a Japanese Neighborhood Where We Could Get to Know Japanese People and Learn Their Customs. Also, I Did Not Like the Idea of Having to Live with the Same US Expatriates That I Would Be Working With.

Thus, When Asked What Type of House Outside of the Three Exxon Housing Compounds Would Be Acceptable to Us, We Said

That It Should Be One That is Located in a Beautiful, Natural Area with Woods, Trails, and Ponds or Streams.

Exxon's Local Representatives Laughed at Our House Preferences and Told Us That No Such Place to Live Was Available to Rent in Tokyo.

But We Then Asked to Meet with a Local Real Estate Agent To Just Try to See If the Agent Could Find Us a House to Rent That Met Our Preferences. And Fortunately, Exxon's Local Representatives Agreed to Do So Even Though They Felt That It Would Be a Useless House Search.

And, Lo and Behold, the Japanese Real Estate Agent Assigned to Work With Us Said She knew of One House to Rent That Might Meet Our Preferences.

So, on the First Day of Our Home Search, She Took Us to Prince Konroji's Estate, Which was Located in a Nice Japanese Neighborhood of Hatsudai, which was just on the Outskirts of Tokyo But Still Within a Short Subway Ride to Downtown Tokyo Where General Sekiyu Seisei Had Its Headquarters Office Building.

When the Japanese Real Estate Agent Drove Us On To the Grounds of Prince Konroji's Estate. We Were Amazed at What We Saw.

First, the Konroji Estate Was Very Large and Surrounded By a High Stone Wall.

Inside the Estate, There was a Large Extremely Nice Mansion Where Prince Konroji and His Family Lived. There Were Three Other Houses. One House was Occupied By One of Prince Konroji's Two Sons. One House was Rented to Outsiders Not Related to Prince Konroji's Family. The Other House Had Been Occupied By Prince Konroji's Other Son Who Had Just Been Transferred By the High-Tech Japanese Company That He Worked For To The United States to Work at Their US Affiliate. And This Was The House That Was Available to Rent.

The House Itself Was Very Modern, with High Ceilings and Large Windows. It Had a Wrap-Around Porch That Overlooked a Japanese Carp Pond with Lots of Beautifully Colored Fish.

It was also Adjacent to ta Hilly Area within Konroji Estate, With Lots of Nice Vegetation and a Short Circular Hiking Trail.

The Carp Pond was Fed By a Stream. And Nearby, There was an Ancient Cave with Two Different Passageways That Led To a Stone Carving of a Buddhist Monk and a Large Serpent.

The Hatsudai Neighborhood was Very Quiet and Quaint, with Very Nice Individual Houses and a Small Shopping Street. It was also Within a Short Walk to the Famous Meiji Shrine Surrounded By a Lovely Park with Lots of Gardens and Flowers.

Both Liddy and I Fell in Love Instantly with the Modern House to Rent in the Beautiful Grounds of the Konroji Estate Along with the Surrounding Neighborhood. And, Even Though the Monthly Rent was Sky High, Exxon Agreed to Pay It After I Offered to Reimburse Them For 25 percent of the Rent.

Who is Prince Konroji? He was Closely Related to the Imperial Family and Grew Up in the Emperor's Palace in Tokyo. He was Assigned to a Variety of Important Tasks Even as a Young Boy. One of His Early Tasks was to Sleep in a Small Room Next to the Emperor's Bedroom and to Notify the Emperor's Medical Staff If He Thought the Emperor was Sick. He Would Go On as An Adult to Serve in Higher-Level Administrative Positions in the Emperor's Palace For Three Different Emperors and Retired As Vice Chamberlain For the Imperial Family.

Before Prince Konroji Left the Imperial Palace, He Wrote a Best-Selling Book Both in Japan and the United States Entitled *The Emperor Wears Western Clothes*. In the Book, He Emphasized That Emperor Hirohito Was a Man of Peace, Who Disagreed with Japan Going to War and Always Advocated For a Peaceful End to the War.

Upon Retirement, as a Reward For Serving Three Different Emperors Extremely Well, He was Given One of the Seven Secret Valleys of Tokyo, Which Became the Konroji Estate. Prince Konroji's Brother, Who Also Served The Same Three Japanese Emperors as Prince Konroji, Was Made Head Priest of Meiji Shrine.

Also, Prince Konroji Made a Big Effort After Retiring to Maintain Good Relations With All of the Members of the Imperial Family.

And, In Fact, On the Days of Prince Konroji's Birthday, The Emperor and Members of His Family Would Visit Prince Konroji's Estate and Wish Him Happy Birthday.

75. Christ is Born on Christmas Eve

Joy To The World!

Our Son, Thomas Nickerson Davis, Was Born on Christmas Eve at a Hospital in a Suburb of Tokyo Owned and Run By a Catholic Order of Nuns.

When I Went to the Hospital, I Saw a Large Banner Above the Door Where Liddy Had Stayed For a Few Days Before Giving Birth and Would Stay For Another Week Saying, "Christ is Born on Christmas Eve."

Both Liddy and Our Newborn Son Were in Excellent Health and Had Survived the Birth Quite Well.

76. BULLET TRAINS—WHY CAN'T WE HAVE THEM IN THE US?

Regarding Train Service in Japan To and From Large Cities From the Northern Tip to the Southern Tip of Japan, the Japanese Government Had Spent Billions of US Dollars In the US Dollar Equivalent to the Japanese Yen to Develop Passenger Train Engines That Could Travel at Speeds of 150 to 200 Miles Per Hour Along With Brand-New Train Tracks and Rail Beds That Were Safe to Handle High Speed Trains.

While We Were in Japan, We Would Quite Often Visit Cities Outside of Tokyo For a Full Weekend of Sightseeing. We Could Never Have Done This In Two Days' Time If Passenger Trains Could Only Travel at Speeds of Forty to Fifty Miles Per Hour.

Another Major Benefit of the New High-Speed Passenger Train Service was That the Trains Had a Track Record of Departing on Time From Major Cities and Arriving at Other Large Cities After a Lengthy Trip a Few Minutes Early But Rarely More than Five Minutes Late. In Fact, If the Bullet Train Was More Than Fifteen Minutes Late to Ones Destination City, The Train Company Would Refund the Full Cost of the One-Way Train Ticket. And Average Delays Had Only Been Twenty-four Seconds Per Trip.

Also, The Bullet Trains Which Traveled on Brand-New Rails and Track Beds Were Extremely Comfortable.

And, The Dining Cars Had Excellent Service and Served Gourmet Food.

I Have Never Understood Why the United States, Unlike Japan and Many European Countries, Has Not Developed High-Speed Passenger Train Service on Safe Track Beds To and From All of Its Major Cities.

77. WONDERFUL TEA GIRLS

In Japan, Large Offices, Including General Sekiyu Seisei, Where I Worked, Employed Tea Girls to Serve Tea and Coffee to the Office Workers, Deliver and Pick Up Mail, and Run Errands For Them.

The Tea Girls Were Known For Their Friendliness, Continuous Smiles, and Very Pleasant Personalities.

When I Returned to Tokyo on My Way Home to Massachusetts From Making a Speech at the Prestigious Asian-Pacific Economic Conference in Singapore, I Visited My Former Japanese Oil Company Where I Had Worked as General Manager For Six Years.

I Arrived at General Sekiyu's New High-Rise Office Building That Was Located Along Side of Tokyo Harbor. When I Took the Elevator to the Top Floor To Meet With the Current Senior Management of General Sekiyu, I Was Overwhelmed By What Happened. As the Senior Management Knew of My Exact Arrival Time, They Arranged For All Forty of the Company's Tea Girls to Welcome Me With Greetings and Applause Just as I Stepped Out of the Elevator.

Also, a Group of Senior Managers That I had Worked With Took Me Out For a Very Nice Japanese Fish Dinner That Night.

I Still Love and Miss Japan and Its Nice People Very Much.

78. Two-Billion-Dollar Merger and Restructuring General Sekiyu

As General Manager of a Joint Venture Japanese Oil Refining Company Owned 50 percent By Exxon and 50 percent By a Japanese Oil Marketing Company, I Quickly Discovered That Oil Marketing Companies in Japan Made a lot More Money Than Oil Refining Companies.

Thus, Early On, I Began Discussions with General Sekiyu, Which was 100 percent Owned By Japanese Shareholders and Which Marketed Most of the Oil Refined By My Company, About the Advantages to Both Companies of Merging Our Two Companies Into One Fully Integrated Oil Company.

The Senior Japanese Management of General Sekiyu Initially Agreed to the Merger, But Only If I Obtained the Concurrence of Japan's Government Ministry of International Trade and Industry, Known as MITI.

As It Turned Out, Obtaining the Approval of the Japanese Government was Very Difficult as They Had Been Opposed to Any Attempts By American Companies to Purchase Japanese Companies.

However, After More Than Two Years of Non-Stop Efforts, I Obtained the Approval of MITI as I was Able to Convince Them That This was a Merger and Not an Acquisition and Would Result in Japanese Shareholders Owning 50 percent of the Combined Oil Company.

We Also Merged the Board of Directors and Departments of the Two Companies and Relocated Our Headquarters Office Staff to the Same Building as General Sekiyu.

The Two-Billion-Dollar Merger and Restructuring Resulted in Many Efficiencies, Better Communications, and Much Better and More Profitable Decision-Making.

Thus, As a Result of the Merger and the Many Other Improvements That I Made in Both the Refining and Marketing Areas, at the End of My Five-Year Expatriate Term of Office, Exxon's Annual Profits From the Joint Venture Oil Company in Japan Improved From Four Million to One Hundred Million USD.

79. MAMA CHERRY AND COPACABANA

In Japan, a lot of Business and Resolution of Problems Are Carried Out Not at the Office From Nine A.M. to Five P.M. But By Attending Japanese Hostess Bars After Work.

My Favorite Hostess Bar Was the Very Large Copacabana Club in the Ginza Entertainment Section of Tokyo, Which Was Owned and Run By Mama Cherry.

The Copacabana Had a Large Dance Floor and a Live Band that Played British and American Rock and Roll Music.

The Hostesses at the Copacabana Did a Wonderful Job of Quickly Taking and Bringing Their Customers' Drink Orders and Were Also Very Bright and Actively Engaged in Conversations to Get to Know and Entertain Their Customers.

The Hostesses at the Copacabana Also Dressed Very Well in Elegant Skintight Dresses, Wore Alluring Makeup, and Were Great Dance Partners.

Also, I was Able After a Couple of Years to Establish a Wonderful Working Relationship with the Interesting and Intriguing Mama Cherry.

In Truth, I Liked to Go to the Copacabana, which was Very Expensive, About Once Every Two Months with Some of My

Japanese Friends Such as Michio Ura, who was My Roommate at Northwestern's Graduate School of Business, Not to Discuss Business Problems, But to Relax, Enjoy the Atmosphere, and Hit the Dance Floor

80. Arrested While Jogging Around Imperial Palace

The Huge Imperial Palace in Tokyo, Which is the Main Residence of the Emperor of Japan and His Extended Family, was in a Large Park-Like Area With a Surrounding Moat and was Only Six Blocks From General Sekiyu's Headquarters Office.

As I Have Always Loved to Jog, I Found it Very Relaxing and Scenically Beautiful to Run Around the Entire Imperial Palace Several Times a Week on its Outer Perimeter Trail.

I Could Also Change From My Business Suit Into My Jogging Gear and Leave My Business Clothes in a Duffel Bag and Place it Under a Park Beach Along with Many Other Joggers at the Starting Point For the Run.

While it was Considered By the Other Joggers to be Fully Safe to Do This. I Did Take My Wallet With Me on the Run

In Japan, Foreign Expatriates Known as *Gaijin*s Are Required to Carry With Them a Green Card, Which is the Japanese Visa That is Required to Work in the Country.

And, Unfortunately, On the One Day of the Year When The Police Frequently Stop Gaijins and Ask to See Their Green Card, I Chose to Run Around the Imperial Palace But Had Placed My Large Visa Green Card in the Jacket of My Suit, Which I had Left in My Duffel Bag Underneath a Park Bench.

And, Lo and Behold, I Was Stopped By a Japanese Policeman

When I had Jogged About Halfway Around the Imperial Palace Who Asked To See My Visa Green Card.

As I Didn't Have it, I Tried to Explain to the Policeman That I had Left It in My Suit Pocket and Placed It in My Duffel Bag Which I Had Put Underneath a Park Bench at the Common Starting Point For Jogging Around the Imperial Palace.

However, the Policeman Was Not Good With English and Did Not Understand My Explanation. And He Asked Me to Write Down the Name of the Company That Employed Me and Its Address. After Doing This, He Told Me That He Would Have To Issue a Warrant For My Arrest and That I Would Be Notified About a Date For My Court Hearing at the Tokyo Police Courtroom.

The Tokyo Police Department Did Contact General Sekiyu and Notified Them of My Arrest For Not Carrying With Me My Green Visa Card and That I Had to Appear For a Court Hearing on the Date and Time That The Police Court Had Chosen.

When the Day of the Court Hearing Came, I Had Arranged for Komiko-San, My Wonderful Japanese Secretary Who Was Excellent in English, to Accompany Me To Be My Translator.

After Arriving in the Lobby of a Very Tall Tokyo Police Building, With a Court Room, We Were Told to Follow a Court Assistant Up the Stairs to the Court Room. But They Did Not Tell Us What Floor It Was On.

The Young Court Assistant Bounded Up the Stairs Ahead of Us and Kept Going For More Than Twenty Floors. However, We Did Not See Him Leave the Staircase at the Floor With the Court Room.

Thus, We Kept Going, and to Our Astonishment, We Ended Up on the Roof of the Tokyo Police Building After Climbing Up Twenty-eight Floors.

We Then Walked Down the Stairs a Few Floors and Ran Into a Tokyo Police Officer. My Secretary Explained in Japanese Our Problem and Where We Needed to Go. And He was Nice Enough to Lead Us Slowly to the Floor With the Police Court Room.

And, After Waiting in the Anti-Room of the Police Court

Room For One Hour, We Were Told That Our Court Proceedings Would Begin.

So, What Happened in the Police Court Room? The Judge Asked Me Over a Hundred Questions For Ninety Minutes Covering Everything About Where I Was Born, All of the Places Where I Had Lived, Where I Went to School, Where I Had Worked, and What Was My Job in Tokyo.

After My Secretary Finished Answering All of the Judge's Questions About Me in Japanese, the Court Assistant Who Was Charged With Writing My Answers to All of the Questions on a Multi-Page Court Form Spoke Up That He Had By Mistake Used the Old Court Form. After Doing So, the Judge Said That He Would Have to Ask Me all of the Questions Over Again.

After Another Ninety Minutes, The Judge Announced That I had Answered All of the Required Questions But Did Not Say Anything Else.

Being Puzzled, I Asked My Secretary to Quietly Find Our If There Would Be Any Fine or Punishment For My Not Having Japan's Visa Work Card in My Possession That Day.

The Judge's Answer Was, "Your Punishment Was Having to Go Through This Long and Tedious Court Hearing."

Thus, My Secretary and I Were Both Relieved and Left the Large Tokyo Police Building With Big Smiles on Our Faces.

And I Took Komiko-San, My Wonderful Secretary, to a Nice Late Lunch at a Popular Tokyo Restaurant.

81. It's a Girl!

Almost Two Years After Tommy Was Born, Christina Parks Davis was Born in November of 1978 at the Same Seibo Byoin International Catholic Maternity Hospital as Tommy, Run By The Franciscan Missionaries of Mary. It was Located in a Park-Like Setting in the Shinjuku Prefecture of Tokyo.

Importantly, It Was Only a Short Taxi Ride From Our House, and Most of the Doctors and Nurses Were Fluent in English.

And Liddy's Mother Flew From Boston to Tokyo and Stayed at Our House For Two Weeks to Take Care of Tommy When Liddy Was in the Hospital and to Help Liddy After She Was Discharged from the Hospital.

Both Liddy and Christie Were In Excellent Health and Had Survived the Birth Quite Well.

82. TOBACCO BANS ARIMAS - KA?

In Japan, I Took to Collecting Beautifully Lacquered Tobacco Boxes That Were First Made in the 16th Century. They Were Used By Male Aristocrats and Members of the Imperial Family to Store Several Different Kinds of Their Pipe Tobacco and to Hold the Very Long and Skinny Japanese Pipes.

They Were Also Displayed as Objects of Art in the Living Quarters of the Japanese Aristocrats and the Imperial Family.

On the Weekends, I Would Quite Often Go Antiquing in Tokyo or Kyoto, Looking For Japanese Tobacco Bans, Antique Furniture, Woodblock Prints, and Scrolls.

Thus, When Entering a Japanese Antique Store, I Would Immediately Ask: "Tobacco Bans Arimas - Ka?" Which Means "Do You Have Any Antique Lacquered Tobacco Boxes For Sale?" If They Answered Yes, I Would Ask to See Them. However, If They Answered No, I Would Leave and Go On To Another Japanese Antique Store.

After Working and Living in Tokyo For Five Years, I Returned to the US with a Dozen Beautifully Lacquered 16th–19th-Century Tobacco Bans.

83. Tailing Twenty-Foot Shark in Truk Lagoon

While in Japan, Liddy and I Went on Quite a Few Vacations to Nearby Pacific Islands.

On One Trip, We Went to the Islands of Guam, Saipan, and Truk, Where There Had Been Many Major Bottles in the Later Stages of World War II Between the Japanese Imperial Army, Air Force, and Navy and US Forces.

The Island of Truk was the Headquarters of the Japanese Imperial Navy and the Main Harbor For Japan's Battleships, Destroyers, Aircraft Carriers, Military Cargo Ships, and Troop Carriers. In Other Words, it was the Japanese Equivalent of Pearl Harbor.

Truk was an Ideal Harbor For the Japanese Navy as the Island Had a Very Large Lagoon That was About Twenty Miles Long and Twenty Miles Wide and With Two Narrow Entrance and Exit Channels to the Pacific Ocean. And the Lagoon Had a Depth of Two Hundred Feet and Was Very Calm.

After Arriving in Truk, We Were Told That the Truk Lagoon, Due To Its Deep and Calm Waters, Was Ideal For Snorkeling and Scuba Diving. And, In One Spot, There was a Five-Hundred-Foot-Long but Still Mostly Intact Japanese Aircraft Carrier Resting on the Sandy Floor of the Lagoon That Had Been Sunk By Torpedoes From US Fighter Bombers in World War II.

So We Signed Up For a Snorkeling Trip To Go and See The Sunken Japanese Aircraft Carrier.

After Jumping Into the Lagoon With Our Snorkeling Gear, Liddy and I Snorkeled in Opposite Directions.

And I Very Shortly Spotted the Sunken Japanese Aircraft Carrier Resting on the Bottom of the Truk Lagoon as the Calm Lagoon Waters were Exceptionally Clear.

But, Lo and Behold, I Spotted an Enormous Shark Swimming Slowly Next to the Bottom of the Japanese Aircraft Carrier. However, Since the Huge Shark was Swimming in the Same Direction As Me, I Decided To Slowly Follow It From What I Thought was a Safe Distance Since I Was Behind the Large Shark on the Surface of the Lagoon, whereas the Shark was Swimming In Front of Me and Close to the Sandy Bottom of the Lagoon, Which was Two Hundred Feet Below Me.

But After Trailing the Large Shark From Behind For a Short Distance, I Suddenly Realized That the Shark Had Somehow Spotted Me and Stopped Swimming. And In Just a Few Seconds, the Large Shark Made a U-Turn and Swam Near the Sandy Bottom of the Lagoon To Where It was Just Underneath Me.

84. POISONOUS FISH AND AN IRON STOMACH

While Working at General Sekiyu in Japan, I was Referred To By Many of the Japanese Workers as "The Henna Gaijin," Which Means "The Strange Foreigner" in English.

And This Was Because Unlike Most of the Other American Expatriates Working For General Sekiyu, I Loved to Eat Raw Fish, Including Poisonous Raw Fish Like Fugo.

Fugo, Which is a Type of Blowfish, and a Japanese Delicacy, is so Poisonous That the Smallest Mistake in its Preparation Can Be Fatal. Fortunately, the Japanese Government Passed a Law That Required That Only Highly Trained and Licensed Chefs in Tokyo Could Serve Fugo. And Special Knives with Wooden Handles and Blades Tempered By a Swordsmith to a Keen Edge were Used to Prepare Fugo. And the Restaurants That Served It Were Considered to be the Finest and Most Expensive in Japan.

At the Few Restaurants in Tokyo That Served Fugo, I Could See Live Fugo Swimming in a Large Tank By the Restaurant Door and Also See on the Entrance Wall a Government License For the Chief Chef at That Restaurant to Serve Fugo.

In Preparing Fugo to Be Served to Customers at the Fugo Restaurants, The Chef Would First Cut Open The Head of the Fugo to Remove Its Brain and Eyes. Then The Chef Would Remove the Skin on All Sides. And, As a Final Step, the Chef Would Remove the Fugo's Ovaries, Liver, and Intestines Which Were Lethal as They Contained the Fugo's Very Strong Poison.

The Tetrodotoxin Poison in the Fugo's Guts is Rapid and Violent and First Causes Numbness Around the Mouth, Then Paralysis and Finally a Quick Death.

Importantly, Because I Had Been Blessed By Having an Iron Stomach, I Never Suffered Any Serious Illness or Death From My Many Tastings of Fugo at Tokyo's Best Restaurants.

85. Village-to-Village Hike With Six-Eight Fijian Chief

On a Prior Trip to Some of the Beautiful Islands of the South Pacific, I Met a Well-known Travel Writer, Who Had Written Many Travel Books on Most of the Islands in the South Pacific.

I Asked Him What Was the Most Interesting Trip That He Had Taken in the South Pacific.

He Told Me That It was a Ten-Day Hundred-Mile Hiking Trip in Fiji With a six-eight Fijian Chief From the Northwestern Tip to the Southeastern Tip of Fiji's Main Island. More Specifically, It was From Nadi to Suva, Which is Fiji's Capital.

I Told the Travel Book Writer That I was Highly Interested in Taking the Same Hike with the Same Fijian Chief That Had Led Him On His Hike. And the Travel Book Writer was Kind Enough to Provide Me with the Chief's Name and How I Could Contact Him.

Several Years Later, After My Marriage to Liddy and Our Moving to Tokyo, I Became Highly Interested In Taking the Long Village-to-Village Hike With the Fijian Chief.

And, After a Six-Month Effort, I Was Finally Able to Make a Contact With the six-eight Fijian Chief and was Able to Arrange For Him to Meet Me in Nadi to Take Me on the Same Hike as the Travel Book Writer in the Following Summer.

Unfortunately, Liddy Could Not Come on the Arduous Hike

as She was Pregnant. However, I Was Able to Make a Reservation For Her to Stay First in a Very Nice Hotel in Nadi and Then at a Luxury Hotel on the Water Near Suva.

The Route of the Ten-Day Hike Was a Diagonal Hike Over the Beautiful High Hills and Mountains and Across Many Streams and Rivers in the Interior of Fiji. Stays Each Night Would Be in Different Fijian Village That Would Also Provide Us With Dinner. However, We Had to Pack Enough Food For Lunch and Breakfast Each Day.

I Was Told By the six-eight Fijian Chief to Bring a Large Supply of Kava Roots to Present to the Chief of Each Village When We Entered the Village as This Was a Strong Historic Custom Which Fijians Followed When Entering and Spending the Night in a Village.

Kava is a Beverage Prepared From a Plant That Grows in Fiji and Some Other Western South Pacific Islands. It is a Popular Social Drink Similar to Alcohol in Western Societies and is Consumed as a Beverage in Fijian Ceremonies to Promote Relaxation.

The Hiking was Arduous as Each Day we Had to Climb Up and Over Mountain Passes and Find Safe Ways to Cross the Streams and Rivers. However, the Landscape was Always Exceptionally Beautiful. And the Streams were Crystal Clear and Blueish-Green in Color Particularly When Flowing Over Sandy or Very Small Lightly Colored Rocks and Pebbles.

On the First Day, When Entering Late in the Afternoon The Village Where My six-eight Fijian Chief and I Had to Spend the Night, We First Met With the Chief of That Village and His Elders in a Good-Sized Thatched-Roof Hut Used For Meetings and Ceremonies.

I First Presented the Village Chief with Some Kava Roots That I Had Brought From Nadi. The Chief Then Had One of His Elders Mash the Kava Roots Into Powder and Then Pour it Into a Very Large Wooden Kava Bowl Filled With Water to Make Kava.

Then, the Village Chief Poured the Kava Into a Gourd For Drinking, Clapped His Hands Three Times, and Then Quickly Drank All of the Kava in the Gourd in One Big Gulp.

The Village Chief Then Offered a Gourd of Kava to Each of the Village Elders.

Then to Welcome My six-eight Fijian Chief and Me to His Village, the Village Chief Had One of His Elders Make Another Large Bowl of Kava From the Village Chief's Own Supply of Kava Roots.

Next, the Village Chief Handed a Gourd of Kava to My six-eight Fijian Chief. My Guide Placed the Kava Gourd on the Floor of the Hut In Front of Where He Was Sitting, Clapped His Hands Three Times, and Then Picked Up the Gourd of Kava and Consumed It With One Big Gulp.

So When the Kava Gourd was Offered To Me, I Set It on the Floor of the Hut in Front of Where I Was Sitting, Clapped My Hands Three Times, and Then Drank It, But in Three Gulps Rather Than One Gulp.

At Each of the Ten Villages That I Stayed in With My six-eight Fijian Chief, The Village Chief and His Elders Provided Us with a Wonderful Dinner of Fresh Fish or Chicken and Lots of Yams, Taro, and Cassava That Have Been the Staple Foods Grown By the Fijian Natives For Thousands of Years.

At the End of Each Dinner, the Villagers Would Entertain Us By Singing and Dancing to Native Songs.

At Night, It was a Long Village Tradition That the Chief of the Village Had to Provide Safe Lodging For His Guests. In Seven of the Villages, I Slept in a Small Thatched-Roof Hut for Visitors. In Two of the Villages, I Was Locked Inside a Yam Hut. And In One of the Villages, I Had to Sleep Under the Large, Primitive Handmade Wooden Bed of the Chief and His Wife.

At the Last Village I Visited, I Was Invited to Dance After Dinner With the Villagers. And I Had Been Told In Advance of My Trip By My six-eight Fijian Chief to Bring a Sulu on the Trip, Which is a Colorful Kilt-Like Wrap-Around Skirt From My Upper Waist to My Ankles that Is Worn By Fijian Village Men When Dancing.

In Addition to Dancing For at Least Twenty Minutes While

Wearing the Sulu. I Learned a Very Unique Fijian Dance Step Which I Still Remember and Can Perform Today.

In Summary, My Ten-Day Village-to-Village Hike with the six-eight Fijian Chief Was a Wonderful and Most Interesting Trip Which I Will Always Remember!

86. My Cat Ruins Dinner with Guam Governor

While in Japan, Liddy and I Took a Short Vacation to Visit the Nearby Micronesian Islands of Guam, Saipan, and Palau.

In Guam, We Got Together With a Former Exxon Cargo Sales Executive, whom I knew Quite Well, Who Had Become The President of the Guam Oil and Refining Company. While I Was in Exxon's Cargo Sales Department, I Helped Start Up the Guam Oil and Refining Company With a Large Loan From Exxon In Return For Obtaining a Ten-Year Contract to Supply Them With 100 percent of Their Crude Oil Requirements From Exxon's Large Crude Oil Exploration and Production Affiliate in Saudi Arabia at a Price Which Was a Little Bit Above the Market Price For Persian Gulf Crude Oil.

My Former Exxon Friend Invited Liddy and Me One Night To Join Him and His Wife For a Group Dinner With the Governor of Guam.

I Had Only Brought One Nice Pair of Full-Length Dress Pants and a Dress Shirt on Our Short Micronesian Island Vacation Which were Appropriate to Wear For a Dinner with the Governor of Guam and His Wife.

However, When I Took My Long Pair of Nice Full-Length Dress Pants Out of My Suitcase, I was Startled To Discover That the Dress Pants Smelled Like Cat Urine.

And I Realized That One of Liddy's and My Two Cats In Our House on Price Konroji's Estate in Tokyo Had Urinated on My Only Pair of Long Dress Pants That I Had Brought To Guam.

While I Tried Very Hard to Wipe Out the Smell of Cat Urine on the Dress Pants With a Wash Cloth, I Was Unsuccessful

Nevertheless, Liddy and I Did Attend the Group Dinner with the Guam Governor.

However, I was Extremely Uneasy the Entire Time For Cocktails and Dinner with the Guam Governor and His Wife and Tried Never to Get Close to Them.

Thus, I Could Never Really Relax and Enjoy Having Cocktails and Dinner as well as Conversations After Dinner With the Governor and His Wife and The Other Invited Guests as One of My Cats Had Ruined My Dinner With the Governor of Guam.

87. Almost Hacked to Death by Hostile Natives in Ponape

Liddy and I Took another Short Vacation to Ponape in The Caroline Islands, Which is Very Mountainous and Known as One of the Wettest Places on Earth With Rainfall Exceeding Three Hundred Inches Every Year.

When Visiting the Tourist Office, Liddy and I were Told About the Beauty of the Very High Lididuhniap Waterfalls with a Wonderful Deep Pool that was Nice for a Quick Swim.

As the Road was Not That Great For Getting There, We Rented a Jeep.

And there was a Small Parking Area at the End of the Dirt and Rocky Road with a Wide Trail Leading to the Waterfalls After a One-Hour Walk.

The Waterfall was Huge, and One Could Hear it From the Parking Area. After a Refreshing Dip in the Pool Underneath the Waterfall and a Nice Lunch that we Had Brought From Town, We Headed Back to Our Jeep.

However, We Chose to Walk Back to the Small Parking Area on a More Beautiful, Unmarked Narrow Trail Rather Than Retake the Wide, Marked Trail Back to the Jeep.

Then, After Starting Up the Jeep and Driving For Only a Few Minutes, About a Dozen Fierce-Looking Natives Wearing only Loincloths Suddenly Appeared on Both Sides of the Primitive Road with Machetes. And They Quickly Began to Cut Down Small Trees so That the Trees Would Fall Across the Road From Both Sides and Thus Force Us to Stop the Jeep.

We Immediately Feared For Our Lives and Thought that the Fierce Natives Might Cut Us Up Into Many Pieces.

Unfortunately, Our Shouted Attempts to Talk to the Fierce Natives Were to No Avail as None of Them Understood Any English.

Then a Small Native Boy of About Ten Years of Age Approached Our Stopped Jeep and Began to Speak to Us in English, Which He Had Learned at School.

The Native Boy Explained that in Returning to the Parking Area From the Waterfalls, We Had Not Taken the Wide Trail Meant For Tourists, But Instead, We Had Taken a Sacred Trail That was Reserved Only For the Chief of the Nearby Tribe and His Family.

Liddy and I Both Apologized and Asked the Native Boy if We Could Visit the Chief of the Tribe and Express Our Deepest Regrets For, By Mistake, Walking on the Sacred Trail That was Reserved Only for the Chief and His Family.

The Native Boy Then Talked to the Fierce-Looking Native Men. And Fortunately, They Removed the Trees That They Had Cut Down From the Road and Allowed Us to Drive a Short Distance in Our Jeep with the Native Boy to a Path That Led To the Tribal Chief's Hut in His Village.

Fortunately, the Tribal Chief was There. And With the Native Boy as Our Interpreter, We Apologized Many Times to the Chief and Stated that We Would Never Walk on His Sacred Trail Again.

The Tribal Chief Seemed to Understand Our Mistake and Asked the Native Boy to Walk Us Back to Our Jeep and To Tell the Native Men That We Should Be Allowed to Proceed on the Dirt and Rocky Road to the Paved Road That Would Take Us Back to the Capital of Ponape.

88. INVITED BY YAP FAMILY TO EXOTIC DINNER ON THEIR DIRT FLOOR

Liddy and I Thoroughly Enjoyed Another Short Vacation Trip From Japan to the Interesting, Unique, and Very Small Island of Yap.

In Yap, We Saw Many Large Pieces of Yap's Stone Money, Which Had Been Used By The Yapese as Far Back as 125 AD, In Most of the Yap Villages That We Visited.

Stone Money is Not the Only Yapese Valuable. Another Highly Valued Form of Money on Yap is Called "Gaw." It is a necklace Formed of Seashells and Whales' Teeth and was Reserved For Chiefs of the Yap Villages.

Another Important Yapese Valuable is "Yap," Which is Shell Money That is Used For Important Events Such as Marriage Proposals and Celebrations, Apologies, and Payment For Local Medicines.

Yap's Most Highly Developed Artform is Dancing and is a Central Part of the Island's Culture. And the Dances Often Tell the Stories of Canoeing to Other Islands, Tribal Conquests, and Religious Events.

The Dancers We Saw Wore Beautiful Costumes with Multicolored Skirts and Ornamental Headdresses and Covered Their Bodies with Flowers and Coconut Oil.

While in Yap, we Made Many Visits to the Visitors Center to

Obtain Information on Where to Visit and What To Do. As a Result, We Managed to Form a Very Good Relationship With a Very Young Yapese Lady Who was Director of the Visitors Center.

Just Before Our Last Day in Yap, the Head of the Yap Visitors Center Invited Us to Have Dinner the Next Night with Her and Her Parents at Their Village Hut.

We Had No Idea What To Expect!

After Arriving at the Village, We Were Invited Inside the Hut of the Head of the Visitors Center and Her Parents. We were Asked to Sit Down on a Very Pretty and Very Large Multi-Colored Cloth Which was Spread Out on the Dirt Floor of the Largest Room in the Hut.

Liddy and I Had a Lovely Time and a Good Back-and-Forth Exchange of Information on What Life was Like in Yap, Japan, and the US.

And We Thoroughly Enjoyed the Fruit Drinks and the Local Homemade Fish and Vegetable Dishes Along with Fresh Fruit and Sweet Cakes for Dessert.

I Will Never Forget Our Last Evening in the Exceptionally Friendly Island of Yap and Would Love to Return to Yap in the Near Future!

89. BECAME BIG FAN OF SUMO WRESTLING IN JAPAN

Sumo Wrestling in Japan is a Unique and Ancient Sport with Lots of Pageantry and is Still Very Popular with the Japanese and the Families of American, British, and Australian Expatriates Working and Living in Japan.

From My Earliest Days of Working at General Sekiyu in Tokyo, if there was One of the Six Sumo Championships Per Year Taking Place, I Would Watch it at General Sekiyu Almost Every Day on Television at the End of the Workday and at Home During the Weekends. This Worked Well as the Lowest-Ranked Sumo Wrestlers Competed in the Mornings and the Early and Mid-Afternoons, with the Highest-Ranked Sumo Wrestlers Competing in the Late Afternoons.

I was Also Given Tickets About Three Times Per Year For Liddy and Me, and Later Tommy, to Attend One of the Sumo Championships at the Ryogoku Kokugikan Sumo Stadium in Tokyo. We were able to Watch the Sumo Matches on Mats Close To the Sumo Ring While Being Served Japanese Delicacies Along with Japanese Beer.

The Sumo Matches Take Place in an Elevated Ring Called the *Dohyu*, Which is Made of Clay and Covered With a Layer of Sand.

The Basic Rules For This Contact Sport Are That When a Sumo Wrestler is Thrown Out of the Sumo Ring or Touches Any Part of His Body Besides the Soles of His Feet on the Floor of the Sumo Ring, He Loses the Match to His Opponent.

Sumo Wrestlers Are Required to Live in Sumo Stables that are Training Camps, Where they Train Under the Watchful Eyes of the Stable Master and Gain as Much Weight as Possible By Eating an Average of Twenty Thousand Calories Per Day.

If Selected at a Very Young Age, They Follow the Training Regimen Dictated By the Stable Master. It is not an Easy Life as They Train From Five A.M. in the Morning, Eat and Drink a Lot, and Sleep a lot.

Their Diet Consists of a Heavy Stew Called *Chunkonabe*, Which is Served From a Giant Pot. They Eat Two Huge Meals a Day and then Sleep a Long Time so that the Food Can Become Fat. They also Drink at Least Six Pints of Beer With Each Meal.

Most of the Top Sumo Wrestlers Weigh at Least Three Hundred Pounds, and a Few Weigh as much as 650 Pounds.

Each of the Six Championships Are Fifteen Days Long and Begin and Conclude on a Sunday.

At Tournament Time, The Sumo Wrestlers Go Through a lot of Preparations With Their Wardrobe and Hair, Which Must Adhere To Historical Rituals and Traditions.

At the Sumo Tournaments, the Sumo Wrestlers Initially Dress in Ceremonial Robes and Then Parade with the Other Sumo Wrestlers Around and Around the Sumo Ring Before the Beginning of the Sumo Matches.

And Then the Sumo Wrestlers Change Into Their Fighting Attire. During the Sumo Matches, Each Wrestler Wears a Loincloth and a Mawashi Belt, Which is Thick and Very Wide and Thirty Feet in Length, which a Wrestler Wraps Around His Midsection Many Times Before Tightening and Knotting it to make it 100 percent Secure.

During the Sumo Match, Each Sumo Wrestler Tries to Use Various Maneuvers To Grab His Opponent's Miwashi, So as To Be Able to Throw or Push His Opponent Out of the Sumo Ring or On To the Floor of the Sumo Ring.

90. CHICKENING OUT JUST BEFORE MY FIRST SUMO MATCH

The Athletic Club That I Belonged To in Tokyo For US, British, and Australian Expatriates Scheduled a Mid-Morning and Luncheon Event With One of the Major Sumo Stables in Tokyo.

I Signed Up for a Sumo Match and was Also Looking Forward to Having Lunch with the Sumo Wrestlers to Find Out Firsthand What They Ate to Increase Their Weight to 300–650 Pounds.

The Leader of My Athletic Club Had Been the Winner of the US NCAA Division I Championship For Lightweight Wrestlers.

For the Sumo Wrestling Events, Our Athletic Club Members Who Had Signed Up for an Exhibition Match With a Japanese Sumo Wrestler Found Out Fortunately that They Were Being Matched Not With the Senior, Very Experienced, and Very Heavy Wrestlers of the Sumo Stable, Some of Whom Were Quite Famous, But With Very Young Freshmen Members of the Sumo Stable who Had Yet to Gain a Huge Amount of Weight.

The American Leader of Our Athletic Club Had the First Exhibition Match and Was Matched Up Against a Young Freshmen Japanese Sumo Wrestler, But One Who Weighed About 250 Pounds, Whereas Our Athletic Club Leader, Who was the NCAA Division I Lightweight Wrestling Champion, Weighed Only 135 Pounds.

I Had No Hopes For the Leader of Our Athletic Club in the First Sumo Match.

To Start Things Off, Both the 135 Leader of Our Athletic Club and the 250 Pound Young Freshmen Japanese Sumo Wrestler Had to Put on a Miwashi, Which is a Very Heavy and Large Waist Belt.

And the Object of the Match was To Try To Grab the Waist Belt of One's Opponent and Throw Them or Push Them On To the Mat Floor of the Sumo Ring. And the Sumo Wrestler Who First Did That was Quickly Declared to be the Winner of the Sumo Match.

To Begin the Match, Both Sumo Wrestlers Had to Each Stand at Opposite Comers of the Sumo Ring, and Then They Usually Moved Very Slowly Towards One Another.

However, Much to My Surprise, the 135-Pound American Leader of Our Athletic Club Quickly Darted From His Corner of the Ring Towards the Young 250-Pound Japanese Freshmen Sumo Wrestler. He Then in a Quick Move Jumped Behind the Japanese Sumo Wrestler and Grabbed the Japanese Wrestler's Mawashi From Behind and in a Twisting Move, Caused the Japanese Wrestler to Fall Down On To the Mat of the Sumo Ring.

Eight Members of My Athletic Club Had Signed Up For a Sumo Match Along With Me. And I Had Asked to be the Last One to Compete with the Young Freshmen Japanese Sumo Wrestlers.

However, None of the Eight Members of My Athletic Club Had Any Wrestling Experience. And All of Them Were Thrown to the Mat of the Sumo Ring By Their Young Freshmen Sumo Wrestler Opponents Within Two Minutes, And Two of My Athletic Club Members Appeared to Be Injured.

Witnessing What Happened Caused Me to Fear That I Would Also Be Injured. So With the Help of an Interpreter, I Explained That I Had Sprained My Ankle the Prior Day and Thus Would Have to Forfeit My Sumo Match With the Young Freshmen Sumo Wrestler.

But To End Things on the Right Note for the Visitors From My Athletic Club, We Were All Invited to Have a Long Lunch With all of the Staff and Members of the Japanese Sumo Stable.

The Lunch Lasted For Two Hours. And We Were Fed With

Unbelievably Large Portions of a Very Thick Stew Along with Lots of Bottles of Japanese Beer.

Most Importantly, I Thoroughly Enjoyed Experiencing What Life was Like at the Japanese Sumo Stable Even Though I Subsequently Found Out That I Had Gained Six Pounds at Their Very Long Luncheon.

91. Breaching Chinese Military Base on a Bicycle

$\mathcal{S}$hortly Before I Was Transferred Back to the US By Exxon, I Realized That While I Had Visited Hong Kong Four Times, I Had Never Been to Mainland China.

So I Booked a One Week Trip to Guilin in Southeastern China, Which is Known as One of the World's Most Beautiful Places, with the Winding Li River Surrounded on Both Sides with Almost a Hundred Idyllic, Sharp Rising Mountains That Have Been Featured For Hundreds of Years in Chinese Scroll Paintings.

And Guilin is Still Inhabited Today By Hundreds of Chinese Artists.

I Planned My Visit in the Spring, When the Mists and Fogs Shroud the Mountains Mystically and the Countryside and Hills are Covered With a Fresh Growth of Beautifully Green Vegetation.

For the First Day of My One Week Visit, I Took a Beautiful, Slow Boat Trip on the Li River.

And the Other Days, I Rented a Bicycle and Took Solo One-Day Cross-Country Trips to Beautiful and Interesting Places and Then Returned at the End of the Day to My Nice Inn in Guilin.

In Quite a Few of My Bike Trips, I Had Difficultly Finding The Places I Wanted to Visit, But Found the Chinese People To Be Very Helpful to Me.

Other Than the Wonderful Scenery, I Thoroughly Enjoyed

Visiting a Red Panda Sanctuary in the Mountains and Exploring Two Mysterious Caves Where I Had to Wear a Helmet and Head Lamp.

I Also Climbed For Two Hours Up a Steep, Vertical, Rocky Mountain, But With the Aid of Steel Cables that Enabled Me to Hook Myself On to Them For the Entire Climb and Thus Prevent Me From Falling Down the Mountain to the Rocks Below. And the Views Once I Reached the Top of the Steep, Rocky Mountain were Stunning.

I Also Particularly Liked Visiting Several Ancient Chinese Tea Houses and was Able to Participate in Tea Ceremonies and the Traditional Chinese Ways of Tea Tasting.

On My Bicycle Routes, I was Always Coming Across Art Stores With Paintings, Pottery, Wood Carvings, and Lacquerware that had been Created Recently by the Many Artists That Lived in the Guilin Area.

During My Last Bicycle Trip, I Decided, After Not Seeing Anything of Interest, to Turn on to a Dirt Road From the Main Road Without Any Idea of Where I was Going.

Shortly After Making the Bicycle Turn, I Saw a Man Sleeping Under a Big Tree About 150 Feet From the Dirt Road.

Then, Suddenly, I Heard a Loud Yell in Chinese. I Turned Around and Saw the Man, Who I Thought Had Been Sleeping Under the Big Tree, Standing Up and Holding a Machine Gun Pointed At Me. And I Noticed For the First Time That The Man Was Dressed in a Soldier's Uniform.

Fearing For My Life, I Stopped and Slowly Turned My Bike Around and Used Sign Language to Try to Communicate to the Armed Chinese Soldier that I had Turned Down the Dirt Road By Mistake.

Then, I Slowly Got on My Bike and Peddled Very Slowly Back to the Main Road.

Fortunately, the Man Dressed as a Soldier Did Not Fire His Machine Gun At Me.

When I Got Back to the Main Road, I Ran Into a Chinese Couple Who Spoke Some English. And They Told Me That the

Dirt Road that I had Turned Onto Led to a Chinese Army Base that was Currently Being Used In the Border Conflict with North Vietnam To the South Of Guilin.

And So Ended One of My Many Close Calls That I Had Experienced While Traveling in Potentially Dangerous Foreign Areas.

92. BACK TO EXXON IN BIG APPLE

After a Little More Than Five Years Working For Exxon in Tokyo, Japan, I was Transferred Back to Exxon's Headquarters in Rockefeller Center, To Become the Corporate Planning Manager and Public Affairs Manager For Exxon's International Division.

As Liddy and I Now Had Two Very Young Children, We Both Thought it Would Be Much Better to Live in a House in a Nice Nearby Suburb of New York City Rather Than Live in an Apartment Building in Manhattan.

After Visits To About Ten Nice Suburbs of NYC That Were Located in Westchester, New York; New Jersey; and Connecticut, We Decided To Try To Find a House in Darien, Connecticut.

Darien Was Only a Forty-FiveMinute Commute Via Express Train Service By the Metro North Commuter Rail Line to the Grand Central Railroad Station in Manhattan on Park Avenue and 42nd Street. And From Grand Central, I Could Walk To and From Rockefeller Center in Only Ten Minutes.

While Darien was a Small Town With Only Twenty Thousand Residents, It Had Many of the Shopping and Other Amenities of Much Larger Suburban Towns.

Most Importantly, Its Public Schools Were Outstanding. And It Bordered Long Island Sound and Had Eleven Public Parks and Two Lovely Public Beaches.

Darien's Property Taxes Were Significantly Lower Than the

NYC Suburbs Located in Westchester County and New Jersey. And It Had the Lowest Crime Rate of All of the Cities in Connecticut.

Fortunately, We Were Able to Purchase a Large, Southern Mount Vernon-Style Home with Pillars Located on 2.5 Acres of Land. In Front of the House was a Huge, Beautiful Pond Which was Deep Enough For Swimming in the Summer and Very Nice for Ice Skating in the Winter. In Back of the House, There Was a Wooden Forever Wild Hill with a Nature Trail.

And the House was Set Back Three Hundred Feet From Middlesex Road, Which Had A Lot of Traffic.

And, of Major Importance to Liddy, The House Was Located Just Down the Road From the Ox Ridge Hunt Club, Which Liddy Quickly Joined Given Her Love For Horses and Riding and Show Jumping Experiences as a Young Girl Growing Up in Rye, New York.

93. Winning Over the Washington Post, NYT, US Government, and Rupert Murdoch

*I*n My New Job as Public Affairs Manager of Exxon's International Division, I was Responsible for Handling All Print and Electronic Media and US Government Inquiries on the Global Industry Oil and Demand Situations Including Responding to All Inquiries During Various Middle East Oil Supply Disruptions.

Historically, Exxon Had Viewed With Suspicion Any Inquiries They Received on the Global and US Industry Oil Demand-and-Supply Situation From Newspaper and Magazine Writers and Television Networks.

And Exxon was Also Extremely Cautious About Handling Any Inquiries They Received on the Global and US Industry Oil Demand and Supply Situation From US Government Agencies Such As The State Department, Energy Department, CIA, Congressional Budget Office, Office of Management and Budget in the White House, and Senators and Congressmen.

In Fact, Exxon's Public Affairs Staffers Were Required to Ask All Media and US Government Representatives to First State Very Precisely What Their Questions Were.

Then, the Public Affair's Staffers Were Required to Contact

Others in Exxon so as to Draft Responses to the Media and US Government Inquiries.

And, As a Last Step, The Public Affair's Staffers Had to Review the Draft Responses to the Media and US Government Inquiries With the Appropriate Senior Executives in Exxon Before They Could Respond to the Inquiries.

Due to the Lengthy Exxon Review Process, There Were Multi-Day Delays Quite Often In Responding to Media and US Government Inquiries. And This Would Often Result in the Media Reporting Information That was Not Correct Since They Had Not Received Exxon's Responses to Their Questions Before They Had To Go To Press or Begin Their TV News Show.

And the Lengthy Exxon Review Process Also Quite Often Resulted in US Government Agencies Making Poor Decisions on How To Respond to An Oil Supply Crisis in the Middle East and North Africa, Since They Had Not Received Any Input From Exxon at the Time That They Had to Make Decisions on How to Respond to the Oil Supply Crisis.

Thus, the Results of the Above Policies and Restrictions that Were Placed on Exxon's Public Affair's Staffers Caused Exxon to Have a Poor Relationship with the Print and Electronic Media and a Lack of a Good Working Relationship With Appointed and Elected Officials in the US Government.

And It Also Resulted in Exxon Receiving Few Positive News Stories From the Print and Electronic Media and, in Some Cases, Negative Press or Reports that Exxon was Unresponsive To Their Inquiries.

Fortunately, With a Lot of Early Support From Pete Wolgast and Brice Sachs, Who Were Members of Exxon International's Senior Management, We Changed the Rules on How Public Affairs Staffers Like Myself Could Respond to Inquiries on the Global Industry Oil Demand-and-Supply Situation From Newspaper, Radio, and TV Reporters; Administrators in US Government Agencies; and Elected City, State, and US Representatives as Follows:

We Adopted a Policy and Practice of Responding To Media

and US Government Inquiries on the Same Day That We Received Them.

I Was Given the Authority to Respond in Most Cases to the Inquiries Without Having to Review the Exact Wording of My Responses With Senior Management at Exxon.

We Developed a Public Version of Exxon's Two-Year Worldwide Industry Oil Demand-and-Supply Outlook on a Quarterly Basis That We Could Share With the Media and US Government Officials.

We Held Quarterly Brown Bag Lunch Meetings With the Appropriate Print, Radio, and TV News Editors and Reporters in Both New York City and Washington, DC, to Review Exxon's Two-Year Industry Oil Demand-and-Supply Outlook and Answer Any Questions That They Had on the Oil Demand-and-Supply Situation.

We Scheduled Quarterly Meetings in Washington, DC, in Which a Senior Executive of Exxon International and Myself Would Present Exxon's Two-Year Industry Oil Demand-and-Supply Outlook With the State Department, Energy Department, Central Intelligence Agency, Congressional Budget Office, and Office of Management and Budget in the White House.

As a Result of the New Much More Proactive Public Affairs Practices That I Implemented Along with Pete Wolgast and Brice Sachs, Exxon's Relationships with the Print and Electronic News Media Vastly Improved Not Only With the *Wall Street Journal* But Also With Very Liberal Newspapers Such as The *New York Times*, *Washington Post*, and Rupert Murdoch's Newspapers in the US, London, and Australia.

We Also Developed Good Relationships For the First Time With News Reporters and Anchors From the Major Television Networks of CBS, NBC, ABC, and With Public Radio and TV Stations.

And Officials in the Major US Government Departments and Agencies Also Felt For the First Time That They Could Call Us Anytime If They Needed Any Information on the World and US Industry Oil Demand and Supply Situation.

In Summary, and Most Importantly, We Witnessed That the US Government Departments and Agencies Made Much Better

Decisions on How To Respond To Various Short-Term and Medium-Term Oil Supply Disruptions in the Middle East When They Had the Correct Information Either Directly or Indirectly From Us.

Also, US Government Officials in Formulating Policies and Making Decisions About How to Respond to Changes in the Global and US Industry Oil Demand and Supply Situation, Were Influenced in the Right Direction By the Information that We Had Provided to The *New York Times*, *Washington Post*, *Wall Street Journal*, and the Major TV and Radio Networks.

94. STABLISHED GOOD RELATIONSHIPS WITH THE TOP ENERGY AND OIL NEWS REPORTERS

Over Just One or Two Years I Was Able to Establish Close Relationships With Some of the Most Outstanding Energy News Reporters in the US.

They Included

1. Tom Friedman, the Three-Time Pulitzer Prize Award Winner and Energy and Middle East Reporter For The *New York Times*.

Later on, at Exxon, When I Established a Speakers Program For Employees, I Invited Tom Friedman To Be One of the First Speakers and Also Arranged the Same Day For Him to Have a One-on-One Lunch Meeting with Exxon's CEO.

2. Hedrick Smith, a Pulitzer Prize Winner and Head of The Washington News Bureau For The *New York Times*, which is Considered the Second-Highest News Editor Position at The *New York Times*.

Incidentally, In 2015 Hedrick Smith Gave a Talk at UMASS Dartmouth, When I Worked as The Business Executive in Residence at the Charlton College of Business, to Promote His New Book on *Who Stole The American Dream*.

During His Talk to Several Hundred Administrators, Professors, and Students, He Mentioned My Name Four Times, and Several

More Times When Answering Questions to Highlight Points He Was Trying to Make.

And, After His Talk, He Gave Me a Copy of His Book and a Short Note Saying, "Good to See You Again After All of Our Years Together On Washington Week In Review & Wishing You Well – Hedrick Smith 11/12/15."

3. Yousef Ibrahim, An Award-Winning International Energy Reporter For The *Wall Street Journal* and Then the Senior Middle East Correspondent For The *New York Times*.

Yousef Was Very Bright, With a Very Diverse and Interesting Background of Being Born in Egypt; Becoming a Coptic Christian; Marrying a Jewish Lady From Israel; and Obtaining a Master's Degree in Journalism From Columbia University.

He Was Also the Only First-Generation Arab Immigrant Who Had a Top News Reporting Job with an American Newspaper. He was Fluent in Arabic, Which Helped Him Develop a Good Working Relationship With Senior Government Officials In all of the Middle Eastern Countries Including Iran and Libya.

In One of His Stories, He Told Me About His Interview With Muammar Qudafi in Qudafi's Tent in the Libyan Desert Which Lasted From Midnight to Dawn.

4. Max Newton, the Head of Business Reporting For The *New York Post* and Rupert Murdoch's Other Newspapers in the US, UK, and Australia.

Max Was Exceptionally Bright. When He Met With Me in Person, He Would Never Take Notes on What I Said To Him in Answering His Questions on the World Energy and Oil Demand/ Supply Situation and Outlook. Nevertheless, He Quoted My Responses a Lot In His Newspaper Articles. And I Never Remember Any Misquotes in All of the Years That I Was Interviewed By Him in Person or Over The Phone.

Max Married His Secretary at The *New York Post* and Invited Me To His Wedding and Reception, Which Liddy and I Both Attended.

When It Came My Turn To Have a Few Nice Congratulatory Greetings With Max and His Wife at the Reception Line, He Asked

Me a Few Questions About The Current Global Energy and Oil Demand and Supply Situation, Which I Quickly Responded To.

And, Lo and Behold, Max Wrote Two Newspaper Articles Based on What I Told Him at His Wedding Reception In No More Than a Minute and Quoted Me Accurately In Both of the Articles.

Also, Given My Highest Respect For Max as An Excellent and Accurate News Reporter, I Arranged For Max to Have a Lunch With Exxon's CEO, Which Went Quite Well.

Lastly, and Perhaps Most Importantly, I Established Excellent Relationships With the Energy Reporters For the Major US and International News Services Such as Reuters, The Associated Press, and United Press International. These News Services Were the Major, and in Most Cases, the Only Supplier of Information on the Global Oil Supply Crisis For Hundreds of Medium-Size Regional Newspapers in the US, Canada, and Europe.

95. Giving Speeches and Appearing On TV

*J*ust Before I Took on the Job of Public Affairs Manager of Exxon International in 1980, The Shah of Iran, Which was a Major Crude Oil Exporter to Asia, Europe, and the United States, was Overthrown In Massive Protests and Worker Strikes and Had To Flee the Country. As a Result, the Imperial Country of Iran Became the Islamic Republic of Iran, Led By Ayatollah Khomeni, the Islamic Religious Leader of Iran.

During the Revolution, the Workers in the Oil Sector Actively Participated in the Islamic Revolution, which Resulted in a Halt in Most of Iran's Crude Oil Production and Exports.

The Loss of Iranian Crude Oil Exports Amounted to 4.8 Million Barrels Per Day.

Also, the Neighboring Crude Oil Producing Country of Iraq, Under Its Leader Saddam Hussein, Invaded Iran in 1980 In Fear that the Iranian Revolution Might Spread to Iraq. And the War Between the Two Large Crude Oil Exporters Lasted Until 1988.

As a Result of the Initial Curtailment of Crude Oil Exports From Both Iran and Iraq, Crude Oil Prices Skyrocketed From $12.50 a Barrel to $34 a Barrel by Mid-1980.

And There Were Fears That the Oil Supply Curtailments From Iran Could Last a Long Time and Cause a Major, Adverse Impact on the Economics of Crude Oil Importing Countries in Europe, Asia, and The United States.

Fortunately, the Much Higher Prices For Crude Oil Resulted in Major Efforts By Large Oil Companies Such as Exxon to Explore For and Develop New Sources of Crude Oil in Alaska, Gulf of Mexico, Canada, and the North Sea. And It Also Resulted in Large Oil Companies Such As Exxon To Develop New Sources of Energy, Such as Coal, Nuclear Power, and Natural Gas.

During This Period of High Anxiety With Regard to Middle East Oil Supplies, Oil Prices, and the Amount of New Sources of Crude Oil and Other Forms of Energy that Could Be Developed, I Became an Expert on The Current Worldwide Industry Energy and Oil Demand Situation; The Outlook For Developing New Sources of Crude Oil and Other Forms of Energy During the Next Two Years; and Whether or Not the New Sources of Crude Oil and Other Forms of Energy Would be Adequate to Meet the Desired International and US Economic Growth Over the Next Two Years.

In Addition to Providing Information on the Current and Near-Term Worldwide Industry Oil and Energy Demand and Supplies to the News Media and US Government Agencies, I Was Frequently Asked to Appear on Radio and TV News Shows, to Answer Questions on the Current and Near-Term Global and US Energy and Oil Demand and Supply Situation and Outlook.

Prior to Taking the Public Affairs Job at Exxon, I Had No Prior Experience In Appearing on TV and Radio News Shows and Handling Difficult and Sometimes Unfriendly Questions. Thus, Exxon Hired One of the Toughest Radio Talk Show Hosts in New York City to Meet With Me Twice a Week For Six Weeks to Help Prepare Me For This New and Very Challenging Assignment.

The Talk Show Host Was Very Helpful to Me in Learning How to Prepare, Act, and Excel In My Appearances on TV and Radio News Programs.

And I Still Remember the Principles that the Tough Media Talk Show Host Emphasized as Follows:

Be Well Prepared in Advance by Identifying the Key Questions that were likely to be Asked and How I Should Respond to Each Question.

Make Sure That I Make the Key Points That Exxon Wanted Me to Make on the Global and US Energy and Oil Demand and Supply Situation and Near-Term Outlook Regardless of What Questions Were Asked By The Media Hosts on Radio and TV.

Be Yourself On Your Personality, How You Conduct Yourself, and How You Dress.

Don't Lose Your Cool!

Other Than Accepting Invitations to Appear on TV and Radio News Shows, I Was Frequently Asked to Give a Talk on Exxon's Worldwide Industry Energy and Oil Demand and Supply Outlook at Energy Conferences Such as the Annual Energy Conference Sponsored By The US Energy Information Agency.

I Also Attended and Spoke at North American Energy Conferences in Quebec City and Saskatchewan.

And I was Invited to Speak at Energy Conferences Sponsored By Universities Such at Northwestern, Columbia, New York University, SUNY, Johns Hopkins, Worcester Institute of Technology, Wharton School of Finance, Smith, Simmons, US Naval Academy, and West Point.

In Addition, I was the Keynote Speaker at a Major Energy Conference Sponsored By Canada's Public Radio and TV Network.

96. Sharing Rockefeller's Caribbean Vacation House with VP and Secret Service

Shortly After Returning to NYC to Work at Exxon in the Spring of 1980, I Attended a Function at the Asia Society and Found Myself Sitting Next to Mrs. John D. Rockefeller Jr.

We Had a Lengthy Back-and-Forth Conversation on How Exxon Was Doing and Our Travel and NYC Interests.

When I Mentioned to Her That I Was in the Early Stages of Planning a Ten-Day Vacation to the Caribbean For Me and My Family During the Upcoming Winter, She Asked If I Would Be Interested in Staying at the Caneel Bay Plantation Resort on the Island of St. John in the US Virgin Islands.

I Told Her That I Had Heard a Lot About How Lovely the Caneel Bay Plantation Resort Was. She Then Asked Me If I Would Be Interested in Staying at Laurance Rockefeller's Estate House When He was Not Visiting the Resort, Which He Owned.

She Highlighted That Laurance Rockefeller's Estate House was on a Private Peninsula With Its Own Private Beach.

I Responded That It Sounded Wonderful and That I Would Love to Stay at Laurance Rockefeller's Estate House.

She Then Told Me to Call the Manager of Caneel Bay and State That She Had Recommended That I Call Him to Find Out If There

Was a Good Time In the Upcoming Winter For a Ten-Day Visit By Me, My Wife, and Our Two Young Children.

The Manager of Caneel Bay Mentioned Several Ten-Day Periods That the Large First Floor of the Estate House Would Be Available.

One of the Ten-Day Periods Was a Perfect Fit For Me and My Family. So I Made a Reservation and Sent a Deposit to Secure It.

The Manager Also Mentioned That the Upstairs of the Large Estate House Had Been Reserved By a Prominent US Citizen and His Wife at About the Same Time Period As Me. But Importantly, The Upstairs Had Its Own Outside Staircase Entrance. And Thus, The Prominent US Citizen and His Wife Would Not Have to Enter the First Floor Where My Family and I Would Be Staying to Gain Access to the Second Floor.

So, During Early November of 1980, I Arrived With My Family For Our Ten-Day Stay. The First Floor of the Estate House Was Wonderful, With a Large Family Room, Dining Room, Kitchen, and Two Bedrooms and Bathrooms. The Large Porch of Our House Was Up a Hill with Wonderful Views of the Ocean. And the Private White Sand Beach was Just a Very Short Walk Down the Hill From the House.

Also, Caneel Bay Had Three Separate Exceptional Restaurants, with One in the Main Quarters of the Resort, One Overlooking a White Sand Beach, and One on the Grounds of a Historic Sugar Mill. And There Was a Large Bar With Music and Entertainment Every Night.

Caneel Bay Was Blessed With Seven Separate Beaches, Tennis Courts, a Boat House, and a Nice Jogging Trail Around the Perimeter of the Resort. Also, the Snorkeling Was Tops!

The Day After We Arrived at Caneel Bay, Liddy and I Noticed Several US Army Helicopters Flying Around Caneel Bay Numerous Times During the Day.

And, Lo and Behold, We Were Told at Dinner By the Manager of the Caneel Bay Plantation Resort That Vice President Walter Mondale and Joan, His Wife, Would Be Arriving the Next Day For a One-Week Vacation and Would Be Staying on the Second Floor of Our Estate House.

And, Soon Enough, Walter and Joan Mondale Arrived After the November 4th Election In One of Three Helicopters, With the Other Two Helicopters Used to Ferry Six US Secret Service Agents From a US Military Base in Puerto Rico to Ensure the Vice President's Safety. The Six Secret Service Agents Stayed in a Small Guest House on the Peninsula That Was Very Closc to the Estate House and Were Replaced Every Eight Hours With Another Shift of Six Secret Service Agents.

Also, On the Same Day, a Much Larger Helicopter Landed With a Good-Sized Armored Jeep For Use By the Vice President and His Wife

And a US Coast Guard Cutter Arrived and Anchored Just Off the Peninsula Where The Mondales and We Were Staying.

The Next Morning After the Arrival of The Mondales, Both Tommy and Christie Woke Up at Six A.M. and Started Making a lot of Noise. Thus, Out of Concern That Their Noises Would Wake Up The Mondales, I Took Tommy and Christie Out For a Long Walk Around the Entire Perimeter of the Caneel Bay Plantation. And Subsequently, Liddy and I Took Turns Getting Up Early to Take the Kids For a Long Walk so as Not to Disturb The Mondales.

Several Days Later, at the End of My Long Early Morning Walk With the Kids, I Heard the Outside Entrance Door to the Second Floor of the Estate House Open.

And, Sure Enough, It was Vice President Walter Mondale. He Came Down the Stairs and Waved To Us.

I Then Asked Him From a Distance If I Could Introduce Tommy and Christie to the Vice President of the United States.

He Let Out a Big Smile, Walked to Us, Shook Tommy's Hand, and Started Up a Nice Conversation.

He Then Took Us to See the Large Armored Jeep Which Was Parked Next to the Guest House with the Six Secret Service Agents.

He Started Up the Jeep and Explained to Us How It Worked.

Then, He Showed Us the So-Called Black Box in the Back of

The Large Armored Jeep. However, the Black Box was Not Black But Was a Silver Aluminum Case About the Size of a Suitcase. And Vice President Mondale Explained That it Contained Only, If Required, Super Secret Communication Electronics That Would Allow the Vice President, in the Absence of the President and While the Vice President Was Away From a US Military Command Center, to Contact the Pentagon About Responding to a Military Attack on the United States By the Soviet Union That Required the Vice President's Authorization to Initiate a Nuclear Counter Attack.

In Conclusion, I Still Relish Being Able to Share Laurance Rockefeller's Caneel Bay Plantation Estate House With the Vice President and His Wife.

And I Felt Very Safe There, as We Were Being Guarded and Protected All Day and All Night By the US Secret Service.

97. Failed Attempt at Polo

*S*oon After Liddy and I Moved To Our New Home on Middlesex Road in Darien, Connecticut, Liddy Became a Member of the Ox Ridge Hunt Club.

The General Manager of the Hunt Club was Tom Goodspeed, who was also a Top Ranked US Polo Player.

Even though I Had a Few Short Horse-Riding Lessons Six Years Earlier, I was Not a Good Horse Rider.

Nevertheless, I Decided to Sign Up With Tom Goodspeed For His Group Polo-Riding Clinic at the Hunt Club.

Early On, I was Able to Handle the Polo Lessons OK.

But Then, Tom Goodspeed Gave Me a Lesson on How to Fall Off the Polo Pony When it Was Galloping Without Getting Hurt.

I Was Scared To Death and Refused To Try To Fall Off the Polo Pony.

And Thus, I Totally Failed in My Attempt to Become a Polo Player.

However, My Failed Attempt at Polo Was Not Due In Any Way to Tom Goodspeed's Skills at Being an Outstanding Polo Player and Instructor.

Tom Goodspeed was Captain of the 1973 and 1974 University of Connecticut NCAA Division I Champion Polo Team.

After Serving From 1977 to 1985 as General Manager of the Ox Ridge Hunt Club, He Became Director of the Los Angeles

Equestrian Center, Which Was one of the Largest US Horse Clubs. He Also Managed and Played on a Professional Top Ranked Polo Team For Ten Seasons and Won the *Polo* Magazine Award in 1995 For "Arena Polo Player of the Year."

And, Last But Not Least, Liddy and I Spotted Tom Goodspeed, Who Had Movie Star Looks, Driving a Convertible in the Rose Bowl Parade in Pasadena with Juice Newton, An Exceptionally Voluptuous American Pop and Country Singer, Songwriter, and Musician. Tom Goodspeed Got To Know Juice Newton Quite Well Because She Stabled Her Horse at the Los Angeles Equestrian Center. And Tom Goodspeed Married Juice Newton Shortly After He Moved to Southern California.

98. SIX-MINUTE MILES ON EXXON'S TREADMILL

One of the Great Fringe Benefits of Being Promoted to The Executive Ranks of Exxon at Their Headquarters in Rockefeller Center was Being Able to Use Their First-Class Health Club in Their Building at 30 Rockefeller Center

The Exxon Health Club Had Several Very Good Fitness Instructors That Designed a Fitness Course Tailormade to the Physical Needs of Each Executive Member.

My Tailormade Course Was As Follows, From the Beginning to the End of My Workout, Which Usually Lasted For Fifty to Sixty Minutes:

Firstly, About Five Minutes of Stretch Exercises.

Then Throwing a Large, Heavily Weighted Leather Ball To a Wooden Board About Twelve Feet From the Floor.

Then, A Dozen Sit-Ups.

Then, About Five Minutes on a Rowing Machine.

Then, Push Ups For a Short Time.

Then, Making the Rounds of Six Upper- and Lower-Body Nautilus Machines.

Then, Ten Minutes on a Bicycle.

And Lastly, Running on a Treadmill, Where I Was Free to Select My Speed and Time on the Treadmill.

I Chose to Run For Just a Few Minutes at a Slow Speed. But

Then I Would Increase the Speed to Where I Was Running Six Minute Miles and Stayed at This Speed for 12-18 Minutes.

Also, the Locker Room and Showers Were First Class.

Thus, I Established a Priority of Trying to Visit Exxon's Health Club For a Workout at the End of the Workday of Three Times Per Week.

Importantly, As a Result of My Workouts at Exxon's Health Club and My Weekend Runs Around Central Park and Hiking Activities, I was in Outstanding Shape.

99. Swim Meets and More Swim Meets

*S*hortly After Moving To Our New Home in Darien, Connecticut, Liddy Enrolled Tommy in a Learn-to-Swim Class at Darien's YMCA.

Tommy Did Very Well in the Learn-to-Swim Class and His Instructor Recommended That Tommy Sign Up For The YMCA's Competitive Swimming Program in Which They Compete in Weekend Swim Meets Against Swimmers From Other YMCAs and Private Swim Clubs in Connecticut and New England.

There Were Also Swimming Championship Meets at the End of the Swimming Season For the YMCAs in Tommy's Area of Connecticut and All of New England.

And, There was a National YMCA Swimming Championship in Fort Lauderdale, Florida.

In Addition, There Were Separate Connecticut, New England, and National Swimming Championships For Swimmers From Both Private and YMCA Swimming Clubs.

Tommy Became a Very Good Competitive Swimmer First in the Seven-to-Eight Age Group and Later Became an Outstanding Competitive Swimmer in the Nine-to-Ten Age Group When He Finished First in the Fifty-Yard Breaststroke at The New England YMCA Championships.

In Tommy's Middle School Years, We Became Aware of the

Outstanding Competitive Swimming Program at the Wilton YMCA, which is Located in the Same County as the Darien YMCA.

Under the Leadership of Tim Murphy, Their Head Competitive Swimming Coach, They

Won the Connecticut Swimming Championships For All Competitive Swimming Clubs Many Times.

Won the National YMCA National Championships at Fort Lauderdale Quite a Number of Times.

Qualified a Dozen Swimmers For the Most Recent US Olympic Swimming Trials To Select the Members of the US Men's and Women's Swim Teams.

Had Janel Jorgeson, One of Their Very Best Swimmers, Win Two Silver Medals at the Olympics.

And, of Major Importance to Many of the Parents of the Wilton YMCA Competitive Swimmers, Many of Their Swimmers Obtained Four-Year Swimming Scholarships at Top National Universities and Were Admitted to Ivy League Universities Because They Could Make a Significant Contribution to the Success of the Universities' Swimming Teams.

Tommy Loved to Compete; Never Missed an Early Morning, Later Afternoon, or Weekend Swim Practice; and Performed Exceptionally Well at Swim Meets While Still Managing to Do His Homework and Achieve Very Good Grades Both in Middle School and High School.

A Few of His Major Competitive Swimming Accomplishments During His High School Years Were as Follows:

In Darien High School's Dual Swimming Meets with Area High Schools, He Almost Always Won the Hundred-Yard Breaststroke and Two Hundred IM Events.

In His Senior Year at High School, He Won the Hundred-Yard Breaststroke and Two Hundred IM Events at the Connecticut High School State Championships. And He Received the Men's High School Swimmer of The Year Award.

While Swimming Fro the Wilton YMCA Swim Team During His Senior Year at High School, He Won the Two-Hundred-Yard

Breaststroke and the Two-Hundred-Yard IM at the YMCA National Championships in Fort Lauderdale.

He Qualified in the Two-Hundred-Yard Breaststroke For the US Olympic Swim Team Trials To Select the Members of the US Swim Team.

During His Last Year of High School, He was Named Men's Swimmer of the Year By Connecticut's United States Swimming Organization.

And, As a Result of Tommy's Competitive Swimming Accomplishments During His Senior Year of High School, Tommy was Recruited By Many Universities and Colleges With Strong National Men's Swimming Teams.

He Accepted a Four-Year Swimming Scholarship to Indiana University, Which was Well Known For its Top Men's Swimming Teams.

His Four-Year Swimming Scholarship Covered 75 percent of Out-of-State Tuition, All Fees, Housing and Meal Costs, Textbook Expenses, Personal Costs, and Travel Costs To and From Our Home.

Liddy and I Loved to Attend Almost All of Tommy's High School, Darien YMCA, and Wilton YMCA Swim Meets.

And, Of Course, One of Us or Both of Us Would Attend Tommy's Championship Meets in Connecticut and New England As Well As The Junior National, Senior National, and YMCA National Championships in Other States.

In Addition to the Fun Part of Watching Tommy Swim and Do Well at Highly Competitive Swim Meets in Connecticut, New England, and Other States, Up Until We Purchased a Car For Tommy In His Junior Year at High School, Either Liddy or I Had to Drive Tommy To and From Early Morning Swim Practices at the Wilton YMCA Five Days a Week Before the Start of the School Day and Again at the End of the School Day and on Saturday or Sunday Mornings.

However, Our Efforts on Behalf of Tommy Were Well Worth It!

100. GRIZZLY ENCOUNTER IN CANADIAN ROCKIES

*D*on, My Younger Brother, and I, Who Both Like to Take Long Hikes, Went on Two Hundred-Mile Backpacking Trips in the Canadian Rockies and One Hundred-Mile Backpacking Trip in Northern California Together With Each of Our Sons, Tommy and Justin.

On the Two Canadian Rockies Trips, Tommy and I Flew into Calgary From New York City, and Justin and My Brother Flew Into Calgary From Los Angeles.

In Calgary, On Both Trips, We First Had a Wonderful Prime Ribs Dinner at a High-End Restaurant.

On the Next Day, We Rented a Car From "Rent A Wreck" and Drove to Banff, Where We Stayed For One Night in a Nice Inn, Had a Good Steak Dinner, and Did Some Last-Minute Shipping For Clothing and Additional Food Supplies.

On the First Canadian Rockies Backpacking Trip, We Started Our Hike From Lake Ohara in the Yoho National Park in the Province of British Columbia and Hiked Southward Primarily in the Banff National Park in the Province of Alberta Towards Banff.

We Ended Our Ten-Day Hike at Another Lake, Where We Were Able to Arrange For a Helicopter Ride Over a Very High Mountain Ridge Back to Banff Where We Had Left Our "Rent A Wreck" Car.

For this Ten-Day Backpacking Trip, We Had to Obtain in

Advance Hiking Permits From the Canadian National Park Service to Hike on Their Well-Maintained Trails and Pitch a Tent at Their Designated Campsites, Which Were Spaced About One Day's Hike From One Another.

Our Breakfasts Consisted of Granola With Powdered Milk, Powdered Orange Juice With Water, and Powdered Coffee with Hot Water.

Our Lunches Were Mostly Peanut Butter and Jelly Sandwiches Along with Cheese and Salami Together With Drinking Water That We Had Obtained From Springs and Streams and Purified With Water Purification Tablets.

For Dinners, We Always Had Soup and a Variety of Dry Dinners That We Cooked on Our Small Camping Stove After Adding Water. And the Dinners Were Topped Off with Each of Us Gorging on Half of a Tasty Cadbury Chocolate, Nut, and Fruit Candy Bar.

We Usually Went To Bed Early In Our Two Respective Tents, with Air Mattresses and Sleeping Bags.

The Hikes Covered a Wide Variety of Terrain Including Climbing Up and Over High Mountain Passes, Going Through Dense Forests, and Crossing Many Streams and A Few Rivers.

We Came Across a Wide Variety of Wildlife on the Backpacking Trips Including Black Bears, Coyotes, Wolverines, Foxes, Elk, Deer, Moose, Mountain Goats, Bighorn Sheep, Pikas, Hawks, Snowshoe Owls, Falcons, Beavers, Rabbits, and Large Snakes.

After Our Ten-Day Backpacking Trip, We Stayed One Night in Banff and Had Another Wonderful Prime Rib Dinner. And the Next Day, We Drove Our "Rent A Wreck" Car To Calgary Early in the Morning so as to Catch Our Two Flights Back to New York City and Los Angeles.

On Our Second Canadian Rockies Backpacking Trip, We Started the Hike at the Huge Columbia Icefield, Covering 325 Square Kilometers, with Ice Depths Up To 365 Meters, and Hiked For Ten Days Northward In the Jasper National Park to the Town of Jasper.

Early in the Backpacking Trip, as We Were just Starting to

Cook Our Dinner, Two Hikers Passed Our Designated Campsite, Going Southward.

They Told Us About Just Seeing a Large Grizzly Bear Several Hours Earlier That was Very Close to the Trail.

After We Finished Dinner, as a Precaution, We Removed all of the Food From Our Four Backpacks, Put the Food in a Large Rucksack, and Hung it With a Strong Rope Over a Large, High Branch of a Tree About a Five-Minute Walk Away From Our Campsite.

Shortly After We all Had Decided to Call It a Day and Climb Into Our Two Respective Tents, I Heard a Growling Noise and Some Heavy Breathing. I Peeked Out of the Zipper Opening to Tommy's and My Tent and was Startled to see a Huge Grizzly Bear Walking Around Our Cooking and Sleeping Area, Doing A Lot of Sniffing.

I Was Scared to Death and Reached For My Long Abercrombie and Fitch Hunting Knife.

And I Whispered to Tommy to Be Absolutely Quiet.

Fortunately, After About Fifteen Minutes of Prowling Around and Sniffing, The Huge Grizzly Bear Left Our Campsite.

And I Quickly Realized that Had We Not Been Told About the Huge Grizzly Bear Sitting Just North of Our Campsite, and Had We Not Removed all of Our Food From the Four Backpacks and Put it into a Large Rucksack and Hung it On a Rope Over a Large Tall Branch of a Tree That was Five Minutes Away From Our Campsite, The Huge Grizzly Bear Most Likely Would Have Enjoyed Having the Four of Us For a Wonderful Feast.

Thanks Be To God For Helping Us Survive!

And, Fortunately, We Did Not Encounter the Huge Grizzly Bear, or Any Other Grizzly Bears, During the Rest of Our Long Hike To Jasper.

101. STEALING WATER FROM HUDSON RIVER

*E*xxon Owned One of the World's Largest Oil Refineries in Aruba, Which is a Dry, Flat Desert-Like Island Off the Coast of Venezuela.

Exxon's Aruba Refinery Needed a Large Amount of Fresh Non-Saltwater For Cooling Purposes To Safely Operate Its Refinery.

However, There Was No Natural Source of Salt-Free Water On the Island of Aruba. So Exxon Had to Rely on Obtaining Salt-Free Water From Two Aruba Government-Owned and -Operated Water Desalination Plants.

The Aruba Government, For Some Reason, Was Not Able to Properly Maintain Its Two Water Desalination Plants.

As a Result, One of the Two Water Desalination Plants Stopped Functioning Properly and Had to be Totally Shut Down. And This was the Water Desalination Plant That Supplied Exxon With Enough Fresh Water to Safely Operate Its Aruba Refinery.

And Water From the Aruba Government's Second Water Desalination Plant Could Not Be Used at Exxon's Aruba Refinery Since the Desalinized Water From This Plant was Required to Supply Aruba's Residents with Fresh Water and was Needed By the Island's Many Large Tourist Resorts That Employed A Lot of Aruba's Islanders with Jobs.

Thus, Unless Exxon Could Obtain a Large Amount of Fresh

Water From Another Source, It Would Have to Shut Down its Very Large Refinery.

So Exxon Very Quickly Tried to Identify Off-Island Sources of Readily Available Fresh Water That Could Be Transported to Its Aruba Refinery.

However, No Readily Available Sources of Large Amounts of Fresh Water for Export Could Be Identified at That Time.

So Someone in Exxon Came Up With a Unique Idea For Obtaining a Free Source of Water From the United States That Could Be Exported By Exxon to Aruba.

The Unique and Unconventional Idea was to Use Some of Exxon's Tankers That Delivered Petroleum Products From Exxon's Refinery in Aruba to Eastern US Ports To

First, Deliver the Petroleum Products From the Aruba Refinery to One or More Eastern US Ports in An Exxon Tanker.

Second, Send the Tanker Out to Sea About Fifty Miles and Clean the Petroleum Residue Out of the Tanker's Cargo Tanks and Pump In Just Enough Saltwater Ballast Water so that the Tanker Could Be Operated Safely.

Third, Send the Tanker Up the Hudson River to Where the River Water was Fresh. Then Discharge the Saltwater Ballast Water From the Tanker's Ballast Water Tanks and Then Go Up the Hudson River a Little Further to Where it Could Pump Clean Fresh Water Into the Cleaned-Out Cargo Tanks of the Tanker.

And Lastly, Deliver the Fresh Hudson River Water to Exxon's Refinery in Aruba So That the Refinery Could Continue to Operate Safely.

However, John Cronin, the Riverkeeper for the Hudson River Fishermen's Association, Noticed Several Large Exxon Oil Tankers Anchoring Well Up the Hudson River and Then Pumping Fresh Hudson River Water Into Its Tankers.

And Then Senior Officials of the Hudson River Fishermen's Association Notified Many US and New York State Government Officials About What John Cronin Had Observed.

As a Result, A Few Days Later, There Were Front Page Articles in the *New York Times* and Other New York Newspapers About Exxon's Tanker Operations in the Hudson River.

And, Shortly Thereafter, There Were Newspaper Headlines About Exxon Stealing Fresh Water From the Hudson River.

And Then There Were Articles Claiming That Exxon's Tankers Were Contaminating the Hudson River By Discharging Ballast Sea Water With Some Petroleum Residue From Their Cargo Tanks Into Areas of the Hudson River That Were Used By Adjacent Municipalities To Supply Their Residents With Clean, Fresh Drinking Water.

Shortly Thereafter, Exxon's Public and Government Affairs Department Was Bombarded Not Just With Phone Calls From the Electronic and Print News Media, But With Multiple Requests From Government Officials to Attend Local, Regional, New York State, US Senate, and the US House of Representatives Hearings to Investigate What Exxon Was Doing With Its Large Oil Tankers on the Hudson River.

As a Result of My Current Job as Public and Government Affairs Manager For Exxon International, Which Owned and Operated Exxon's International Oil Tankers That Were Observed Loading Fresh Hudson River Water Into Their Tankers, I Was Called Upon to Oversee How Exxon Should Respond to This Major Crisis.

Given the Magnitude of This Major Government and Public Relations Problem, I Devoted Myself Full Time To

Drafting Exxon's Immediate Response To Inquiries From the Print and Electronic News Media.

Drafting Exxon's Immediate Response To Administrative and Elected Government Officials in New York State As Well As Environmental Organizations and Members of the Senate and House of Representatives.

Formulating a Plan For Exxon To Resolve This Crisis For Review By the CEO of Exxon and Other Senior Exxon Management Officials.

Fortunately, I Was Able to Develop a Plan of Action For Exxon

Which Didn't Totally Eliminate the Damage to Exxon But Which Reduced the Damage Significantly Over a Period of Time.

My Plan Was as Follows:

Immediately Cease Sending Exxon's Tankers Up the Hudson River For Any Purpose.

Identify Other Worldwide Sources of Fresh Water Which We Could Pledge To Use For Our Refinery in Aruba Even Though They Were Costly.

Directing Exxon's Engineering Experts to Undertake Studies to Demonstrate That Discharging Ballast Sale Water Into the Hudson River Downstream of Where the Fresh Water Was Taken Did Not Cause Any Problems Given That the Minor Amounts of Salt Water and Infinitesimal Amounts of Petroleum Residue Discharged Into the Hudson River Were Totally Diluted By the Much Large Amounts of Rapidly Flowing Hudson River Water.

Offering To Fund Multi-Million Dollar Grants to Environmental Organizations in New York State.

And, Lo and Behold, I Received a Significant Year-End Exxon Bonus Based on My Efforts to Minimize the Lasting Damage to Exxon From the Hudson River Crisis.

102. GRAHAM GUND'S MASSACHUSETTS SUMMER HOUSE

Liddy's Parents Gifted Their Properties on Mishaum Point in Massachusetts To Each of Their Four Children After They Had Purchased Clark Island in Maine As Their Vacation Home.

Vicky Tabor Received Her Grandmother's Summer House and Associated Land. Bert Nickerson Received His Grandmother's Artists Studio and Associated Land. And Chris Morgen and Liddy Each Received a Three-Acre Undeveloped Lot on the West Side of Mishaum Point.

After Returning to the US From Japan, Liddy and I Decided to Build a Summer House on Our Three-Acre Lot, Which is One of the Highest Lots on Mishaum Point and Has Wonderful Views of Buzzards Bay, The Mishaum Point Dock, and the Many Beautiful West Side Sunsets.

Warren and Jane Shapleigh, Who Built a New Award-Winning Summer House on the West Side of Mishaum Point, Invited Liddy and I to a Small Cocktail Party at Their House to Meet Graham Gund, Their Famous Architect From Cambridge, Massachusetts.

At the Cocktail Party, We Made an Appointment With Graham Gund To Meet Us at Our Lot To Obtain His Views on Where to Site Our House and What the House Should Look Like.

At the Meeting With Graham Gund, He Brought a Step Ladder and Climbed Up On it in Many Places To Find Out What the Views

Were Like So As To Select the Best Site For Our New Summer House.

Graham Gund Fell In Love with the Location of Our Lot and Offered To Prepare an Architectural Design For Our New Summer House.

We Gave Graham Gund the Go-Ahead to Proceed with the Architectural Design. And Three Months Later, Graham Gund Called Me To Say That He Would Prepare a Small Wooden Model of His Ideas For What the House Would Look Like. I Said Great, and We Set a Date For a Meeting With Him at My Office in Rockefeller Center When He was Planning to Be in New York City on Other Business.

Graham Gund Came To My Office With a Small Wooden House Model of His Plans For What Our Summer House Would Look Like. He Sat Down on a Chair on the Other Side of My Desk. He Then Held Up the Small Wooden House Model and Very Slowly Turned it Around While He Explained in Detail His Ideas On What the House Would Look Like.

I Noticed That the Glue on the Small Wooden House Model was Still Wet. When I Asked Graham Gund Why The Glue was Still Wet, He Responded That He Had Just Finished Making the Small Wooden House Model Over the Last Two Days While Staying at the Manhattan Apartment of Ann Swain Landreth, His Publicity Agent and a Partner of a Prestigious Public Relations Firm, Whom He Subsequently Married.

Liddy and I Both Liked the Design of the Small Wooden House Model Very Much. So We Signed a Contract With Graham Gund to Develop a Detailed Architectural Plan For Our House.

Several Months Later, Liddy and I Met with Graham Gund at the Office of the Architects Firm That He Founded in Cambridge, Massachusetts, to Review His Detailed to a Roof Deck. The Roof Deck Provides a Magnificent 360-Degree View of the Peninsula of Mishaum Point. The Bedrooms are Nestled In Under the Large Hipped Roof Punctuated with Multi-Shaped Dormers Playfully Providing Focused Views and Air.

Our Graham Gund Summer House Was Also Featured In *House Beautiful*, With Lots of Beautiful Color Photographs; Two Books; and The Boston Museum of Architects.

In Furnishing Our Summer House, We Spent a Lot of Time Shopping For Antique American Country and Summer House Furniture with the Help of a Home Furnishing Consultant From Philadelphia That was Recommended By Graham Gund.

103. Niece Wins Oscar for Best Supporting Actress

Mira Sorvino, My Sister's Oldest of Two Daughters, was a Whiz Kid in High School and College in Every Respect. She was Almost Straight A's in High School in New Jersey and was Accepted By Harvard, Where she Graduated in 1989 With High Honors and a Degree in East Asian Studies. She also Spent Her Junior Year Abroad in China, Where She Became Fluent in Mandarin Chinese.

Mira's Favorite Extracurricular Activities Were Acting and Singing. In Both High School and at Harvard, Mira Starred in Many Plays and Musicals.

After Graduating From Harvard, Mira Accepted an Editing Position with a Major Book Publishing Company in Manhattan.

However, Her Love was Still Acting. So She Obtained Roles in Two Movies and Then a Major Role Six Years After Graduating From Harvard in a Woody Allen Film Titled *Mighty Aphrodite*. In the Film, Mira Portrayed a Happy-Go-Lucky Prostitute Friend of Woody Allen.

For Mira's Role in *Mighty Aphrodite*, She Received a Golden Globes Award and Then An Oscar Academy Award For Best Supporting Actress.

Shortly After Receiving The Oscar, Mira and Lorraine, My Sister, and Mother of Mira Came to Our House in Darien, Connecticut, and Sang Several Lively and Fun Duets Together In Front of Liddy, Liddy's Mother, and Me.

Nine Years After Receiving the Oscar and Performing in Lots of Movies and TV Shows, Mira Married Chris Backus in 2004 in a Beautiful Wedding Ceremony, Which Liddy and I Attended, at a Private Villa Estate on the Isle of Capri in Italy.

Mira and Chris Now Have Four Wonderful Children, With Ages Ranging From Nine to Seventeen and Live in Malibu, California.

104. CHRISTIE STARS IN HIGH SCHOOL AND POST 53

C hristie, Our Daughter, Did Extremely Well Academically at Darien High School, Which is Acknowledged as the Best Public High School in Connecticut.

Liddy and I Never Had to Prod Christie to Study Hard and Do Her Homework in the Afternoons, Evenings, and Weekends.

On Her Own, Christie Came Up With Her Own Unique Test Preparation System.

First, She Would Find Out Well in Advance When the Major Tests Were Scheduled For Each of the Courses That She Was Taking Each Semester in High School.

About One Month Before Each Major Test, She Would Do a Broad Review of the Course Materials in the Textbook For the Course and Her Classroom Notes.

Then, About Two Weeks Before the Major Test Date, She Would Do an In-Depth Review of the Course Materials in the Textbook and Classroom Notes.

And Finally, Just a Day or An Evening Before the Major Test, She Would Do a Second In-Depth Review of the Course Materials.

Her Efforts Paid Off as She Graduated From Darian High School With the Fourth Highest Grade Point Average in Her Graduating Class.

Regarding Christie's Efforts to Decide Which College or

University to Attend After Graduating From High School, Most of Her High-Achieving Friends at Darian High School Wanted to Attend a Top Small Liberal Arts College in New England Such As Amherst, Williams, Bates, Bowdoin, Colby, and Middlebury.

However, Christie, Being Somewhat of a Contrarian, Decided to Focus Her Admission Efforts on Being Accepted at Top Large US Universities.

Christie Ended Up Deciding to Attend the University of Michigan, Where They Accepted Her For the Highly Prestigious Honors College of Liberal Arts.

The University of Michigan Ranks Among the Very Best in The United States in Many Fields of Study, Mainly Because it Attracts Some of the Biggest Names in Academia To Teach and Do Research in Ann Arbor.

The University of Michigan Honors College is Limited to the Top 1,400 Liberal Arts Students Out of a Total Undergraduate Enrollment of About Twenty-five Thousand Liberal Arts Students. And It is Considered to be the Best Honors Program in the US, Since It Has Small Classes and Offers More Special Honors Classes and Has More Seminar Rather Than Lecture Courses.

And It Also Has Special Academic Advisors For Every Honors College Student. For Example, Christie's Academic Advisor Would Take Christie and the Other Honors College Students Assigned To Her Advisor Out For a Pizza Dinner on Sundays Every Two Weeks.

Also, the Honors College Has Its Own Graduation Day Recognition Program.

Regarding Christie's Extracurricular Activities at Darien High School, She Decided to Join Post 53, Which Provided Emergency Ambulance Services To People in the Darien Area That Were Injured in Automobile or Other Accidents.

The Twenty Darien High School Students in Post 53 Were Responsible as a Group For Operating Three Fully Equipped State-of-the-Art Ambulances Twenty-four Hours a Day For 365 Days Each Year.

Post 53 Had Its Own Ambulance Building Which Housed the

Three Ambulances, And the Twenty Darien High School Students in Post 53 Took Turns Being Assigned to the Ambulance Building at Nights and the Weekends. During the School Day, One or Two Ambulances Were Kept at Darien High School.

In Addition to Being Employed as a Post 53 Ambulance Worker, the Post 53 High School Students Also Raised Money Via a Big Memorial Weekend Festival to Maintain and Service the Ambulances.

Most Importantly, Being a Member of Post 53, Charged With Responding Quickly to Save the Lives of Injured People, Raised Christie's Self-Esteem and Confidence in Herself Considerably.

And It Helped Her a lot in Getting Accepted at Top Universities Such as the University of Michigan.

105. EXXON—THE BEST AND BRIGHTEST!

I Spent Twenty-five Years Working For Exxon in Rockefeller Center; Houston, Texas; Tokyo; and New Jersey and Concluded That Their Professional Employees Were the Best and Brightest!

When Comparing Exxon's Return on Capital Employed and Stock Appreciation Over My Last Ten Years There, Both of these Measures of Company Performance Were Higher Than Any Other Major United States or International Energy and Oil Company.

In My Opinion, Exxon's High Performance Resulted From Their Very High Standards In Who They Hired From Universities to Work Initially For Exxon at Their Headquarters in Rockefeller Center.

Exxon's High Standards Were As Follows:

They Only Hired University Graduates With a Master's Degree in Business Administration.

They Only Recruited Graduates From the Top Ten MBA Universities in the US.

The Top Ten Were Harvard, Columbia, New York University, Wharton School of Finance at the University of Pennsylvania, Michigan, Northwestern, Indiana, Chicago, Stanford, and Massachusetts Institute of Technology.

When Recruiting at the Top Ten MBA Universities, Exxon Always Sent a Very Senior Manager From Their Headquarters Office in Rockefeller Center Along with a Graduate From the MBA

School Where They Were Recruiting Who Had Completed About Five Years of Service For Exxon in Rockefeller Center.

For Example, When I was Interviewed By Exxon at Northwestern For a Job at Exxon's Headquarters Office in Rockefeller Center, They Sent Jack Bennett, who was a Senior Official in Exxon's Treasurer's Department.

Jack Bennett Interviewed MBA Students Over Two Days Who Had Expressed a High Interest in Working For Exxon at Their Headquarters Office in Rockefeller Center and Who Had Been Recommended as a Top Candidate For a Job at Exxon By the Dean of Northwestern's Graduate School of Business.

As Another Example of Exxon's Very High Degree of Selectiveness In Deciding Who to Hire For Their Corporate Headquarters in Rockefeller Center, I Was the Only Graduate MBA Student at Northwestern of the Twenty MBA Students that Jack Bennett Interviewed That Was Subsequently Invited With All Expenses Paid to Visit Exxon For a Full Day of Job Interviews at Exxon's Headquarters Office in Rockefeller Center.

106. "Restructure, Shrink, or Perish"

Liddy and I Decided To Move in August of 1997 To Our Beautiful Summer House on the Water in Mishaum Point, Which is Located in South Dartmouth, Massachusetts.

Both of Us Wanted to Work, So Within a Month of Moving to Mishaum Point, We Each Started Looking For a Job.

Liddy Landed a Great Job in Only a Month's Time of Becoming the Manager of Davoll's General Store in the Russells Mills Area of South Dartmouth.

Davolls is One of the Oldest General Stores in the United States, and the Oldest General Store in Massachusetts, Dating Back to 1793. It Sells Women's Clothing, Gift Items, Antiques, Books and Stationary, Byars Choice Dolls and Other Collectibles, Sandwiches, and Non-Alcoholic Drinks. And It is Famous For Its Childrens Candies. It is also a Popular Gathering Place Early in the Morning For Politically Minded Nearby Residents To Gather and Talk Local, State, and National Politics While Enjoying a Cup of Coffee and a Donut.

Regarding My Job Search, I Would Go to the Dartmouth Public Library Early Every Morning and Read the Help Wanted Sections in the *Boston Globe*, *Providence Business Journal*, *New Bedford Standard Times*, and The *Wall Street Journal*.

I Set a Goal of Responding to Three Help Wanted Ads a Day

For Jobs in Finance, Business Consulting, Business Foundations, and Large Non-Profit Organizations.

At the End of Each Workday, I Would Take the Three Drafts of My Response Letters To Organizations That Were Offering a Job of Interest To Me To a Very Competent Lady in a Secretary's Office in the Berkshire Hathaway Mill Building in the South End of New Bedford. At the End of the Next Workday, I Would Pick Up the Three Letters That My Secretary Had Typed For Me, Put Them in an Envelope Along with My Excellent Resume, and Deliver Them to the Post Office that was Located Across the Street.

As a Result of My Very Aggressive Job Search Program, Which I Began in September of 1997, By Mid-December I Had Been Invited For Job Interviews With a Dozen Organizations Located in Various Parts of Massachusetts and Providence, Rhode Island.

And I Ended Up Receiving Full-Time Job Offers From Several, Large Financial Advisory Firms, An Executive Search Company, Several Fundraising Firms, The Marketing Departments In Several Large Companies, and An Energy Consulting Company.

Just Before Christmas. I Accepted a Job as Restructuring Director For ESAI Energy, Which is a National and International Energy Consulting Company Headquartered Just North of Boston.

ESAI's Owner and President was Ed Krapels, Whom I Knew Quite Well From My Time as Public and Government Affairs Manager of Exxon International. I Would See Ed Krapels Many Times at Energy Conferences in the US and Canada, Where We Were Both Speakers.

At ESAI, I Was Quickly Given a Lot of Consulting Assignments with US and International Oil and Energy Companies and Government Energy Specialists Such as Those In Japan, With the Ministry of International Trade and Industry, and Those in France, With ELF, a Government-Owned Energy Company.

Right Away, I Undertook a Major Study to Identify the Ten Best US and International Oil and Energy Companies in Terms of Their Return on Capital Employed and Return to Shareholders in the Form of Stock Appreciation Over the Past Ten Years.

After Identifying the Ten Highest-Performing Oil and Energy Companies, I Identified the Most Important Business Strategies and Areas of Investment Focus That These Companies Identified and Focused On That Resulted In Their Exceptional Business and Financial Performance.

And Gathering This Information Required My Obtaining and Reading Each Company's Quarterly and Annual Reports For the Prior Ten Years and Contacting the Ten Companies With Any Questions That I Had on Their Business Strategies and Areas of Investment Focus.

The Ten Highest Performing US and International Oil and Energy Companies Were Exxon, BP, ARCO, Amoco, Chevron, Mobil, Texaco, Shell, Sun, and Tosco.

When Comparing the Most Important Business Strategies and Areas of Investment Focus That Led to the Very High Business and Financial Performance By Each of the Ten Highest-Performing US and International Oil and Energy Companies, There Were Many Differences, and None of the Companies Pursued the Same Business Strategies and Areas of Investment Focus as Any One of the Other Companies.

Thus, My Major Message Was That There Are Many Different Ways to Achieve Very High Levels of Performance in the Oil and Energy Industry.

For Example:

Exxon's Focus Has Been On Investment Discipline, Asset Management, and Relentless Efficiency and Productivity Improvements Including a 45 percent Cut in Its Workforce.

BP's Focus Was To Involve Everyone From Top to Bottom in Identifying New Ways To Improve Performance and To Delegate More to Business Units, Increase Accountability, and Reduce Corporate Hierarchy.

Tosco Focused on Being Alert For Cheap Acquisition Opportunities By Purchasing Unwanted Refineries and Gas Stations.

ARCO's Focus Was Geographic Concentration in Existing and

Contiguous Markets Via Acquisitions and Construction of New Gas Stations.

Sun Implemented a Major Turnaround Plan To Restructure Its Organization Into Seven Independently Run Business Units, a Shared Service Organization

For Staff Functions, and a Much Smaller Headquarters Staff.

Shell and Texaco Combined Their Downstream Operations in Europe.

Amoco Focused on Being the Number One Gasoline Marketer in Its Thirty-Three-State Area and On Decentralization By Going From Three Large Companies to Seventeen Separate Business Enterprises and Subsequently to Seventy Business Groups.

Mobil Merged with Exxon.

Chevron Set Much Higher Goals For Cost Reduction, Return on Capital Employed and Safety and Sold Marginal Refining, Marketing, and Producing Assets.

At the End of My Research to Identify the Top Ten US and International Oil and Energy Companies in Terms of Financial Performance Along With the Business Strategies and Areas of Investment Focus That Led To Their Success, I Wrote a Book Titled *Restructure, Shrink, or Perish*. My Book was Privately Published by ESAI Energy, the Consulting Company I Worked For, and Sold For Twenty-five Thousand Dollars a Copy To the CEOs of Many US and International Oil and Energy Companies.

To Publicize My Book, I Gave a Talk at a Large Energy Conference in Washington, DC, Hosted By the Brookings Institute and Johns Hopkins University Titled "Restructure, Shrink, or Perish."

Based on My Well Received Speech in Washington DC. I Was Invited With All Expenses Paid To Give a Keynote Address on "Restructure, Shrink, or Perish" at a North American Energy Conference at the Villa De Quebec Castle in Quebec City.

And Subsequently, I Was Invited With All Expenses Paid to Give a Keynote Address on "Restructuring: Shrink or Perish" at the Major Annual Asian Pacific Economic Conference in Singapore, Which Was Attended By Many Presidents, Prime Ministers, and

Other Senior Government Officials From Asian Countries and Other Countries That Border On the Pacific Ocean.

And, Lo and Behold, I Was Voted To Be the Second-Most Interesting Speaker By the Government Officials Who Attended the APEC Conference.

107. CANDLELIGHT DINNERS WITH MOTHER-IN-LAW

Soon After Starting My New Job at ESAI Energy, I Experienced For the First Time the Long Commute By Car Five Days a Week Back and Forth to ESAI Energy, Which is Located North of Boston in Wakefield, Massachusetts.

Unexpectedly, Liddy's Mother in Lincoln, Massachusetts, Offered to Let Me Stay at Her House, Where She Was Living Alone, on Monday Nights and Also to Join Her On Monday Nights For Dinner.

I Readily Accepted Her Kind Invitation as Her House was Located Only a Fifteen-Minute Drive To and From ESAI's Headquarters Office in Wakefield, Massachusetts.

So, Every Monday Night, I Would Stop at a Wine Store on the Drive From Wakefield to Her House in Lincoln and Purchase a Very Good Bottle of Red Wine.

Liddy's Mother Would Pre-Cook the Dinner Before I Arrived and Then Heat It Up Just Before Out Scheduled Dinnertime.

Before Dinner, We Would Watch the Network Evening News For Thirty Minutes While She Enjoyed a Gin Martini and I Enjoyed a Vodka Tonic She Had Prepared For Me.

Also, Before Turning In For the Night, Liddy's Mother Would Set Out Some Granola and Fresh Fruit Along with Some Coffee For Me to Heat Up For My Breakfasts on Tuesday Mornings.

A Big Thank You to Liz Nickerson, Liddy's Kind and Thoughtful Mother!

Also, to Further Reduce My Long Weekly Commutes, Ed Krapels, ESAI Energy's President, Allowed Me to Work From Home on Wednesdays.

Thus, I Was Able to Reduce the Long Car Commutes From Liddy's and My House on Mishaum Point to ESAI Energy's Headquarters in Wakefield, Massachusetts, From Five Round Trips to Three Round Trips Per Week.

108. Obtaining Prestigious Job as Executive Director of the Greater New Bedford Industrial Foundation

After I had Been Working for ESAI Energy, I was Offered and Accepted a Job as Executive Director of the Prestigious Greater New Bedford Industrial Foundation.

The Industrial Foundation was a Private Non-Profit Job Creation Organization Founded in 1955 to Provide Jobs For Unemployed Workers in the Greater New Bedford Area.

At the Time of Its Founding, New Bedford's Unemployment Rate was 20 percent.

The Industrial Foundation's Job Creation Idea was to Buy Land for an Industrial Park, Develop It, and Sell Lots to Companies For New Plants and Associated Offices.

However, Initially the Industrial Foundation Didn't Have Any Money. So They Launched a Private Fundraising Campaign and Raised $550,000 From Five Thousand Individuals, Which was Equivalent to Four Million in Current Dollars as of 1998.

In 1959, the Industrial Foundation Purchased Fifty Acres of Woodlands in Northern New Bedford Adjacent to Route 140, Which is Now Part of the New Bedford Business Park; Constructed Two

Roads; Brought In Utilities; and Sold Six Lots to Six Companies For New Plants With Associated Offices.

In 1961, the Industrial Foundation Held a Sunday Open House at the Industrial Park, Which was Attended By Thirty Thousand Area Residents to View the Six New Plants.

The Industrial Foundation Repeated the Same Expansion Process Many Times By Purchasing Woodlands Adjacent to the Land They Already Owned in the Industrial Park, Building New Roads, Extending Utility Lines and Pipes, and Selling Lots to Companies For Plants and Associated Offices.

At the Time I Joined the Industrial Foundation as Its Executive Director, They Had 125 Trustees Who Met Annually and Fifteen Executive Committee Members That Met Once a Month.

However, They Only Had One Full-Time Employee as an Executive Secretary and Relied on the Staff of the New Bedford Economic Development Council to Manage and Market the Industrial Park.

109. Developing a Turn-Around Plan For the Industrial Park

When I Started My New Job On May 18, 1998, As Executive Director of the Grater New Bedford Industrial Foundation, I Quickly Discovered That No New Sales of Land in the Industrial Park Had Been Made By the Staff of the New Bedford Economic Development Council in the Previous Ten Years.

The Industrial Park Had Been Deteriorating Year By Year, And There Were Lots of Maintenance, Appearance, Utility, Traffic, Safety, Security, Regulations, Wetlands, and Marketing Issues That Needed To Be Quickly Addressed and Resolved.

Two of the Three Largest Companies in the Industrial Park Were Planning to Close Their Plants in the Park Within Nine Months, With One Company Planning to Build a Replacement Plant in New Jersey and the Other Company Planning to Build a Replacement Plant in South Carolina.

Initiating a Park Security Patrol Service During the Evenings, Weekends, and Holidays.

Strengthening the Zoning Regulations For the Industrial Park Including the Development of Strong Anti-Nuisance Covenants.

Hiring C.B. Richard Ellis, the World's Largest Commercial Real Estate Brokerage Firm, to Help Me Market the Park.

I Presented the Above Eleven-Point Improvement Plan to the

Industrial Foundation's Executive Committee at Their Monthly Meeting on July 6th.

They Wanted a Month to Think About It.

And, Fortunately, at the Next Monthly Meeting of the Executive Committee on August 3rd, They Approved My Entire Park Improvement Plan Without Any Exceptions.

Shortly Thereafter, I Met Separately With Each of the Companies in the Industrial Park to Inform Them About the Industrial Foundation's Plans to Implement a Major Improvement Plan For the Industrial Park.

Our Improvement Plan Was Well Received by the Park Companies. And Many of the Park Companies Volunteered to Serve on the Park Committees to Help Finalize the Details of Some of the Improvement Plans.

And the Two Large Companies That Were Planning to Move Out of the Industrial Park Cancelled Their Plans to Do So.

110. Forty-three Purchases, Twenty-four Expansions, Twenty-six Leases and Three Thousand New Jobs

*I*n My First Five Years as Executive Director of the Greater New Bedford Industrial Foundation and as Developer, Manager, and Marketer of the New Bedford Industrial Park, I was Able to Raise Millions of Dollars From Federal, State, and Local Sources Along with Money From the Sale of the Industrial Foundation's Land in the Park to Cover the Costs of Implementing all of the Park Improvements in My 1998 Improvement Plan, Along with Additional Improvements That I Subsequently Identified.

These Major Park Improvements Included

1. Building Six New Roads So As To Make Available More Land to Sell.
2. Repaving all of the Older Roads with a Lot of Help From New Bedford's Public Infrastructure Department.
3. Establishing and Updating a Large Company Directory Sign at a Paved Vehicle Pull-In Area Just After the Park Entrance With All of the Park Companies Listed Along with a Map of the Park Showing Where Each Company was Located.

4. Planting Seasonal Flowers in the Spring, Summer, and Fall, Along with Small Flowering Trees in the Newly Constructed Park Median Strips on the Two Major Entrance Roads to the Park.

5. Completing a Wetlands Flagging of the Entire Park so that We Could Identify the Locations and Boundaries of all of the Developable and Saleable Upland Acre Lots in the Park.

6. Increasing the Annual Maintenance Expenditures For the Park by 700 percent.

7. Hiring Don Vigeant's Maintenance Company, Which was Located Close to the Park, to Visit the Park Every Day to Identify Any Maintenance and Repair Needs on the Public Roads and Alongside the Public Roads that Needed To Be Taken Care Of Immediately and to Supplement the City of New Bedford's Snow-Plowing Work in the Winter Months.

8. Recruiting Northstar Learning Centers, Which is a First-Class Early Childhood Education and Development Organization, to Build and Operate a Day Care Facility in the Park For the Young Children of Park Employees.

9. Attracting Two Machine Shops, a Bank, and Subsequently Two Fast Food Restaurants and a Gas Station to the Park.

10. Completing in Several Stages Major Improvements in the Park's Telecommunications Services By Adding T-1, T-3, DSL, Cable, and Wireless Facilities.

11. Improving Traffic Safety at the Entrance to the Park By Erecting Stop Signs, Constructing Traffic Islands, and Painting Directional Arrows on the Roads, So As to Slow Down the Vehicles Entering, Exiting, and Passing By the Park.

12. Initiating a Park Security Service with Marked Security Vehicles to Patrol the Park During the Evenings, Weekends, and Holidays, so as to Provide Better Security Protection for Employees of the Park Companies that

Worked During Those Times and Significantly Reduce Pilferage and Break-ins of Park Company Buildings.

13. Expanding the Zoning Regulations For the Park, Including the Development of a Strong Anti-Nuisance Clause and Putting Those Regulations in the Deeds of Park Companies.

The Anti-Nuisance Clause States That "No Park Project May Go Forward Which Poses Any Significant Risks, Hazards, or Problems to the Land in the Park, Other Companies in the Park or Nearby Residents of the Park, Such As Fire; Explosion; Dust, Noise; Odor; Unhealthy Air Emissions; Ground Water Contamination; Soil Contamination; Adverse Wetlands Impacts; Adverse Endangered Species Impacts; Or Unsightly Operations."

During My Sixteen-Year Tenure at the Park, I Turned Away Twenty-nine Companies That Wanted to Buy, Build, or Lease a Facility in the Park For Nuisance Reasons.

14. Contracting with Rick Borden, Who was a Senior Vice President of Real Estate for the Industrial Division of CB Richard Ellis, Which is the World's Largest Commercial and Industrial Real Estate Brokerage Firm, To Help Me Market the Park.

15. Obtaining State Master Plan Approval For Development of the Park Thus Eliminating the Need for Lengthy and Costly State Permitting By Companies Wanting to Construct a New Facility or Expand Their Existing Facility in the Park.

16. Helping Companies Obtain Local Government Permits From New Bedford or Dartmouth in Sixty Days or Less For New Buildings and Expansion Projects.

17. Helping New Companies or Existing Companies That Were Planning New Building Projects in the Park To Obtain State, City, or Town Tax Incentives; State Workforce Training Grants; and Assistance From New

Bedford's Career Center Staff in Hiring Qualified New Workers.

18. Assisting Companies in Obtaining Bank Financing For New Buildings, Building Additions, and Equipment Purchases.

19. Helping Companies Sell Their Surplus Land in the Park and Lease Their Surplus Building Space.

20. Surveying All Park Companies on a Yearly Basis To Obtain Their New Ideas on How to Further Improve the Park.

As a Result of the Above Twenty Major Park Improvements, Along with Considerable Help From Rick Borden of CB Richard Ellis, During My Park Tenure From 1998 to 2014, There Were Forty-three Purchases of Land or Buildings in the Park; Twenty-four Building Expansions; and Twenty-six Leases of Space in Park Buildings.

And Most Importantly, Companies in the Park Grew From Eighteen to Forty-nine, and Good-Paying Jobs Increased From 1,500 to 4,500.

And the Park Became the Hottest Industrial Park By Far in Massachusetts During My Last Ten Years of Developing, Managing, and Marketing the Park, and Became the Second-Largest Industrial Park in Massachusetts.

Some Examples of the Many Excellent Companies that Moved Into the Park or Expanded Their Existing Facilities in the Park During My Tenure Are as Follows:

Zapp Precision Steel From Germany Built a New 77,000 Sq. Ft. Plant Which is Regarded as the Most Beautiful Steel Plant in the World, With No Belching Smokestacks But with Horizontal Assembly Lines and a One-Hundred-Foot Vertical Assembly Line all Within Clear View of Their Elevated Board of Directors Room, with One, Long Floor-to-Ceiling Glass Wall Facing the Assembly Lines.

Titleist, Which has 50 percent of the Worldwide Market For

Golf Balls, Built a New 254,000 Sq. Ft. Plant in The New Bedford Side of the Park and Expanded Its Plant in the Dartmouth Side of the Park Several Times to 169,000 Sq. Ft.

AFC Cable, Which Has Its Worldwide Headquarters in the Park and Has 40 percent of the North American Market For Armored Electrical and Communications Cable, Built a New 240,000 Sq. Ft. Plant and Headquarters Office in Addition to Its Other Large Facility in the Park.

Five Star Surgical Built a New 38,000 Sq. Ft. Medical Instruments Manufacturing and Headquarters Office Facility.

Symmetry Medical Acquired an 82,000 Sq. Ft. Facility For the Manufacture of Orthopedic Medical Devices and Relocated Its New Products R&D Division From Its Headquarters In Indiana to the Park.

Reinhart Foodservice, a Food Supply Company, Purchased and Expanded an Existing Park Facility to 116,000 Sq. Ft.

Lighthouse Masonry Built a Beautiful New 30,000 Sq. Ft. Headquarters Office and Supply Facility, Which is Regarded as the Most Attractive Building in the Park.

Aerovox Electronics Built a New 137,000 Sq. Ft. Plant and Headquarters Office Building.

Ahead Inc., a Maker of Golfing Hats and Clothing, Built a New 93,000 Sq. Ft. Plant and Headquarters Office Building.

Horacio's Welding and Sheet Metal Acquired, Renovated, and Expanded an Existing Park Facility to 36,000 Sq. Ft. For Its Plant and Headquarters Office.

111. Creating New Bedford's Global Learning Charter School

After Only Being In My New Job For One Year as Executive Director of the Greater New Bedford Industrial Foundation and as Developer, Manager, and Marketer of the New Bedford Industrial Park, Some Community Leaders in New Bedford Invited Me to Take Part In Their Early Discussions About Creating a Charter School in New Bedford and Deciding What Type of School It Should Be.

I Readily Accepted Their Invitation as I Believed That Having Excellent Schools is the DNA of Economic Development and Preparing Children For Successful Careers. And Thus, It Is So Important For the Children in New Bedford to Have Access to Excellent Schools.

In New Bedford, the Elementary Schools Were Performing Quite Well Based on Their Students' Achievement Scores on State-Mandated Yearly Tests For English, Math, and Science.

However, the Students in New Bedford's Three Middle Schools Were Getting Poor Scores on the State Tests. And New Bedford's High School Suffered From Low Four-Year Graduation Rates and Unsatisfactory Test Scores.

After Lots of Meetings and Discussions with the Community Leaders About the Type of Charter School That was Most Needed, We Decided To Focus On Starting Up a Charter School Which Would Be Both a Middle School and a High School For Grades Six to Twelve, so as to Address the Most Pressing School Improvement Needs of New Bedford's Children.

In Order to Create an Outstanding Charter School, We Believed It was Necessary to Identify and Then Contract With One of the Best School Improvement Consulting Firms in the United States, so as to Guide Us in the Right Direction In Terms Of Establishing a Motivational School Mission; Hiring an Outstanding Executive Director and Two Principals; Recruiting Highly Qualified Teachers; Selecting the Curriculum For Each Grade; and Identifying the Type of Teaching That Would Be Most Effective With New Bedford's Children.

Fortunately, We Were Able to Contract With the Education Development Center in Newton, Massachusetts, to Have Their President and Two Senior Vice Presidents Guide Us In Preparing the Opening of the Charter School as well as Overseeing and Guiding the Teacher's Classroom Performance For Three Years Or More After Our Initial Startup.

I Also Found Out From the Education Development Center That Gary Jacobs, the Son of Irwin Jacobs, Who was Born and Went to School in New Bedford and Then Obtained a PhD From MIT and Formed a Multi-Billion Dollar Company to Make Operating Software For Cell Phones, Started Up a High-Performing Charter High School in San Diego.

In Its First Year, Gary Jacobs High Tech High School Achieved the Second-Best Math Scores of all of the Public High Schools in California. As a Result, Bill Gates, From the Gates Foundation, Found Out About High Tech High's Success and Gave Them a $6.5 Million Grant to Replicate High Tech High's Performance Practices in Nine Other Public High Schools in the United States.

After I Contacted High Tech High, Gary Jacobs, Irwin Jacobs, and the Principal of High Tech High Flew to New Bedford to Meet With the Global Learning Charter School's Newly Formed Board of Trustees, Headed Up By Me, to Evaluate Whether or Not to Select Our Charter School, Which Was Scheduled to Open Within a Year, as One of Their Nine High Tech High Replication Schools.

Fortunately, They Were Impressed With Our Plans For the New Charter School in New Bedford and the Fact that the Prestigious Education Development Center Would Be Guiding and Overseeing Our School Opening and Our Teaching Practices For Three or More Years.

Thus, High Tech High Announced in 2002 That They Had Selected the Global Learning Charter School as One of Their Nine Replication Schools. And, As a Result, They Would Be Involved in Training Our Administrators and Teachers and Evaluating Our Performance. And They Would Also Provide Us With a Significant Multi-Year Startup Grant.

In September of the Same Year, The Global Learning Charter School Opened With 250 Students In Grades Six to Eight and Then Grew Year By Year to Four Hundred Students in Grades Five to Twelve. And All of the Students Were Selected By a Lottery.

In Our First Informational Meeting, With Large Numbers of Parents and Children, As a Result of all of the High-Tech, High-Publicity About Their Selection of Us as a Replication School, The Lines For Getting Into Our School Building Were Three Deep All the Way Around a Very Large New Bedford City Block.

Some of the New Innovative Concepts Initiated Right From the Beginning of The Global Learning Charter School Were

Grouping Students of All Ability Levels To Be Taught Together In the Same Classes.

Implementing Differentiated Instruction so as to Meet the Different Education Needs of Each Student Within the Same Classroom.

Initiating a Major Effort To Meet With Churches and Social Service Organizations So That the GLCPS Student Body Would Mirror the Racial, Socio-Economic, and Bilingual Breakdown of New Bedford.

Establishing Themes For the Curriculum of Career Awareness, Global Citizenship, Technology Literacy, and Life Skills and Integrate Them Into the Basic Subjects of Math, English, Social Studies, Science, and Performing Arts.

Launching a Nationwide Search For an Outstanding Executive Director and Two Principals.

Recruiting Outstanding Teachers That Shared the Global Learning Charter School's Mission From Massachusetts and Rhode Island Schools.

Emphasizing Project-Based Learning As Well As Developing Outstanding Presentation, Writing, and Teamwork Skills; Having An Outstanding Executive Director, Two Principals, Administrative Staff, and Teachers, As Well As Fully Implementing the Innovative Teaching Concepts, Resulted in Excellent Performance By the GLCPS Students in Both the Middle School and High School.

With Reference to the GLCPS High School:

It is Currently Ranked By the US News and World Report as Being in the Top 3 percent of All Public High Schools in The United States In Terms of Performance.

On the Most Recent Tenth-Grade State of Massachusetts MCAS Test Results, the Percentage of GLCPS Students Meeting or Exceeding Expectations Was 84 percent For English Compared to 24 percent For New Bedford's Main High School; 83 percent For Science Compared to 33 percent For New Bedford's Main High School and; 64 percent For Math Compared to 20 percent For New Bedford's Main High School.

The GLCPS Had a Four-Year High School Graduation Rate in 2019 For All Students of 94 percent Compared to 65 percent For New Bedford's Main High School.

While the State of Massachusetts Only Allows Individuals to Serve on the Board of Trustees of Charter Schools For a Maximum of Ten Years, I Served as Chair of the Board of Trustees For the GLCPS In Its First Three Years and As Chair of the Board of Trustees In My Last Three Years as a Member of the Board of Trustees. And, In My Other Four Years on the GLCPS Board of Trustees, I Served as Chair of the Finance Committee.

However, Since Having to Retire From the GLCPS Board of Trustees After My Ten Years of Service, I Have Continued to Be Actively Involved In Monitoring and Helping to Further Improve the Performance of the GLCPS. In Fact, Steve Furtado, Who Is Executive Director of the GLCPS, Mentioned That He Receives More Phone Calls From Me In Many Years Compared to Most of the Current Members of the GLCPS Board of Trustees.

At the Time of My Retirement as Chair of the GLCPS Board of Trustees, I Received the Following Appreciation Letter From the GLCPS Board of Trustees:

Dear Tom,

There is one simple inexorable fact: the New Bedford Global Learning Charter School owes much of its existence and much of its success to your vision and dedication. When there was no Charter School, you helped forge a coalition of community members to make it a reality. In those early days when the school was on the verge of chaos, you were there to keep it steady. Whenever Finances became an issue, you were there to guide our path. When our mission was unclear, you continually pressed for excellence and an extended school day. When we were uncertain as to whom we served, you reminded us of our commitment to inner city families and, you continually reminded us that our students should and could be successful in their pursuit of college.

Your boundless energy and laser vision kept us on track. We are not sure that we could successfully count the endless number of hours that you have dedicated to the Charter School during the past ten years. You have managed to "talk the talk" and "walk the walk" when it comes to supporting your ideas that education is at the foundation of our City and the foundation of business. You have demonstrated that business leaders, such as yourself, have an obligation to support and engage themselves in our school's progress and betterment.

Finally, this Board of Trustees, on behalf of the Global Learning Charter School and its Families, thanks you for your long years of unselfish service. We wish you well, good health and continued engagement in the life of our school and community.

Sincerely,

Pam Cruz

Global Learning Charter School Board of Trustees

112. MAN OF THE YEAR!

The *Standard-Times*, Based in New Bedford, Is the Largest of Three Daily Newspapers Covering the News In the Twelve Cities and Towns Located In the South Coast of Massachusetts.

At the End of Each Year, the Editors and Senior News Reporters of the *Standard-Times* Discuss and Then Select the Man and Woman of The Year For Each of the Twelve South Coast Cities and Towns. And, In Addition, They Select a South Coast Man and Woman of The Year.

After Having Served For Only Three and a Half Years As Executive Director of the Greater New Bedford Industrial Foundation and as Developer, Manager, and Marketer of the New Bedford Industrial Park, As Well As Being Involved In New Education Initiatives To Create a Charter School and Reduce the Dropout Rate at New Bedford High School, I Was Selected By the *Standard-Times* as South Coast Man of The Year.

Attached Is The *Standard-Times* December 30, 2001, Article and Photograph of Me as The South Coast Man of The Year For 2001 and Another Major *Standard-Times* Article and Photograph of Me Published on January 7, 2001.

113. Mayor Kalisz and Leontire

When I Took Over My New Job on May 18, 1998, in New Bedford as Executive Director of the Greater New Bedford Industrial Foundation and as Developer, Manager, and Marketer of the New Bedford Industrial Park, Mayor Kalisz Had Just Started as the Mayor of New Bedford in January of 1998.

Mayor Kalisz Went On To Serve as Mayor For Three Two-Year Terms, Totaling Six Years. And While the Subsequent Mayors of New Bedford Were Very Helpful to Me and the New Bedford Industrial Park, Mayor Kalisz was By Far the Most Helpful.

Mayor Kalisz Recognized Right Away That Further Growth in the New Bedford Industrial Park Would Generate Lots of Good-Paying Jobs For Residents of New Bedford Regardless of Whether the New Company Located in the New Bedford or the Dartmouth Side of the Industrial Park.

Mayor Kalisz was Also Very Helpful in Getting the Other Departments in the City of New Bedford to Cooperate With Me In Improving the New Bedford Industrial Park By Expanding the Roads; Repaving the Older Roads; Expanding the City's Water and Sewer Lines; Improving the Traffic Safety at the Entrance To the Park; Bringing More Advanced and Faster Telecommunication Services to the Park; Granting Faster Permits To Companies Planning to Build a New Facility or Expand Their Existing Plant in the Park;

and Approving City Tax Incentives For Companies Planning to Build a New Facility or Expand Their Existing Facility in the Park.

And Mayor Kalisz was Most Helpful in Meeting Face to Face Early On With Companies From Outside the New Bedford Area, Another State, or a Foreign Country That Were Considering Building a New Facility in the Park to Help Sell the Advantages of the Industrial Park and Answer Any Questions That They Had.

Also, George Leontire Was Most Helpful in Fully Supporting and Assisting with all of the Planned Improvements to the Industrial Park and In Helping to Attract New Companies to the Park.

George Leontire Had Many Important Roles in the City of New Bedford's Government. He was City Solicitor. He was the Mayor's Campaign Manager and Chief Political Advisor. He was the Mayor's Right-Hand Man, Left-Hand Man, and Troubleshooter For Resolving Major Issues and Problems. And Even Though George Leontire Did Not Have the Title of Economic Development Director For the City of New Bedford, He Was In Fact the Head of Economic Development For the City.

Despite the Multiple City Jobs Handled By George Leontire, He was Always Very Accessible For Me. When I Needed to Meet with George Leontire, I Would Slowly Walk Past His Office, Which Always Had the Door Open Unless He was Meeting With Someone. And George Would Always Wave Me Regardless of Whether He was on the Phone or Not.

And Most Importantly, George Leontire was Extremely Bright and the Ultimate Multitasker.

What I Also Admired About Mayor Kalisz was that Even Though I was Viewed By Many as an Outsider to New Bedford in My Early Months on My New Job, Mayor Kalisz Invited Me to Sit at His Table at His First Annual State of the City Address. He Also Acknowledged Me at Many of His Press Conferences and Invited Me to Meet His Family and Enjoy a Hot Chocolate In the Major's Office During the City's Annual New Year's Eve Festivals.

And When I Would Pitch Mayor Kalisz in the Mayor's Office on a Major New Improvement to the New Bedford Industrial Park

That I Needed the City's Help On, Rather Than Saying That He Needed To Discuss My Proposed Improvement to the Industrial Park With Several Others in His City Government Before Responding To Me, He Would Stand Up, Extend His Hand Towards Me, and Shake Hands With Me.

And Thus, As a Result of Shaking My Hand, I Knew I Had Mayor Kalisz's Full Support For My Proposed Improvement to the New Bedford Industrial Park.

Also, I Always Remember George Leontire's Advice To Me When I Met with Him During My First Week in New Bedford.

It was, "While New Bedford Has All of the Problems and Challenges of Larger Major Cities, It is Small Enough Where One Person Can Make a Positive Difference."

And, Just Like Mayor Kalisz and George Leontire, I Also Made a Positive Difference.

114. LOVING THE CITY COUNCIL

In New Bedford, I Never Remember Even Losing One Vote at My Meetings With the New Bedford City Council.

Importantly, This Was Due To Two Factors.

First, Everything That I proposed to the New Bedford City Council For Their Approval Was About Further Improving the New Bedford Industrial Park or Welcoming a New Company to the Park or Helping an Existing Company Expand Their Plant in the Park was in the City of New Bedford's Best Interests.

Second, And Equally Important, I Treated Every One of the Eleven City Councilors with My Utmost Respect By

Sending Them a Written Copy of My Proposal Two to Three Weeks in Advance of the City Council Meeting.

Then, Contacting Each City Councilor By Phone or In Person To Find Out if They Had Any Questions or Issues With My Proposal.

Answering Their Questions, Resolving Any Issues With My Proposal, or Revising My Proposal to Address Their Concerns Within a Week of the City Council Meeting.

Showing Up at the City Council Meeting About One Hour Before It Started to Answer Any Further Questions That Any of the Eleven City Councilors Had on My Proposal.

Thanking Each City Councilor For Their Vote in Support of My Proposal at the End of the City Council Meeting.

115. SEE'S CANDIES WINS FRIENDS AT CITY AND TOWN HALLS

With Regard to My Proposals For Further Improving the New Bedford Industrial Park and Obtaining Site Plan and Building Plan Approvals For a New Company Building a Plant in the Park or an Existing Company Expanding Their Plant in the Park, I Needed to Obtain in Advance Approvals From the Conservation and Planning Departments and Commissions in the City of New Bedford or the Town of Dartmouth.

And, In Many Cases, I Also Needed Input From Those Two Departments in Developing My Proposals and the Company's Building Proposals.

And, In Most Cases, I Would Meet In Advance With the Department Heads and Senior Staff of the Above Mentioned Departments To Review My New Plans For Further Improving the Industrial Park, A New Company's Plans For Building a Plant in the Park and Existing Plans To Expand Their Plant in the Park.

In My Reviews With the Various Permitting Departments, I Would Also Seek Out Their Suggestions On My Proposals For Improving the Industrial Park and the Company's Proposals For Building or Expanding a Plant in the Park.

And, In Some Cases, I Would Revise My Proposals For Improving the Industrial Park or Obtain the Agreement of the Company To

Revise Their Building Plans to Reflect the Helpful Suggestions From the Departments in New Bedford or Dartmouth.

But What Helped Me the Most in Obtaining Input, Help, and Permitting Approvals From the Department Heads and Staff of the Key Departments That I Worked With In New Bedford and Dartmouth was My Annual Practice of Personally Delivering To Each Department a Very Large Box of See's Delicious Nuts and Chews Chocolates Every Year About a Week Before Christmas.

And That's How I Made So Many Friends in the Key Departments That I Worked With in New Bedford and Dartmouth.

116. Kissing Up to Governors

Shortly After Mitt Romney Was First Elected in November of 2002 as Governor of Massachusetts, I Invited Him to Come to New Bedford To Speak to Business Leaders From the South Coast of Massachusetts on What His Priorities Were in His First Hundred Days of Being Governor of Massachusetts, Starting in January of 2003.

He Accepted My Invitation and Requested That I Work Hard to Obtain a Large Turnout in What Has Always Been a Heavily Democratic Area of Massachusetts.

I Did So and, Lo and Behold, Since Mitt Romney was known as the Savior of the US Olympics and a Highly Successful Venture Capitalist in the Boston Area, I Filled One of the Largest Conference Halls in New Bedford With a Standing-Room Crowd of Mostly Senior Business Leaders From the South Coast of Massachusetts.

Mitt Romney Gave a PowerPoint Personal Computer Presentation of His Highest Priority Plans For His First Hundred Days of Being Governor.

After Romney's Presentation and Question and Answer Session Had Ended, I Was Overwhelmed With Lots of Extended Thank Yous From Governor Romney About the Great Job I Did in Getting Several Hundred Business Leaders to Attend the Meeting With Him.

Shortly Thereafter, Governor Romney Appointed Me To Be On

His Newly Established Governor's Economic Development Advisory Committee, Which He Named "The Innovation Institute."

I Readily Accepted the Governor's Invitation, Along With About Sixty Other Senior Leaders From the Business Community, Universities, Consulting Companies, and Think Tanks in the Greater Boston Area and Elsewhere In the State. Although, I was the Only Member From the South Coast of Massachusetts.

We Met Once a Month For Three Hour Meetings In Various Large Hotels In Boston and Cambridge and Had Very Lively and In-Depth Discussions With Regard to Trying to Identify New Initiatives That Had the Potential For Significantly Improving Economic Development in the State of Massachusetts.

During Romney's Five Years as Being Governor of Massachusetts, We Identified Four Major New Initiatives all of Which Were Overwhelmingly Accepted By Governor Romney and Implemented By His Senior Staff.

They Were

Implement a $1 Billion Bio Tech Incentive Program to Recruit New Biotech Companies to Massachusetts and Cause Existing Biotech Companies to Expand Here Rather Than Elsewhere.

Create a New Advanced Manufacturing Center to Promote and Share Information on New, Advanced Manufacturing Systems That Had a High Payout For Efficiency, Increasing Production in the Same Amount of Space, Reducing Energy Needs, and Lowering Costs.

Bringing Advanced Telecommunications Infrastructure To the Entire State.

Establishing a Massive Computer Data Storage Center Powered By Cheaper Electricity From a Nearby Waterfall and Shared By the State Government, Major Universities, and Massachusetts High-Tech Firms.

After Romney Retired From Being Governor of Massachusetts at the End of 2007, Each of the Two Governors That Succeeded Romney Were Responsible For Reselecting the Members of The Innovation Institute.

However, Because I Attended All of the Meetings and Made

Strong Contributions to the Work of the Innovation Institute, I Was Reselected By Each of the Two Succeeding Governors to Romney Even Though About 65 percent of the Members Were Not Reappointed Each Time By the New Governor.

Importantly, Governor Romney was also Very Impressed With All of the Improvements That I Made to the New Bedford Industrial Park and the Very High Growth In Quality Companies and Good-Paying Jobs That Resulted From My Improvements to the Industrial Park,

As a Result, He Approved My Request to Provide a $1.5 Million State Infrastructure Grant To Construct Two New Roads in the Dartmouth Side of the Industrial Park.

117. APRIL VACATIONS IN BRITISH VIRGIN GORDA, GRENADA, ST. LUCIA, AND THE GRENADINES

Liddy and I Scheduled Seven- to Eight-Day Visits To the Caribbean In Many Years Starting On April 15th, which was the First Day That the Resorts Lowered Their Sky-High Winter Rates By 25 to 40 percent.

Most Recently, We Stayed at the Calabash Hotel in Grenada, which is Very British and has Won Many Awards For Its Ambience and Rhodes Restaurant.

We Stayed On the First Floor of a Small Two-Story Cottage With Two Suites on the First Floor and Two Suites on the Second Floor.

Our Suite Had a Very Nice Patio with Closeup Views of the Beach and Bay. It Also Had a Large Separate Sitting Room and Bedroom.

A Special Feature of Having a Suite at the Calabash Hotel was that One of the Resort's Private Maids Would Take Our Order For Breakfast the Night Before and Prepare It the Next Morning in a Small Kitchen Attached To Our Cottage. She Would Set Up Our Table on the Patio and Bring Us the Wonderful Breakfast That We Had Ordered.

Our Private Maid Would Also Bring Us Delicious Hors d'oeuvres Just Before Dinner Every Night.

In Grenada, We Loved to Visit Its Capital, Which is Extremely

Beautiful, with a Large Harbor Surrounded By Hills On Three Sides With a Wide Variety of Pretty, Pastel-Colored Houses.

There were Many Historic Government Buildings and Churches in Grenada's Capital Along with a Colorful Outdoor Fruit and Vegetable Market.

We Also Liked To Take a Hike to a Beautiful Waterfall in One of Grenada's National Parks, Which Was Blessed With a Deep Swimming Pool at the Bottom of the Very High Waterfall.

And We Always Had Lunch Each Day at One of Grenada's Many Fine Restaurants Specializing in Local Dishes and Fresh Seafood.

Also, In One Year, After Spending Three Days in Grenada, We Took a Seven-Day Cruise on a Large Classic Nineteenth-Century Clipper Sailboat, Which Anchored Each Day at a Beautiful Island in the Grenadines and Then Sailed Each Night to Another Island. In Total, We Were Able to Visit, Explore, Snorkel, and Have Lunch at the Most Beautiful Grenadine Islands From Grenada to St. Vincent.

Another of Our Favorite places to Visit in the Caribbean Was British Virgin Gorda Where We Stayed at the Biras Creek or Bitter End Resort, Which Are Accessible Only By Boat.

At Both of These Resorts, We Could Snorkel, Climb Two High Mountains with Beautiful Views, Have a Barbeque Lunch on the Beach; Go On a Sunset Sail, and Take Half-Day Excursions on a Boston Whaler at No Cost To Visit Nearby Small Islands For Snorkeling and Hiking.

Also, the Bitter End Had a Great Rock and Roll Dance Party with a Live Band Every Monday Night For Its Guests and Resort Staff Along with Visitors From Other Resorts on British Virgin Gorda.

Unfortunately, Both the Bitter End and Biras Creek Resorts Were Badly Damaged and Mostly Destroyed By Hurricanes Maria and Irma in 2017.

And, So Far, Neither Resort Has Been Fully Restored and Opened For Vacationers.

Other Caribbean Islands That We Visited For Three to Four Short But Enjoyable Stays Were Nevis, St. Kitts, and Dominica.

We Also Stayed Many Times on the Island of St. Lucia at the Anse Chastanet Beach Hotel, with Views of the Island's Two Very High Pitons, One of Which We Climbed To the Top. St. Lucia Also Had a Beautiful Botanical Park with a High Waterfall and Many Exotic Flowering Bushes. And the Snorkeling at the Resort's Beach was Outstanding.

118. LOVING THE ISLE OF CAPRI

Liddy and I Experienced the Isle of Capri in the Gulf of Naples For the First Time When We Attended Mira Sorvino's Wedding to Chris Backus in July of 2004.

And Since Then, We Have Been Back Many Times In April for Eight-Day Vacations.

We Always Stayed at the Hotel Luna, Which is a Lovely European Hotel Bordered By the Augustus Gardens and with Excellent Views of the Famous Faraglioni Rocks That Jut Out a Hundred Meters Above the Intensely Blue Sea. And Their Gourmet Restaurant is Tops.

There Were Many Interesting Things to Do in Capri. We Loved to Hike For Miles on Various Coastal Cliff Trails Overlooking the Ocean.

We Also Visited Several Famous Villas of the Roman Emperors.

And We Liked to Hang Out in the Mornings For a Cup of Coffee or In the Evenings For a Glass of Wine or Two in the Piazzetta Umberto Town Square While Gawking at all of the Interesting Europeans and Movie Stars Passing Back and Forth Through the Town Square.

Other Major Attractions For Us Included Taking a Small Boat Trip Around the Island; Entering the Blue Grotto; Walking Through the Beautiful Augustus Gardens; Eating at Old Italian Restaurants; Strolling Through the Beautiful Villa San Michelle in Anacapri;

Entering the Baroque Church of San Michele Arcangels, with Its Mosaic Tiled Floor Depicting Adam and Eve in Paradise; and Taking a Cable Car to the Top of Mount Solara For Its Wonderful Views From Six Hundred Meters Above the Sea.

And We Also Enjoyed Window Shopping at the Luxurious Shops and Boutiques Near the Town Square.

Other Activities That Liddy and I Most Enjoyed Were Shopping Every Morning at Three or Four Small Food and Wine Shops For Our Picnic Lunches and Strolling Along the Very Narrow and Up-and-Down Historic Cobblestone Lanes, Which Passed By the Smaller Villas With Gardens where the People of Capri Lived.

A Unique Feature of the Many Small Villas was That There was a Pretty, Colorful Mosaic Tile Adjacent to Each Villa's Entry Gate with the Name and Street Number For the Villa Along with a Picture Portrayal of the Villa.

119. Multiple Hiking Trips in Swiss Alps

Since Moving to Massachusetts, Liddy and I Have Always Enjoyed Taking Many Seven- to Ten-Day Hiking Trips During September in the Swiss Alps.

Our Favorite Spot to Base Hiking Trips From Has Almost Always Been Zermatt. To Get There, We Fly From Boston to Geneva or Zurich, Then Board an Excellent Swiss Express Train at the Airport to a City Located North of Zermatt, and Then Board a Local Swiss Train to Take Us to Zermatt.

In Zermatt, We Have Always Stayed at the Hotel Alpenblick, Which is Located on the Outskirts of Zermatt's Commercial District. It Is Owned and Run By a Large Swiss Family That Includes a Grandmother who Oversees the Placements For the Breakfast Buffet; Mother-In-Law Who Runs the Check-In Counter; Son Who Oversees the Lunch and Dinner Dining Room, Kitchen and Bar; and Several Grandchildren Who Sometimes Serve as Waiters and Waitresses.

We Have Been Fortunate to Always Receive a Large Nice Room On the Top Floor of the Hotel With a Balcony That Looks Out at the Matterhorn.

We Always Take Day Hiking Trips in All Directions By First Boarding a Cable Car or Train to Take Us to a Much Higher Altitude Stop Where We Start and End Our Hike for the Day.

Before Starting the Trip, We Have a Big Breakfast at the Alpenblick and Then Shop at a Nearby Food and Wine Store For Our Lunch Supplies.

And When We Return to Zermatt On the Cable Car or Train, We Have a Nice Hot Bath at Our Hotel and Then Have a Drink at the Bar Followed By a Tasteful Dinner.

On Several Trips, We Also Planned Four-Day Hiking Trips Where We Hiked From Zermatt to the First Mountain Inn, Climbed a Mountain Peak the Next Day, Spent a Second Night at the First Mountain Inn, Hiked Over a Very Long Mountain Pass To a Second Mountain Inn Where We Spent the Night, and Hiked Back to Our Hotel in Zermatt After Having a Gourmet Lunch at Another Mountain Inn.

The Swiss People That We Came In Contact With Were Always Very Friendly and Helpful Towards Us Regardless of Whether They Were German Swiss, Italian Swiss, French Swiss, or Pure Swiss.

In Zermatt, We Also Enjoyed the Outdoor Concerts and the Various Nice Hiking Clothing Shops and the Davis Store, Where We Always Bought One or Two Things for Each of Us. Liddy and I Still Have Our Umbrellas With the Davis Name Displayed in Large Letters As Well As Several Davis Ball Point Pens and a Davis Hat.

Like the Taj Mahal, I Never Got Tired of Looking at the Matterhorn!

120. Christmas Trips to Pump Room In Chicago

On My First Visit to the National Biotech Trade Show in Chicago as Part of The Governor of Massachusetts Sales Team, to Attract New Biotech Companies to Build Research and Manufacturing Facilities in Massachusetts, I Stayed with Most of the Other Members of the Governor's Sales Team at the Ambassador East Hotel in the Historic 19th-Century Brownstone Section of Chicago Just North of the Michigan Avenue Shopping District and Rush Street, with its Many Jazz Bars and Steakhouses.

The Ambassador East Hotel, Which is Now Named The Ambassador Hotel, Has Been and Still is a Popular Place Where the Movie and TV Stars Stay When They Are Visiting Chicago.

It is Also the Home of the Pump Room's Large Bar and Restaurant, Which was the Site For America's First Early Morning Talk Radio Show Which Highlighted the News Headlines, Sports Scores, and Weather and Also Featured Interviews with Movie, TV, and Music Stars.

At My First Visit, I Fell in Love with the Ambiance of The Ambassador East Hotel and the Opportunities to Gawk at the Visits By the Young Fashion Crowd to the Pump Room on Friday Night and the Visits By the Movie and TV Stars Along with Major Politicians on Sunday Night For Mixing With One Another.

The Pump Room Served Drinks and Food to a Large Number of

Famous Celebrities Who Were Regular Customers Including Frank Sinatra, John Barrymore, Marilyn Monroe, Oprah Winfrey, Judy Garland, Bette Davis, Beverly Sills, Natalie Wood, Paul Newman, Humphrey Bogart, Lauren Bacall, Vincent Price, John Steinbeck, Ronald Reagan, Helen Hayes, Clark Gable, Sammy Davis Jr., Jerry Lewis, Dean Martin, Elizabeth Taylor, Lena Horne, Joan Crawford, Tallulah Bankhead, Audrey Hepburn, Liza Minelli, Robert Redford, Eddie Fisher, Peggy Lee, Mick Jagger, Vivien Leigh, Dolly Parton, and More Recently Tom Davis.

Also, In the Pump Room, There is a Large, Elevated Booth in One Corner of the Restaurant and Bar with Comfortable Sitting Chairs, a Dining Table, and Four Telephones Named Booth #1 Which was Reserved For Frank Sinatra when He was in Town.

So, When Tommy, Our Son, Landed a High Yield Bond Fund Management Job After Graduating From Indiana University with JP Morgan in Indianapolis Just South of Chicago, and Christie, Our Daughter, Landed a Job After Graduating From the University of Michigan with a PhD as Assistant Professor of Anthropology at Western Illinois University in Macomb, Illinois, Just West of Chicago, I Suggested to Liddy, Tommy, and Christie That We All Get Together For a Pre-Christmas Family Visit at the Ambassador East Hotel in Chicago.

Everyone Agreed With My Plan. And After Our First Pre-Christmas Visit Together at The Ambassador East Hotel, Everyone Fell in Love with All of Our Many Interesting Activities in Chicago.

These Included Shopping on Michigan Avenue, which is the Chicago Equivalent of Fifth Avenue in Manhattan; Going to The Lincoln Park Zoo; Visiting the Unique Museum of Science and Industry; Having Lunch at Billy Goats Tavern and Dinner at Gibson's Steakhouse; Having a Glass of Wine After Dinner Every Night in the Pump Room; and Taking a Walk in the 19th-Century Historic Brownstone Section of Chicago to View the Wonderful Christmas Decorations.

So Every Year Since Our First Pre-Christmas Davis Family Get-Together in Chicago, We Have Followed the Tradition of First

Spending Four Days Together in Chicago at The Ambassador East Hotel and Then Visiting Tommy's Home in Indianapolis For Three Days at Christmas Every Other Year and Christie's Home in Macomb For Three Days at Christmas Every Other Year.

121. Fourth Presbyterian Church on Michigan Avenue

When I Attended Northwestern's Graduate School of Business in 1961 and 1962 That was Located Just North of Downtown Chicago, I Heard About An Outstanding Preacher at the Nearby Fourth Presbyterian Church on North Michigan Avenue, Who Had Just Been Named By *Time* Magazine as One of the Top Ten Preachers in the United States.

So I Attended a Sunday Service and was Extremely Impressed with the Outstanding Sermon of the Award-Winning Preacher.

And Subsequently, I Never Missed a Sunday Morning Service and Sermon By the Award-Winning Preacher at the Fourth Presbyterian Church During My Entire Remaining Time at Northwestern's Graduate School of Business.

And Many Years Later, when Liddy and I Started Our Pre-Christmas Get-Togethers In Chicago with Tommy and His Two Twin Sons and with Christie and Her One Son, Liddy and I Attended a Pre-Christmas Sunday Service at the Fourth Presbyterian Church, which had Grown to 5,500 Members and was Housed in a Beautiful, Historic Gothic Church Building on North Michigan Avenue.

We Were Overwhelmed By the Outstanding, Interesting, and Reflective Sermon By Pastor Shannon Kershner, Who Has Also Been Named By a National Magazine as One of the Top Ten Preachers in America, And When the Prior Head Pastor at the

Fourth Presbyterian Retired After Twenty-five Years of Service, Shannon Kershner was Selected as the New Head Pastor from 260 Preachers From All Over the United States.

One Totally Unique Practice of Pastor Shannon Kershner was That When She Was Trying to Highlight an Important Point or Points in Her Sermon, She Would Break Into Song with Her Wonderful Operatic Soprano Voice and Sing the Important Point or Points That She Was Making.

Thus, at Every Subsequent Pre-Christmas Visit By Liddy and I to Chicago, We Made It a Priority to Attend a Pre-Christmas Service at the Fourth Presbyterian Church When Shannon Kershner was Preaching.

122. Dancing with the Stars
and the Blond Bombshell

*E*ver Since My Early High School Days, I Loved to Dance to Rock and Roll Music. In Our House in Evanston, Illinois, I Would Purchase Rock and Roll Records and Play the Records While Dancing to the Rock and Roll Music in Front of a Large Mirror on the Second Floor Hallway of My Family's House.

I Would Also Go to Evanston Township High School's Dance Parties with Sharon Eves and Go to the Evanston YMCA Plantation Room After Home High School Basketball Games to Dance to Rock and Roll Music. And I Was Also Invited to Many Dance Parties at the Houses of My High School Friends.

And Throughout My College Days and Work at Exxon in Manhattan, I Would Seek Out Rock and Roll Parties and Go To a lot to Dance Discos.

However, Unbelievably, My Best Rock and Roll Dance Experiences Occurred After Reaching the Ripe Old Age of Sixty-five.

For Instance, When I Went to San Diego, Which is the Dance Capital of the US, to Attend the Annual National Biotech Trade Show, or To Meet with the Principal and Senior Administrators of High Tech High Which Had Chosen the Global Learning Charter School in New Bedford as One of Their Affiliated Charter Schools, I Would Almost Always Go To One of the San Diego Dance Clubs After Dinner For An Hour or Two of Rock and Roll Dancing.

In Downtown San Diego, There Are Seven Dance Clubs, and Each Major Suburb of San Diego Also Has a Dance Club.

And On Shelter Island in San Diego, Where I Always Stayed In a Hotel While Attending the Annual Week-Long Biotech Trade Show or Meetings with the Staff of High Tech High, There was an Outstanding and Very Large Dance Club Named "The Backstage Club."

The Backstage Club was Owned By Famous Movie and Music Stars and Had a Live Music Group Playing and Singing Rock and Roll Songs Almost Every Night of the Week.

Thus, After Dinner, I Would Visit the Backstage Club Most of the Time to Hit the Dance Floor Before Going to Bed at My Hotel, Which was Only a Five-Minute Walk From the Backstage Club.

And I Wasn't Shy About Asking Ladies, None of Whom I Knew, to Dance With Me.

One Evening About Ten Years Ago, When I Walked Up to the Backstage Club, There was a Huge Crowd and a Long Line to Get In. And There was a Hundred-Dollar Cover Charge Just To Enter the Dance Club.

Then, I Found Out That They Were Having a "Televised Southern California Rock and Roll Dancing With The Stars Contest" to Raise Money For Local Charities.

And the Rules For the Southern California Rock and Roll Dancing With The Stars Contest Were As Follows:

The Only Rock and Roll Dancing Performers Selected In Advance Were Six Female and Six Male Southern California Movie and TV Stars.

Any Male Attending the Backstage Club Could Try to Entice a Female Attendee To Be Their Partner For An Important Introductory Dance, Providing They or Their Female Partner Were Not a Professional Dancer, Did Not Know Each Other, and Did Not Know Any of the Twelve Movie and TV Stars.

To Begin the Event, the Male and Female Dance Partners Would Hit the Dance Floor For an Important Introductory Dance.

After the Long Introductory Rock and Roll Dance, Each of the

Six Male and Six Female Movie and TV Stars Would One After Another Select Their Partner For the Southern California Rock and Roll Dancing With The Stars Contest Just From the Attendees Who Participated In the Introductory Dance.

Then, There Were Ten Rock and Roll Dances, with One Dance Couple Eliminated at the End of Each Dance By a Panel of Three Judges Based on the Magnitude of the Applause or Lack of Applause For Each Couple By the Large Number of Spectators Sitting or Standing on the Three Sides of the Dance Floor.

When There Were Only Two Dance Couples Remaining, the Two Finalist Couples Would Dance Separately To a Rock and Roll Song Selected in Advance By Each of the Movie and TV Stars.

And, Finally, the Very Large Audience was Asked to Cheer For Who They Thought Was the Best Rock and Roll Dance Couple, with the Three Judges Deciding on the Winner Based on the Magnitude of the Applause For Each of the Two Finalist Couples.

Right Away, After Entering the Backstage Club and Paying the Hundred-Dollar Cover Charge, I Decided That I Would Like to Participate in the Southern California Dancing With The Stars Rock and Roll Contest, Rather Than Just Watching the Dance Contest.

So I Quickly Had a Beer and Surveyed the Crowd to Decide Which of the Many Attractive Ladies There I Should Ask to Be My Dance Partner.

I Became Fixated With Two Very Attractive, Tall Twin Brunette Ladies with Beautiful Green Eyes Standing Close to the Dance Floor and Acting Like They Wanted to be Part of the Rock and Roll Dance Contest.

So I Approached Them and Asked Whether One of Them Would Like to Be My Dance Partner.

One Said Yes. So I Succeeded In the First Step of the Rock and Roll Dance Contest, which was to Obtain a Female Attendee Partner For the Introductory Dance.

However, I Had No Idea of Whether My Female Partner Would Be a Great Rock and Roll Dancer.

Fortunately, I Discovered in the First Few Minutes of the Long

Introductory Dance That My Tall, Attractive Brunette Dance Partner With Beautiful Green Eyes was an Exceptional Rock and Roll Dancer.

At the End of the Long Introductory Dance, On a One-By-One Basis, The Six Male and Six Female Movie and TV Stars Selected Their Dance Partners From the Attendees Who Participated in the Long Introductory Dance.

And, Lo and Behold, The First Male Movie and TV Star to Choose a Dance Partner Chose My Tall, Attractive Brunette Dance Partner In the Introductory Dance.

And, Unbelievably, I was Chosen By the Third Female Movie and TV Star to Have a Choice as Her Dance Partner For the Rock and Roll Dancing With The Stars Contest.

My Partner was a Star on an Early Morning TV Show in Los Angeles That Highlighted the News Headlines, Sport Scores, and the Weather Forecasts and Also Interviewed Music, Movie, and TV Stars and Political Officials.

She was a Beautiful Blond with an Overflowing Personality and was Blessed with a Very Top-Heavy and Sexy Figure.

She Had Also Given a lot of Thought in Advance about How to Appeal to the Audience who Would in Effect Be Choosing the Champion Rock and Roll Dance Couple Based on Their Applause or Lack of Applause.

So, Very Quickly, She Suggested that Both of Us Should Be Introduced to the Audience Not By Our Real Names But By Names That Would Be Popular with the Audience.

Thus, She was Introduced to the Audience as "The Blond Bombshell," and I was Introduced as "Touchdown."

We Both Danced Exceptionally Well Together and Had a Lot of Great Rock and Roll Dance Moves.

And We Were Attracted to the Audience By the Fact that My TV Star Partner was in Her Thrities and I was in My Sixties.

And We Were Both Natural Dancers and Danced Together as if We Had Been Rehearsing Our Rock and Roll Dance Steps For Months.

Thus, We Were Chosen By the Magnitude of the Applause That We Received From Each of the First Ten Dances to Not Be One of the Couples Who Were Eliminated After Each of the First Ten Dances, But Instead Were Chosen By the Audience To Be One of the Two Finalist Dancers.

The Last Two Dances in the Rock and Roll Dancing With The Stars Contest Were For Each of the Two Finalist Couples to Perform a Separate Dance to a Rock and Roll Tune Selected in Advance By the Two Movie and TV Stars, Who Were Finalists.

The First Finalist Couple Was My Tall, Attractive Brunette Dance Partner With the Beautiful Green-Eyes For the Introductory Dance and Her Male TV Star Partner.

And They Did an Excellent Rock and Roll Dance With Back Flips that Were So Good That I Told My Partner That We Could Never Do Better Than Them.

The Blond Bombshell Strongly Disagreed and Stated That If I Followed the Rock and Roll Dance Choreography That She Had Selected, We Would Have More Appeal with the Audience as Follows:

Initially, We Would Both Stand at Opposite Corners of the Dance Floor.

Then I Would Dance Slowly to the Middle of the Dance Floor and Then She Would Start Dancing to the Middle of the Dance Floor, Showing Off All of Her Sexy Moves as if She Wanted Me.

However, I Would Reject Her and Do an About Face and Return Quickly to My Corner of the Dance Floor.

Next, She Would Dance Slowly to the Middle of the Dance Floor and Then I Would Start Dancing to the Middle of the Dance Floor, Showing Off all of My Dance Moves and Acting Like I Really Needed Her.

However, She Would Reject My Overtures, Turn Around Quickly, and Return to Her Corner of the Dance Floor.

As the Finale to Our Dance, We Both Danced at the Same Time to the Middle of the Dance Floor and Twirled Around Each

Other Many Times as If We Like Each Other a Lot, And Then We Warmly Embraced Each Other and Kissed Each Other a Lot.

At the End of Our Dance as Finalists, the Applause We Got From the Audience Was Unbelievably Loud and Lasted a Long Time with Lots of Catcalls. And, As a Result, the Three Judges Declared the Blond Bombshell and Touchdown as the Winners of the Southern California Rock and Roll Dancing With The Stars Contest.

Then, There Were Many Shouts From the Audience For Us To Do a Curtain-Call Rock and Roll Dance, Which We Did.

And Based on Even a Louder Applause and Shouts From the Audience, We Did Two More Curtain-Call Rock and Roll Dances.

The Southern California Rock and Roll Dancing With The Stars Contest was Filmed Live That Thursday Night and Then Shown on TV Saturday Night in California and the Adjacent States with Excellent Ratings and a Much, Much Better-Than-Expected Viewing Audience.

I Will Never Forget This Wonderful Dancing Experience and My Last Dance with the Blond Bombshell!

123. Dance Gig with Naomi Watts

On My Last Visit to the National Biotech Trade Show in San Diego, Before Retiring After Sixteen Years of Being Executive Director of the Greater New Bedford Industrial Foundation and the Developer, Manager, and Marketer of the New Bedford Business Park, I Made Several Visits After Dinner to the Backstage Club For a Few Rock and Roll Dances.

On My Last Night in San Diego When I Visited the Backstage Club, I Saw a Beautiful Blond Sitting on the Other Side of the Dance Floor From Me.

Without Knowing who the Beautiful Blond was, I Bounded Across the Dance Floor and Asked Her For a Dance With Me.

She Immediately Said Yes, and We Danced Exceptionally Well Together For Three Long Rock and Roll Dances.

After a Short Embrace and a Kiss, the Beautiful Blond Asked Me to Follow Her to Her Table So As to Meet Her Partner.

I Did So But Did Not Know Who the Beautiful Blond Was.

Her Male Partner Announced to Me Right Away That They Were Known in Hollywood as the Janis Joplin and Allen Ginsberg Couple.

I Responded That I Had Seen Janis Joplin and Allen Ginsberg Perform at a Very Large Theatre in Greenwich Village, with Janis Joplin Belting Out Songs and Allen Ginsberg Following Her By

Sitting With His Legs Crossed on the Stage, Playing a Guitar and Reading Poetry.

We Had a Nice Conversation For Just a Few More Minutes; However, I Left the Backstage Club Not Knowing Who The Beautiful Blond or Her Male Partner Were, Although I Assumed That They Were Both Movie Stars Since They Had Told Me That They Lived Together in Hollywood.

When I Returned to Mishaum Point From San Diego, I First Quickly Went Through My Mail.

To My Astonishment, On the Cover of September 2014 *Town and Country* magazine was a Large Color Photo of the Beautiful Blond, Who Was None Other Than Naomi Watts, the American Movie Star From Australia.

And, Per the Article in *Town and Country* magazine, Naomi Watts' Partner was Liev Schreiber, the American Movie Star From California.

And Naomi Watts, In the Article, Highlighted Her Love to Dance By Always Being the First One to Hit the Dance Floor and the Last One to Leave the Dance Floor at Parties.

Very Recently, Naomi and Liev Parted Ways. And Naomi Has Been Devoting Much of Her Life to Caring For Her Two Sons, Alexander and Samuel, While Still Starring in Quite a Few Movies.

124. PERFORMING WITH 1950S ROCK AND ROLL GROUP

Just Two Years Ago, Liddy and I Attended a Rock and Roll Music Concert at the Zeiterian Theatre In New Bedford By a Rock and Roll Music Group From New York City That Played and Sang 1950s Rock and Roll Songs Such As "Rock Around the Clock," "Shake Rattle and Roll," and "Blue Suede Shoes" etc.

The Attendees at the 1950s Rock and Roll Music Concert Completely Filled the Zeiterian Theatre's Two Thousand Seats. In Addition, There Were Several Hundred More Attendees Standing in the Aisles or at the Back of the Theatre.

I Loved the Music Group's Rock and Roll Music Songs and Wanted Badly to Dance To Them.

So, at the Start Of Their Last Rock and Roll Song, I Raced Down the Side Aisle and Bounded Up the Stairs Onto the Stage and Did a Rock and Roll Dance Gig For the Entire Song and Managed To Cover the Entire Stage From Front to Back and Side to Side With My Many Dance Moves.

The Audience Loved Me and Applauded and Screamed Loudly Shortly After I Had Began My Dance Gig.

After My Dance Gig, the Two Directors of the Zeiterian Theatre Approached Me. Rather Than Criticizing My Unscheduled Dance Gig on the Stage, They Praised Me and Stated That It Was Obvious That the Audience Also Loved My Rock and Roll Dancing.

Importantly, I Also Received Excellent Reviews By Several Regional Newspapers and the Local Radio and TV Station. And Fred Kalisz, the Former Mayor of New Bedford, Said That Everything He Heard About My Surprise Performance Was Very Positive.

Also, When I Looked Out at the Audience, I Did Not See Anyone Who Looked Younger Than Sixties in Age. And. This was Because the Rock and Roll Music Group From New York City Played Only 1950s Rock and Roll Songs.

125. FETED IN DC FOR THREE DAYS

*I*n 2013, Seven Countries Decided To Have a Special Three-Day Event in Washington, DC, to Honor Important Living Explorers From Their Countries.

And I Was Selected By the Explorers Club to Be a Part of the United States Group to Participate In the Event.

Liddy and I Enjoyed Participating In all of the Planned Activities in Washington, DC.

On Friday Night, We Had Dinner at the Personal Residence of the Portuguese Ambassador to the United States.

On Saturday Night, We Attended a Formal Black-Tie Dinner at the Willard Hotel Near the White House, and I Had My Picture Taken Next to a Live Cheetah.

And Sunday Brunch was at the Prestigious Cosmos Club. Sitting Across the Table From Liddy and Me was a Lady From Texas Who Won the Powder Puff Derby For Women. This Involved Flying Solo on a World War I-Era By Plane Without Any Instruments From Long Beach, California, to Portland, Maine, with Three Refueling Stops.

In Between Meals, There Was a Special Visit to the White House and Smithsonian Museum and Many Events to Hear Accounts and See Films of Expeditions By Living Explorers.

126. Thomas G. Davis Solar Farm

And Just Before Retiring in 2014 From My Job as The Developer, Manager, and Marketer of the New Bedford Business Park, I Sold an Isolated Lot on the Dartmouth Side of the Park to Sun Edison For a Very Large Solar Panel Farm. The Electricity Generated By the Solar Farm was Sold to the City of New Bedford at a Discounted Price

And, At a Well Attended Press Conference to Celebrate the Completion of the Solar Farm, Sun Edison and Officials From the City of New Bedford and Town of Dartmouth Announced That They Were Naming the Solar Farm as the "Thomas G. Davis Solar Park" in My Honor and Erected a Large Sign of the Thomas G. Davis Solar Park at the Entrance to the Solar Farm.

127. Would You Believe a Monument?

*I*n 2014, at the End of My Last Year as Executive Director of the Greater New Bedford Industrial Foundation, I Was Honored at the Industrial Foundation's Well-Attended Annual Meeting at a Large Titleist Golf Ball Plant on the New Bedford Side of the New Bedford Business Park.

At the Annual Meeting, The Chair of the Greater New Bedford Industrial Foundation and an Executive Vice President From Titleist That was In Charge of Titleist's Three Facilities In the New Bedford Business Park Unveiled a Large, Stone Monument Honoring Me That was Placed In a Median Strip Across the Street From the Large Titleist Plant at the Intersection of Two Major Entrance Roads In the New Bedford Business Park.

The Large Monument Read:

HONORING

THOMAS G. DAVIS

EXECUTIVE DIRECTOR

GREATER NEW BEDFORD INDUSTRIAL FOUNDATION

1998–2014

I Only Had One Question When Liz Isherwood, the Chair of the Industrial Foundation's Board of Trustees, Spoke About the Large, Engraved Stone Monument Honoring My Sixteen Years of Dedication to Increasing the Number of Quality Companies and Good-Paying Jobs In the New Bedford Business Park.

It was, "Can I Be Buried Under the Monument?"

And Liz Isherwood Responded, "Tom, That Why We Put It There."

And Liz Added That "The Industrial Foundation Wanted a Way to Honor Tom For All Of His Years of Service and the Work He Did in Modernizing, Beautifying, and Growing the New Bedford Business Park By Making the Large Stone Monument as Permanent as Possible and Engraving It With Tom's Name Would Be a Good Way of Doing That."

I Responded That "I Was Overwhelmed and Very Grateful For the Stone Monument and Other Honors That I Received, Which Included Being Elected as a New Member of The Industrial Foundation's Board of Trustees."

128. CITY COUNCIL RESOLUTION HONORING THOMAS G. DAVIS

At My Last Meeting In 2014 With the New Bedford City Council Before Retiring From My Job As Executive Director of the Greater New Bedford Industrial Foundation and as Developer, Manager, and Marketer of the New Bedford Business Park, They Held a Special Meeting to Honor My Many Accomplishments.

Every City Councilor Rose to Speak About My Many Accomplishments.

And Linda Morad, Councilor at Large, Presented Me with a Written Resolution Signed By All Eleven City Councilors and It Read As Follows:

1. Whereas, When Thomas G. Davis Along With His Wife Elizabeth Moved to Their Summer House in Dartmouth, Massachusetts, Thomas G. Davis Wanted to Continue to Work and Sought a Job In the Public Service Area and Was Hired as Executive Director of the Greater New Bedford Industrial Foundation, a Non-Profit Job Creation Trust Focused On Increasing Employment In the Greater New Bedford Area By Convincing New Companies To Locate Here and By Causing Existing Companies To Expand Here Rather Than Somewhere Else; and

2. Whereas, As the Developer, Manager and Marketer of the New Bedford Business Park, Thomas G. Davis Developed and

Implemented a Major Plan to Modernize and Beautify Every Aspect of the Park; and

3. Whereas, Mr. Davis's Efforts Over the Last Sixteen Years Resulted In An Increase In the Number of Companies in the Park, From Eighteen to Forty-Five and a Tripling of Good Paying Jobs, From Fifteen Hundred to Forty-Five Hundred and the Catapulting of the New Bedford Business Park to Become the Second Largest Industrial Park In Massachusetts in Terms of Jobs; and

4. Whereas, Thomas G. Davis Is Also Very Active In Education In New Bedford. Including the Founding of the Global Learning Charter School and Serving as Chair or Treasurer For Ten Years and Participating In Multiple Other School Improvement Initiatives and Advocacy Efforts; and

5. Whereas, For His Efforts In Bringing Together Educators, Business Leaders and Local Elected Officials As Well As Leading the Turnaround Effort That Resulted in the New Bedford Business Park's Expansion and Success, Producing Thousands of New Jobs For Area Residents. Thomas G. Davis Was Selected as Southcoast Man of the Year By the *Standard-Times*:

Now, Therefore, Be It Resolved, That the New Bedford City Council Hereby Honors Thomas G. Davis. Executive Director of the Greater New Bedford Industrial Foundation on the Occasion of His Retirement From the Industrial Foundation, Recognizes His Many Accomplishment and Achievements, Thanks Him For His Many Years of Hard Work on Behalf of the Residents of This City and Extends Its Best Wishes For Many Years of Happiness and Success and Hopes That He Will Continue to Remain Involved In Economic Development and School Improvement Initiatives in New Bedford.

And, To My Surprise, Just Before The End of the City Council Meeting, the President of the City Council Rose and Proposed to Name a Planned New Road in New Bedford Business Park "Toms Way." And the Motion was Swiftly Approved By a Unanimous Vote.

Most Importantly, During My Sixteen Years as Executive Director of the Greater New Bedford Industrial Foundation and as Developer, Manager, and Marketer of the New Bedford Business

Park, The New Bedford City Council Was So Helpful to Me In Many, Many, Many Ways.

And I Could Not Have Succeeded Without Their Help, Support, and Cooperation.

129. HI PROFESSOR!

When I Announced In the Spring of 2014 My Planned Retirement in the Fall of 2014 as Executive Director of The Greater New Bedford Industrial Foundation and Developer, Manager, and Marketer of the New Bedford Business Park, I Was Immediately Approached By the Esteemed Charlton College of Business at UMass Dartmouth to Become Their "Business Executive in Residence."

Because of My Extensive Business Relationships Not Just Locally on the South Coast But in the Entire State of Massachusetts As Well As Rhode Island, They Believed That I Could Help Existing Business Students Obtain Internships and Graduating Business Students Obtain Full-Time Jobs With Quality Companies.

I Started Work in January of 2015 and Very Quickly Came Up With a Vastly Improved New Plan For Obtaining Internships and Full-Times Jobs For Students From the Charlton School of Business.

I Based My New Internship and Full-Time Job Placement Plan on the Best Practices of Boston College, Boston University, UMass Amherst, Bentley, and Bryant, All of Which Had Excellent and Successful Programs For Helping Their Business Students Obtain High-Quality Internships and Full-Times Jobs.

The Most Important Internship and Job Placement Improvements That I Initiated and Implemented Are As Follows:

1. Scheduled Joint UMD Engineering and Business Job Fairs.
2. Participated In Campus-Wide Job Fairs at UMD.
3. Invited Large Companies to Come to Campus to Conduct Back-to-Back Half-Hour Job Interviews With Graduating Business Students.

   They Would Send Their Job Description Writeups to Us Forty-five to Sixty Days Before the Interview Date, Which We Would Post on a Very Large Bulletin Board.

   And We Would Send the Resumes of the Interested Business Students Who Had Signed Up To Be Interviewed to the Company Recruiters Two Weeks Before the Interview Date.
4. Offered Companies Opportunities to Make Information Presentations on Campus By a Senior Executive and a Recent Business School Graduate with Three to Five Years of Work Experience at the Company.
5. Completed a CCB Job Placement Notebook Containing The
   a. Names of the Sixty-five Companies with Five to Eighty-eight CCB Graduates Currently Working For Them.
   b. Names of the Thirty-five Companies with Two to Four CCB Graduates Currently Working For Them.
   c. Names and Job Titles For the CCB Graduates Working For the Companies Listed Above.
   d. Companies and Organizations Providing Internships For CCB Business Students From 2012 to 2016.
   e. Names, Titles, Emails, Phone Numbers, and Addresses For the Human Resources Contacts For Business Internships and Full-Time Jobs In Each of the Companies Listed Above.
6. Initiated with a Senior Marketing Professor a For-Credit Internship Opportunities Course That Was Taken By Sixty-six Students During My First Year.

7. Provided Handouts to CCB Students to Help Them Develop Winning Resumes, Know the Best Things To Say In Their First Interview, and Identify Sources For Internships and Full-Time Jobs.
8. In My First Year, I Met With 150 CCB Students –Two to Four Times Each To Help Them Develop Winning Resumes and Obtain Internships and Full-Time Jobs.
9. Conducted Group Seminars on Developing Winning Resumes and How to Shine at Interviews.
10. Conducted In the Fall a One-Page Survey of the Current Years CCB January and June Graduates to Determine For those Seeking a Permanent, Full-Time Jobs, How Many Found Jobs, and With What Companies or Organizations and With What Job Title.

And, Most Importantly, In My Last Year at CCB, I Helped 103 Graduating Students Obtain Full-Time Jobs and 203 Current Students Obtain Internships.

Unfortunately, After Spending Two Highly Successful Years at UMD's Charlton College of Business, Helping Hundreds of CCB's Students Obtain Professional Internships and Full-Time Jobs With Quality Companies and Organizations, Three Major Negative Events Caused Me to Make a Very Difficult Decision to Resign From CCB on December 31, 2016.

The Three Negative Events Were As Follows:

1. The President of the Entire University of Massachusetts System Announced in a Front-Page Story in the Boston Globe on Thanksgiving That He Was Terminating the Services of Divina Grossman as Chancellor of UMass Dartmouth Without Notifying Her in Advance That He Had Decided Not to Renew Her Employment Contract and the Reasons Why He Was Doing So.

   I Had a Wonderful Relationship With Divina Grossman, During All of My Two Years at CCB. She was a Major Supporter of My Efforts To Significantly Improve the Internship and Full-Time Job Placement Efforts at CCB, And She Always Invited Me to Attend Her Major Events and Would Always Publicly Recognize Me and Announce My Presence at These Events.

2. A Group of Senior Professors at CCB Petitioned the Provost of UMD to Terminate the Employment Contract of Angappa Gunasekaran, Known as Guna, Who was Dean of the Charlton College of Business.

    And, Unfortunately, Guna's Employment Contract Was Terminated.

    Guna Was My Boss at CCB and Fully Supported All of My Efforts To Help CCB's Students Obtain Good Professional Internships and Full-Time Jobs With Quality Companies.

3. Based on My Survey of the Career Counseling, Internship Coaching, and Job Placement Services of Four Massachusetts Universities, Other Than Harvard and MIT and One Rhode Island University with Outstanding Business Schools, I Found That They Had Five to Fifteen Full-Time Professional Employees In Their Business School Career Center. Thus, I Recommended That CCB Establish a Job Placement Center Staffed Initially By a Full-Time Director of Job Placement Services with a Title of Associate Dean Along with Three Full-Time Professional Administrators.

    However, My Recommendation, Despite Being Approved by CCB's Business Advisory Board, to Increase the Number of Full-Time Professional Employees To Four at CCB Devoted to Career Counseling, Interview Coaching, and Job Placement Services From Just Me Along with the Part-Time Services of Another CCB Staffer who was Working on His PhD, was Rejected By the Provost of UMass Dartmouth For Budgetary Reasons.

    Nevertheless, To This Very Day, I Miss Very Much

Not Working at the Charlton College of Business at UMass Dartmouth.

I Loved the Day-to-Day Interactions with Students and the Immense Satisfaction From Helping Students Obtain Professional Internships and Full-Time Jobs with High-Quality Companies.

I Also Admired My Nice Office on the Second Floor of the New and Very Impressive Charlton College of Business Building and the Beautiful Campus and Having to Walk Across the Very Large, But Well Maintained Green Field to Reach Other Campus Buildings.

And Starting Early On and Continuing For Two Years, I Loved It When Many of the Female CCB Students Would Greet Me with a Very Loud and Friendly, "Hi, Professor," When They Passed By Me on Campus.

130. Closing $3.5 Million Land Sale to Maine Coast Heritage Trust

Liddy and Her Two Sisters Were Gifted 147 Acres of Land on Clark Island From Their Parents Who Purchased Clark Island in 1985 From a Quarry Company That Had Ceased Their Quarry Operations.

The Land Gift Excluded the Land For the Nickerson House Lot on the Southern Portion of the Island and a Large Conservation Easement Lot Located Northeast of the Nickerson House Lot. After Liddy's Parents Passed Away, the Ownership of This Land Was Transferred to the Clark Island Trust with the Future Beneficiaries of the Trust Being the Children and Grandchildren of the Three Sisters.

Even Though Clark Island is Privately Owned, a Large Number of Nearby Residents to Clark Island Like to Walk Across the Causeway and Take Walks on the Clark Island Road, Often with Their Dogs. However, They Stop Well Short of the Nickerson House Lot, Due to a Large Sign From the Nickerson Family on a Tree Trunk Asking Them to Turn Around.

Also in the Summer Months, Some of the Visitors Including Their Children Like to Take a Swim in the Large Quarry, which Fills Up with Rain and Salt Water To One Hundred Feet of Depth and Can Be Accessed Only By Following a Short Trail to a High, Rocky Cliff Ledge Where They Need to Jump Into the Quarry Water.

However, It is Very Difficult to Climb Out of the Quarry Water On To The Very High and Very Slippery Moss Covered Granite Cliff Ledge.

And Chris Morgen, One of Liddy's Two Sisters, Who Lives in Germany Along with Her Husband and Seldom Visits Clark Island, Became Very Concerned That The Three Sisters Could Face a Multi-Million-Dollar Lawsuit If a Visiting Child Were to Drown in the Quarry.

As a Result, The Three Sisters, In the Summer of 2013 When They Were All on Mishaum Point in Massachusetts, Decided to Have a Private Meeting Among Themselves at a Nearby Restaurant to Discuss Whether or Not to Retain the Ownership of Some or all of Their Land on Clark Island Including the Large Quarry Lot.

And They Decided at Their Private Meeting To Try To Sell a Significant Portion of Their Land on Clark Island Including the Large Quarry Lot to a Maine Land Trust For a Nature and Hiking Preserve.

And They Appointed Me to Represent Them in Contacting the Prestigious Maine Coast Heritage Trust and Landvest, Which is a National Real Estate Brokerage Firm With an Office in Camden, Maine, to Initiate Discussions with MCHT and Landvest About the Possibility of Selling a Major Portion of Their Clark Island Land to MCHT For a Hiking and Nature Preserve.

However, The Three Sisters Did Not Want To Sell The Nickerson House Lot; The Caretaker's House Lot; The Causeway From the Mainland to Clark Island; and The Road on Clark Island From the Causeway to the Nickerson House Lot.

Beginning in the Fall of 2013, I Initiated Meetings in Boston and Maine First Just With Landvest And Then in the First Half of 2014 With Both Landvest and MCHT.

And, During the Early Period, I Had More Than Twenty-five Emails and Other Communications with the Tabors, Morgans, and Liddy About What Land to Sell and What Land to Retain Along with What Restrictions Should The Three Sisters Place on the Use of the Land on Clark Island By Visitors to MCHT's Hiking and Nature Preserve.

In the Early Fall of 2014, Steve Walker, The Project Manager for MCHT, Wrote a Letter to The Three Sisters Expressing MCHT's Interest In Purchasing the Eighty-Six-Acre West Lot and the Twenty-Four-Acre East Lot; Having an Appraisal Done on the Market Value of That Land Since They Are Required as a Non-Profit Organization in Maine Not to Pay More Than the Appraised Value For Any Land They Purchase; and Drafting a Purchase Option Agreement For Review By The Three Sisters.

And, In November of 2014, The Three Sisters and I Received a Letter From Steve Walker Proposing That MCHT Be Given a Two-Year Option To Purchase the West Lot and the East Lot, Totaling 110 Acres For $3.1 Million.

By The Way, The Maine Coast Heritage Trust was Founded By Peggy Rockefeller, the Wife of David Rockefeller, Who Served as Chair of the Board of Trustees For the First Fifteen Years. I Got to Know David and Peggy, as well as Several Senior Rockefellers and Some of Their Wives, During My Later Years of Working For Exxon in Rockefeller Center.

In the Next Six Years, I Personally Spent Hundreds of Hours and Generated and Feet of Files In Negotiating and Completing the $3.5 Million Sale of 124 Acres of Liddy's. Her Two Sisters and The Clark Island Trust's Land on Clark Island to The Maine Coast Heritage Trust For a Hiking and Nature Preserve Open to the General Public, And The Closing on The Clark Island Land Sale to MCHT Took Place on July 1, 2020. Importantly, 30 Percent of the Land on Clark Island Has Been Retained By Liddy and Her Two Sisters and The Clark Island Trust For Their Wonderful House Lot at the Southern End of Clark Island; The Caretaker's House Lot at the Northern Tip of Clark Island; The Causeway Access to Clark Island From the Mainland; The Road From the Northern Tip to the Southern Tip of Clark Island; and A Buffer Zone Between The Three Sisters' House Lot and the MCHT Land.

Also, The Three Sisters, The Clark Island Trust, and I Had Many

Face-to-Face Meetings with MCHT to Obtain Their Agreement to Multiple Restrictions on the General Public's Visits to Their Hiking and Nature Preserve, Including Not Being Able to Drive Their Vehicles Onto Clark Island. Instead, They Will Park Them in the Craignair Inn Parking Lot on the Mainland and Walk Across the Nearby Causeway to Clark Island.

Also, and Most Importantly, There Are Many New Major Benefits to The Three Sisters and Their Offspring From the Sale of Some of Their Land to MCHT:

1. MCHT Will Do a Much Better Job of Maintaining the Existing Hiking Trails and Will Also Create and Maintain a Few New Hiking Trails.
2. There Will No Longer Be a Major Liability Risk If a Visitor's Child Drowns in the Large Quarry Since the Large Quarry Will Be Owned By MCHT.
3. The Three Sisters Real Estate Taxes From the Town of St. George For Their Land on Clark Island Will Be Reduced By At Least 75 percent and Possibly By As Much As 95 percent.

131. ALL-AMERICAN SON, RACE CAR DRIVER, AND LEVERAGED HIGH YIELD BOND FUND MANAGER

*I*f Only I Had Two Words to Describe Thomas Nickerson Davis, My Forty-Four-Year-Old Son, It Would Be the "Go-Go Guy."

He Took a Love to Competitive Swimming When He Was Only Seven Years Old at the Darien, Connecticut, YMCA and Later at the Wilton, Connecticut, YMCA and Never Stopped Competing Until He Had Graduated From the University of Indiana.

While In Elementary and Middle Schools, He Participated In Local and Regional Swimming Meets With Other YMCAs. And He Competed Every Year in the YMCA and the United States Swimming Championships For Connecticut and the New England YMCA Swimming Championships in Providence, Rhode Island.

And He Won His First New England Breaststroke Championship When He Was Ten Years Old.

In High School, He Won Many Dual Meets In the Breaststroke and IM Events and Also Won Those Two Events His Senior Year at the Connecticut High School Men's Swimming Championships.

And He Received the Men's Connecticut High School Swimmer of The Year Award.

He Also Competed Nationally in the YMCA Swimming Championships in Fort Lauderdale, Florida, and In His Senior

Year Won Gold Medals in the Two-Hundred-Yard Breaststroke and Two-Hundred-Yard IM Events and a Silver Medal in the Hundred-Yard Breaststroke.

And, During His Senior Year in High School. He Competed in the US Junior and Senior National Swimming Championships. He Also Qualified to Compete In the US Swimming Trials to Select the Members of the US Olympic Team. And He was Named Men's Swimmer of the Year By Connecticut's United States Swimming Organization.

In Applying to Universities, He Received a Large Number of Swimming Scholarship Offers and Chose to Join the Indiana University Men's Swimming Team, Which Has Always Been One of the Top Men's College Swimming Teams in the United States.

And. Lo and Behold, He Received All America Honors His Freshman Year at the Division I National Men's Swimming Championships in Austin, Texas.

After Graduating From College and Obtaining a Top Job as a High Yield Bond Analyst and Manager at a Prestigious Bond Mutual Fund Company in a Suburb of Indianapolis, He Still Wanted to Race Competitively.

However, He Chose to Compete in Different Sporting Events From Day One and Still Competes Locally, Regionally, and Nationally in Racing Events In a Wide Variety of Sports. These Events Have Included Bike Races, Mountain Bike Races, Triathlons, Motorcycle Track Races, Indianapolis-Style Car Races, and Racing His Own Porsche.

Also, Tommy, Despite Spending a Lot of Time Going to Daily Swimming Practices Both Before Breakfast and After School Each Day, as Well as Traveling To and Competing in Lots of Local, Regional, State, and National Swimming Meets and Championships, Realized the Vital Importance To His Future Working Career of Obtaining Very Good Grades In a Wide Variety of Subjects In School.

Thus, Despite His Very Difficult and Time-Consuming Swimming Schedule, He Placed a Very High Priority of Attending

All of His Classes Each Day and Allocated Enough Time To Do His Homework Every Day.

And His Exemplary Work Ethic Has Continued In His Professional Wall Street Career, Resulting In His Receiving Many Promotions and Large Yearly Bonuses.

Currently, Tommy was Recently Promoted to Be Executive Director of Leveraged High Yield Bond Funds For J.P. Morgan and Has a Lovely Office on the Top Floor of the Highest Office Building in Downtown Indianapolis.

Tommy Has Also Become a Very Good Family Man With Natalie, His Lovely Wife Who Also Graduated From Indiana University, and With Nick and Henry, His Very Bright and Energetic Nine-Year-Old Twin Boys.

So, Let's Hear It For the Go-Go Guy!

132. PhD Daughter, Highly Rated Professor, and Author of Anthropology Books

*I*f I Only Had Two Words to Describe Christina Parks Davis, Liddy's and My Forty-Three-Year-Old Daughter, It Would Be "Miss Academia."

Starting Very Early In Her Elementary School Years and Continuing On In Her Middle School, High School, and University Years, Christie Always Placed a Very High Priority On Doing Exceptionally Well in School.

Christie Developed an Excellent System For Preparing For Important Exams Which She Formulated On Her Own With No Input Or Prodding From Her Parents or Others.

About a Month Before a Test, She Would Do a Broad Review of the Textbook and Her Lecture Notes That She Would Be Tested On. And About Two Weeks Before a Test, She Would Do an In-Depth Detailed Review of the Textbook and Her Lecture Notes That She Would Be Tested On, And She Would Conduct Another In-Depth Detailed Review of the Course Materials Two Days and One Day Before the Test.

As a Result of Her Efforts, She Received Excellent Grades Throughout Her Schooling Years, and Particularly at Darien High School and The University of Michigan.

At Darien High School, Which is One of the Top High Schools in Connecticut, Christie's Grade Point Average Was 4th Highest In Her Graduating Class.

As a Result, She Was Accepted at the University of Michigan In Their Honors College For Liberal Arts Students Which Is Limited to 1,500 Students Out of a Total Liberal Arts Enrollment of About 25,000.

Christie Obtained Excellent Grades at the University of Michigan.

After Graduating With High Honors From the University of Michigan, She Wanted to Pursue a PhD Degree in Graduate School After Working In a Teaching Job For a Few Years, And She was Hired By the Hello School in Japan to Teach Conversational English to Adults.

Next, She Returned to the United States and Enrolled at The University of Chicago, Where She Received a Master's Degree in Social Sciences.

Then, to Pursue Her Career Goal, She Enrolled In the University of Michigan's PhD Program For Anthropology Students.

While at Michigan, Christie Received a Fulbright Scholarship To Teach and Conduct Research For Three Years, Starting in 2007 For Her PhD Dissertation at Two High Schools In Kandy, Sri Lanka, on the Interactions, Conversations, and Social Practices of the Multi-Ethnic, Multi-Religious, and Multi-Linguistic High School Students While a Brutal Civil War Which Began in 1983 Was Still Going On Between the Northern and Eastern Tamil Tigers, Who Were Primarily Muslims and the Sinhalese Sri Lankan Government, Whose Followers Were Primarily Buddhists.

After Receiving Her PhD Degree, Christie Taught Anthropology Classes at Columbia University as an Adjunct Assistant Professor.

And Then, She Was Hired By Western Illinois University as an Assistant Professor of Anthropology and Recently Promoted to Become a Full Professor of Anthropology.

Regarding Christie's Academic Achievements After Graduating From the University of Michigan with a PhD in Anthropology and

Becoming a Professor of Anthropology at Western Illinois University, They Are Numerous:

She Has Always Been Rated As Excellent By Her Students at Western Illinois University, Who Are Required to Fill Out a Written Performance Evaluation of Their Teachers at the End of Each Course.

The Prestigious Oxford University Press Published Her First Book on *The Struggle For a Multilingual Future in Sri Lanka* in 2020. It is Currently Being Used In South Asia Anthropology Classes at Stanford, Oberlin, NYU, Indian Institute of Technology, and Jaffna University in Sri Lanka.

Her Second Book Was Just Published in August 2021 On *Language, Education and Identity In South Asia.* It Included Chapters Written By Christie and Ten Other Prominent Anthropologists and was Edited By Christie and a Senior Anthropology Professor.

Christie Also Completed Fifteen Research Papers, Wrote Ten Articles and Chapters For Five Books.

Christie Attends Several Major National and International Conferences on Anthropology Each Year and Is Always One of the Major Speakers at These Conferences.

Christie is Book Review Editor For the Journal of Linguistic Anthropology and Is Active In Five Anthropology Organizations.

Christie is Also Married to Canaan Albright and Has a Very Bright, Energetic, and Personable Eight-Year-Old Son Named Kingston.

Let's all Have a Big Round of Applause For Miss Academia!

133. Wonderful Marriage To Liddy For Almost Fifty Years

When I First Met Liddy in Manhattan, I Was Very Impressed With Her Background.

She Graduated From the University of Arizona with a Bachelors Degree in Anthropology.

Her First Job After Graduation Was Working For the American Museum of Natural History in Manhattan. And Shortly After She Began Her Museum Job, She Was Hired By Margaret Mead as One of Her Two Assistants at the American Museum of Natural History.

Since Liddy was an Expert in the Peoples of the South Pacific and Had Traveled to Many of the Primitive South Pacific Islands, She Was Given the Job By Margaret Mead of Both Designing and Overseeing the Implementation of the Museum's First Peoples of the Pacific Exhibition Hall. And She Did an Excellent Job of Deciding What to Exhibit and Where to Exhibit Each Item in the Exhibition Hall.

I Got to know Both of Liddy's Parents Early On and Liked Them Very Much. Liddy's Father Had Recently Retired as Chairman and CEO of Mobil Oil. And He Also Served on a Number of Boards Including Rockefeller University, Raytheon, and The Metropolitan Life Insurance Company. And He Had Served As Chair of Harvard University's Board of Overseers, Chairman of the Federal Reserve

Bank of New York, and Chairman of President Johnson's Business Council.

Liddy's Mother Graduated From Sarah Lawrence College and Was the Daughter of the Chairman of the National City Bank of New York.

And Liddy Had Two Sisters and One Brother.

Liddy and I Became Engaged to be Married in the Fall of 1972, When We Were Both in the Midst of Planning and Buying Equipment and Supplies For Our Winter Mount Everest Exhibition in December of 1972.

And We Were Married On May 5th of 1973 In a Very Nice Wedding Ceremony at a Church in Lincoln, Massachusetts, and a Reception at Liddy's Parents' Home in Lincoln.

Most Importantly, I Have Had a Wonderful Marriage With Liddy For Almost Fifty Years In So Many Ways:

She Has Been a Wonderful Mother to Tommy and Christie, Our Two Children, and is Still in Close Touch With Both of Them.

She Is An Excellent and Creative Cook and Loves to Cook For the First-Time Recipes For Main Courses That She Has Seen in the *Red Book of Cooking* and The *New York Times* Food Section.

She Loves to Go on Hiking Trips With Me In Regional Parks, National Parks, and Switzerland and on Trips to the Caribbean and Isle of Capri In the Late Winter Months.

She Has Been a Wonderful Partner With Me In Our Exotic Trips to the South Pacific Islands and Tierra del Fuego.

And, Like Me, She Enjoys Dancing to Rock and Roll Songs at Events in Greater New Bedford, Such as the Lloyd Center of The Environment Clambakes and the Prince Henry Society Christmas Parties.

I Always Liked to See Liddy Riding and Jumping Horses at The Ox Ridge Hunt Club in Darien, Connecticut, Where She Won Many Medals and Ribbons.

I Was Also Very Proud of the Excellent Job Liddy Did as Manager of the Historic Davoll's General Store in the Russells Mills Village of South Dartmouth For Sixteen Years.

And We Both Love to Go Out to Dinner Together Twice a Week at Interesting Restaurants in South Dartmouth, Westport, New Bedford, Newport, and Providence, Rhode Island. And, Once a Year, We Have a Big Treat Dinner at the Famous No. 9 Park Restaurant In Boston Across the Street From the State Capital.

Lastly, I Am Confident That Liddy and I Will Lavishly Celebrate Our 50th Wedding Anniversary and Will Live Long Enough to Celebrate Our 60th Wedding Anniversary.

134. STILL REMEMBERING AND ADMIRING MY PARENTS

Both of My Parents Were Very Helpful to Me Early On In My Childhood In Many Ways.

My Father Grew Up In Ann Arbor, Michigan, as the Son of a Very Successful Businessman Who Owned a High-End Men's Clothing Store in Downtown Ann Arbor. His Mother was Very Active In the Democratic Party, Both Locally and At the State and National Level.

My Father Graduated From the University of Michigan With Bachelors and Master's Degrees and From Columbia University with a PhD in Education Administration.

He First Worked as a History Teacher and Football Coach at a High School in Southwestern Ohio and Was Promoted Very Quickly After Obtaining His Master's Degree at Michigan To Become Principal of the High School.

He Then Served in Mayor La Guardia's School Administration Department in New York City, Became Deputy Secretary For Education in Vermont, and Was Secretary of Education For Puerto Rico. He Then Held Senior Administrative Positions at George Washington University and the University of Illinois, Chicago.

In His Last Job, Which He Held For Twelve Years, He was a Lobbyist For the National Education Association in Washington, DC.

My Mother Grew Up In a Poor Farm in Michigan. She Attended Many Universities By First Working to Save Money and Then Enrolling In a University For One to Two Years Until Her Savings Ran Out and Then Repeating This Process Many Times. And, In the Process She Attended Western Michigan, Wisconsin, Indiana, and Colorado University to Obtain Her Bachelor's Degree and Finished Up at Columbia University With a Master's Degree in Teaching English.

She First Taught English at Ann Arbor High School Until She Married My Father.

While Carrying Out All of the Motherly Duties For Me and My Sister and Brother, She Wrote More Than One Hundred Human Interest Articles For National Magazines and Taught English in High School as a Substitute Teacher.

In Washington, DC, She Founded the Washington, DC, and Virginia Branches of the National League Of American Pen Women, With Margaret Truman and Two Other Women. She Was Elected As An Officer and Attended All of the Pen Women Meetings, Which Were Held in The White House.

Later in Life, My Mother Taught Effective Writing Courses For US Government Employees in Washington DC, and Virginia.

So, How Did My Parents Influence Me In the Right Direction and Help Me In My Boyhood Years?

Regarding My Father, He Instilled In Me a Great Love For the Outdoors and Outdoors Activities. In Vermont, He Took Us On Short Trips to Climb Mountains. In Bethesda, Maryland, He Took Us On Weekend Outdoor Camping Trips In a Large State Park In the Mountains of West Virginia. And For Summer Vacations, He Would Rent a Cottage On the Outer Banks of North Carolina For Swimming, Fishing, and Boating. In Illinois, During Part of the Summer, He Would Rent a Primitive Cabin in Door County, Wisconsin, That Was Halfway Down a Thousand-Foot Granite Cliff Overlooking Lake Superior. In Addition to the Above, He Took Us On a Four-Week Trip By Car to Visit the Major National Parks

Located West of the Mississippi River and Attend the US National Rodeo Championships in Cheyenne, Wyoming.

Also, My Father Instilled In Me a Strong Desire to Go to College. Every Year, in the Fall, He Would Take Me to a Football Game at a College that We Hadn't Visited Before. We Would Arrive on Campus at Mid Morning, Take a Walking Tour of the Major Campus Area, Eat Lunch at a Campus Hangout, and Attend the Entire Football Game. And I Would Always Come Back Home with a Pennant From the University Which I Tacked On To My Bedroom Wall. So After Making These Campus Visits For Ten Years, My Bedroom Walls Were Covered With Colorful University Pennants.

My Mother Was So Helpful To Me In Getting Accepted For Admissions to Outstanding Universities and In Obtaining a Good Full-Time Professional Job After Graduating From Northwestern With an MBA in Finance.

Given That My Mother Was An Outstanding Human Interest Writer, She Would Review the One or Two Essays That I Had to Write in Applying For Admissions to Undergraduate Schools, Law Schools, and Graduate Business Schools. She Would Make Many Revisions, Additions, and Deletions to My Draft Essays. And The End Result Was That I Was Accepted For Admissions By Many Elite Universities Including Harvard Graduate Business School; Virginia Law School; Yale Law School; Northwestern Graduate Business School; Michigan; Cal-Berkley; Wharton School Of Finance, Indiana; New York University; and a Number of Other High-Quality Universities.

And My Mother's Detailed Editing of My Essays Also Helped Me Obtain Two Major College Scholarships That Covered 75 percent of the Total Costs of Attending The University of Michigan and the Northwestern Graduate School of Business.

My Mother Also Spent a Lot of Time Reviewing and Revising My Bio That I Was Using To Obtain a Full-Time Professional Job as a Financial Analyst or Security Analyst After Graduating From Northwestern's Graduate School of Business.

As a Result of My Mother's Efforts, I Obtained Fifteen Full-

Time Job Offers From High-Quality Companies Located in New York City, Minneapolis, Chicago, Cleveland, and Detroit. And, In Fact, Several Head Interviewers Commented To Me That My Bio Was the Most Interesting One That They Had Ever Read.